Praise for *Cracking the Healthcare Leadership Code*

Transformational leadership is core to success in any field, especially healthcare. The stakes are high because attracting, retaining, and developing the best leaders will have the greatest amount of impact on patient care and their l[...] CO of a large community hospital v[...] system. Through practical experienc[...] ook, he did an incredible job of buil[...] for the organization being ranked as one of the leading hospitals in America.

Steve Wanamaker
CEO and Publisher,
CDO Magazine

Dr. Kevin Joseph quickly became a champion for our communities—West Chester and Liberty Townships, the emerging epicenter for business between our two major markets, Cincinnati and Dayton. As a practicing ER physician and chief executive officer of up-and-coming UC Health West Chester Hospital, Kevin's unique skill set, passion for patient care, and support of our communities positioned Kevin and West Chester Hospital as a regional and national leader and provided a glimpse into the future of healthcare leadership.

With his one-of-a-kind perspective, Kevin provides the reader a balanced look at leadership, healthcare, and the importance of having a purpose in what we do. His real-world tips throughout the book emphasize his expertise from vast experiences that are transferable to all professionals in any industry. If you are looking for real-world insights into leadership today and into our future, I recommend reading *Cracking the Healthcare Leadership Code*.

Joseph A. Hinson, IOM
President and CEO,
West Chester • Liberty Chamber Alliance

While the principles outlined in *Cracking the Healthcare Leadership Code* are geared toward the healthcare industries, the strategies presented would be applicable toward leadership in any discipline.

Dr. Joseph understands some universal truths motivating and influencing others—I took a similar approach during my years in law enforcement leadership and can confirm it gets results. The book is an enjoyable, thought-provoking read, which should be required for any manager serious about improving their skills as an effective leader. Having known and worked with Dr. Joseph for over 25 years, I can attest to his living the concepts detailed in his book.

Lieutenant Doug Ventre
Retired Commander,
Cincinnati Police Department SWAT Team

Kevin Joseph does an excellent job of bringing us back to the basic tenets of leadership. This is the kind of book everyone should read. It's great for new leaders and emerging leaders, and it's a wonderful refresher for senior leaders. It's filled with smart tactics—important reminders of all the little things that should be hardwired into our leadership style and that we need to use more often.

Lee Ann Liska
Chief Operating Officer, Vanderbilt University Hospital,
Vanderbilt University Medical Center

Our workforce has changed, and we must evolve as leaders. Great leadership is no longer optional. We must engage people, inspire them, connect them to a larger sense of purpose, and make sure they know that they have a voice. Kevin Joseph gets this. His ideas are applicable to everyone, from a small organization with limited resources to a large hospital or business. In the end, your success comes down to how you treat people and how they see you as a leader. Employees want to know you care, and Kevin shows you how to make that loud and clear.

Craig Oaks
Vice President, Human Resources

I have had the great fortune to work directly with and for Dr. Kevin Joseph over the past years. He is an exceptional transformational healthcare leader. He practices what he is preaching and brings incredible positive energy and passion to the work. I learn from Kevin every day and am glad he has taken the time to share some of the key elements of his humble, effective, and great leadership style.

Jeff Norton
Vice President
Institute for Safety, Reliability and Clinical Performance Improvement

Research in psychological safety shows that when we minimize emotional tension, we maximize brain power and get the best outcomes for our patients. Dr. Kevin Joseph has created both a strategic and a tactical guide for reducing the power imbalance within organizations so that fear is reduced and psychological safety flourishes. As the chief medical officer at TriHealth, he was able to drive some amazing outcomes. TriHealth reduced serious preventable harm to patients by 70 percent. The number of anonymous event reports declined by 79 percent, indicating that caregivers and providers were feeling safer in reporting harm. In fact, in every measure that we use, TriHealth is better because of Kevin and his ideas.

Craig Clapper
PE Executive Advisor,
SSM Health—Center for Clinical Excellence

I love how Kevin tells his personal story about finding his purpose early on. I also love how he talks organizations through what they can do to help people find and live *their* sense of purpose (and he gives lots of specifics). We know that when people's hearts are on fire, things change. While Kevin is obviously in a hospital setting, I can't wait to implement his ideas at the Boys and Girls Club. I am excited to get started and share this message with my team!

Patti Alderson
Founder and CEO,
Boys and Girls Club, West Chester and Liberty Townships

CRACKING THE

HEALTHCARE
LEADERSHIP
CODE

CRACKING THE

HEALTHCARE
LEADERSHIP
CODE

How Purpose, Humility,
and Accessibility Can
Transform Your
Organization

Kevin J. Joseph, MD, MBA

ACHE Management Series

27 26 25 24 23   5 4 3 2 1

Library of Congress Cataloging-in-Publication Data is on file at the Library of Congress, Washington, DC.

ISBN: 978-1-64055-391-0

The paper used in this publication meets the minimum requirements of American National Standard for Information Sciences—Permanence of Paper for Printed Library Materials, ANSI Z39.48-1984. ∞ ™

Manuscript editor: Sharon Sofinski; Cover designer: James Slate; Layout: PerfectType

Found an error or a typo? We want to know! Please e-mail it to hapbooks@ache.org, mentioning the book's title and putting "Book Error" in the subject line.

For photocopying and copyright information, please contact Copyright Clearance Center at www.copyright.com or at (978) 750-8400.

Health Administration Press
A division of the Foundation of the
    American College of Healthcare Executives
300 S. Riverside Plaza, Suite 1900
Chicago, IL 60606-6698
(312) 424-2800

This book is dedicated to all healthcare workers in ambulatory care, acute care, post-acute care, extended care, pre-hospital care, and all other settings. Whether you are directly interacting with patients or not, you are a caregiver. You are serving others through a very noble profession. With every difficult day, remember that all your efforts and sacrifice are leaving a legacy by changing the lives of others.

Contents

Foreword

I was so excited to have the opportunity to write the foreword to this book. Healthcare leadership is my lifelong passion. And being the right kind of leader has never mattered so much.

Our world has undergone a major disruption in the past few years. People's attitudes toward work have been changing for decades, and companies have been slowly adapting. But COVID-19 and its aftermath—including the talent shortage—have upped the urgency. The stakes are huge.

A new type of organization is taking shape from the chaos. I call it the Human Capital Ecosystem™, which is a framework my firm uses to help clients attract, retain, and engage talent. Basically, the employee is at the center of everything. All the components in the ecosystem—from selection and onboarding to supervisor relationships, skill building, and career development (and more)—work together to fully engage and empower that employee.

One reason we're helping clients shift to this model is that today's employees expect it. They want more autonomy. They want professional development. (Training and development is crucial because having the right skill set empowers people—they feel confident when they are highly competent.) They want strong relationships with leaders who genuinely care about them. They want their work to have purpose. And they want a flatter hierarchical structure so their ideas can be heard, explored, and put into practice.

This is why I appreciate Kevin Joseph's thoughts on breaking down the power gradient. The old-school industry hierarchy—with senior leaders and physicians at the top and everyone else below them—works against creating the kind of culture today's talent, especially younger people, insist on. Thankfully, this has changed drastically and continues to change, and there is plenty we can do to keep moving in the right direction.

Flattening the power gradient is not only what employees want; it also gets the best results. An increasingly complex industry and external environment calls for cultures of collaboration. No single person, however smart and capable, could ever have all the answers. Only with the free flow of ideas, with everyone working at full capacity, can we arrive at the best possible solutions.

And, of course, there's the safety issue. Kevin references the Tenerife disaster, in which the airline industry's rigid power gradient led to a subordinate's unwillingness to challenge the captain, which in turn led to a deadly runway collision. In healthcare, we also hold lives in our hands. It's so important that people feel free to speak up when they see a potential issue.

All of this is why organizations need to invest in creating a different kind of leader—one who can get people to the table in a way that enables full access to the brains, skills, and perspectives we're paying for.

Sometimes leaders work hard to find and hire the most talented people—and then block their freedom to use that talent. They "lead" in a way that shuts people down, that undermines the collaboration needed to get to the right solution. They carry their authority in a way that pushes people away from the challenge at hand, rather than drawing them to it.

No one does this on purpose. I have worked with many leaders over the years, and almost without exception they have wonderful intentions. They care, very much, about doing right by their organizations. Yet we all have our shortcomings and blind spots (certainly including myself). This is why self-awareness is so critical. Before we can effectively lead others, we need to get our insides right.

For instance, if we happen to be the kind of leader who has a strong need to be right or have our idea always be the one that's chosen, it's important to know this about ourselves. We must notice when that need to win is triggered so we can catch ourselves, back off, and refocus on the priority at hand, which is listening, learning, and thinking clearly so that together we can arrive at the best solution.

We need to be constantly aware of how people experience us as leaders. Approachability is so important. It's what allows us to build the kinds of relationships that make people feel okay about giving honest feedback.

The bottom line is that leaders can no longer be authority figures. We need to be more like facilitators, setting the right example, empowering people with plenty of training and development, and making sure conditions are right for them to use their talents and knowledge to the fullest. Kevin does a great job of giving practical tips leaders can use to break down the power gradient so they can fulfill this goal.

So yes, we need to know *ourselves* so we can work on our shortcomings. But it's equally important that we know *our people.*

Strong leader–caregiver relationships are vital. We need to invest heavily in them. Great relationships don't "just happen." As Kevin points out, intentionally making regular meaningful connections with caregivers not only breaks down the power gradient and builds trust, but it also gets people engaged and aligned with our mission and makes them want to stay. I agree.

I feel so strongly about meaningful relationships that my firm has created a framework to help leaders build them. It's called Relationship Rounding™. It's based on the well-known practice of consistently setting aside time to ask specific questions of individual employees to gather actionable information. Our version is focused mainly on making meaningful human connections (not just checking off boxes). It helps us demonstrate to employees that we care about them, really get to know them on a personal level, and check in on their well-being. (This last one is especially important right now, with burnout and mental health issues at an all-time high.)

However you go about it, the ability to build these kinds of relationships is no longer a "nice-to-have" for leaders. It's a "must-have."

In healthcare, we ask people to do really hard things. We need to make regular deposits into what Stephen Covey called the emotional bank account, so that when we need to make the inevitable withdrawals (e.g., asking them to work long, tough hours during a pandemic), the foundation of trust and mutual respect will be in place. Rather than leaving or disengaging, they will rise to the occasion.

Finally, I love Kevin's emphasis on *purpose* and *service.* He comes back to them again and again throughout this book. These concepts are intertwined and inseparable. The healthcare industry exists to serve others. That is its purpose. The mission to serve patients is at the center of every job in every healthcare organization—from nurse to surgeon to cafeteria worker to transporter to financial professional. This is the great equalizer and, ultimately, why hierarchy doesn't matter.

Anyone who takes a job in healthcare is accepting this premise: "This—serving others—is my purpose." The way I see it, they are answering a calling. The leader's role is to help that person stay connected to that calling, on good days, tough days, and every day. It's not always easy, but if we want to do the best possible job of caring for the patients who place their trust in us, keeping that calling top of mind is necessary.

Thank you, Kevin, for the opportunity to write the foreword to *Cracking the Healthcare Leadership Code.* And thank you, reader, for answering the call to get better and better at becoming the kind of leader we need today. Your organizations, coworkers, patients, communities, and the entire industry thanks you for doing this work. We are grateful.

—Quint Studer
Author of *The Calling: Why Healthcare Is So Special*

Preface

THERE'S NEVER BEEN a more pressing need for leadership training in healthcare. Our industry has a long history of transitioning unprepared people into leadership positions, and the problem has only intensified in recent years. Extreme burnout is rampant, and turnover at all levels has never been greater. These issues are resulting in unprecedented changes in leadership. For new or transitioning leaders to succeed, they must not only have the necessary aptitude, attitude, and ability but must also adopt a new approach to leadership. It is just as imperative for established leaders to rapidly evolve their leadership philosophy and style to thrive in this new environment with all of its challenges.

There's nothing remotely simple about the world we are navigating right now. At all levels, every leader—new, transitioning, or established—needs to find their footing in this new healthcare landscape. I don't pretend to have all the answers. But I know what has worked for the organizations I've led (and, just as importantly, what hasn't worked)—and I *definitely* know how it feels to be blindsided by a sudden leadership transition and healthcare transformation.

A mere two and a half years after I finished my training to be an emergency medicine physician—a time when I was focused on honing my clinical skills and delivering exceptional care—I was provided the unexpected opportunity to be the medical director of an emergency department. I accepted the offer, which I couldn't refuse. Another two and a half years later, I received a call from the CEO of the healthcare system on a Friday evening to join him for dinner on Sunday. At the conclusion of dinner, he stated that the following morning he was going to appoint me to be the president and CEO of the hospital.

While the first promotion was daunting, the second one was truly terrifying. How was I qualified to run a hospital when I was still a relatively inexperienced medical director? Although I was fairly educated with a doctorate in medicine, a bachelor degree in biomedical engineering, and residency training in emergency medicine and was back in school to receive a master's degree in business administration, I was woefully ill-prepared. Not a single hour of my education provided even a hint of leadership training, which was evident in my approach, my failures, my inefficiency, and frankly, my lacking personal health and professional joy.

The precarious position in which I was placed, as well as my experiences in several subsequent senior leadership positions, have formed the backbone of this book. Today, it is rare to find leadership training in traditional educational tracks, including residencies and fellowships. Often, leadership is taught (if at all) as a set of tactical skills such as running a meeting, creating a dashboard, or completing an evaluation. However, the great majority of leadership skills are not tactical or discrete. For example, how does a leader inspire others, foster teamwork, and encourage innovation? It is difficult to effectively teach these critical skills in a lecture format because they are highly experiential. Even for the tactical skills, being good at them requires experience. Someone can learn how to logistically run a meeting, but are they able to engage others in the meeting to feel comfortable in candidly expressing their thoughts and challenging the most senior person in the room?

Unfortunately, many of these learning experiences about how to be a great leader come through failure and tough lessons. The opportunity to experience these lessons is not even guaranteed, and it is unknown when (or if) a leader will encounter them. This book was written to share lessons from failure so that you can avoid them and to share stories of success so that you can replicate them.

I firmly believe that one of a leader's most important responsibilities is not to create followers but rather to create other leaders. My goal in writing *Cracking the Healthcare Leadership Code* is to create other leaders, further develop the skills of current leaders, and give those who are already exceptional leaders a different perspective to consider or something new to try. My promise to leaders at every level is that there is something in this book that will catch your attention and, hopefully, shift your thinking in a way that changes you, those around you, and the entire culture for the better.

—Kevin Joseph, MD, MBA

The Power Gradient Toolkit

POWER GRADIENT IS a term used to describe the difference in power between two individuals. The difference can be real, such as the difference between a chief executive officer and a manager. It can also be a perceived difference, such as the one between an experienced team member and a newly graduated individual in the same department who both have the same function.

It has been proven repeatedly in many industries, including healthcare, that a larger power gradient corresponds to a greater chance for error. At the bedside, errors can result in safety events that can cause harm or even death to a patient. In addition, large power gradients decrease team member retention, innovation, and shared opportunities for operational improvements. Such decreases ultimately have a negative effect on the success of the organization.

Given the critical significance of addressing the power gradient, I have partnered with Reliability for Life Group (R4L) to develop a toolkit to assist leaders of all levels in reducing the power gradient. It is written as a supplement to chapter 6, "Breaking Down the Power Gradient."

Inside the toolkit you will find the following:

- A list of key concept definitions related to the "power gradient" topic
- An introduction highlighting the effects and consequences of steep power gradients, including an outline of a

three-tiered comprehensive framework (Organization, Leaders, Team Members)for breaking down the power gradient

- Six calls to action: activities supported by researchers, field engineers, and healthcare practitioners to reduce the power gradient in an organization. Simple tools are aligned within each of the six calls to action to start your journey toward breaking down the power gradient in your organization.

The toolkit can be used in several ways:

- As a resource for your leadership team to gain situational awareness of the effect of power gradients
- As a snapshot, highlighting where your organization is with each call to action and what to do next—or as a blueprint to guide you in choosing your next priorities
- As an orientation piece for new leaders
- As a refresher for your leadership team

The Power Gradient Toolkit can be downloaded for your use by visiting ache.org/HAP and searching for this book's order code (24891). A digital version can also be found at www.R4LG.com.

Acknowledgments

To my wife Heather and children Anna and Jameson: Thank you for your patience. There are no words strong enough to adequately express my love for you. You are my joy and treasures.

To my parents, who have built my character focused on integrity, humility, work ethic, love, passion, and purpose: I am forever grateful, and I consider myself a great parent if I am only a small fraction as good at parenting as you have been (and continue to be) with your children and grandchildren.

To the following people who saw something in me that I didn't see myself, then believed in me and took a chance on me: Art Shoukis, David Stern, and Jim Kingsbury. I wouldn't be where I am today without your trust and support.

To three people I consider mentors, either through direct conversation or simply learning from their publications: Quint Studer, Marc Bard, and Michael O'Brien. Your guidance has been instrumental in my growth.

To all my colleagues I studied with as an engineering and medical student, and to everyone I have ever worked with as a physician or healthcare executive: No matter your role, I have learned and grown so much from you all.

To my close friends who have always supported me in so many ways.

To the team at DeHart & Company: This book would not have been written without you. Working with you has been such a joy, and I am looking forward to what we can create together in the future.

To Him, without whom nothing is possible.

CHAPTER 1

Finding and Maintaining Purpose

IN MANY WAYS, this whole book is about purpose. While we'll discuss many aspects of healthcare leadership, they all flow from and connect back to this central idea: When we wholeheartedly know what we're created for and why we do what we do, we're more likely to flourish and thrive. And by *we*, I mean both organizations and individuals.

I have come to believe that helping others discover, tap into, express, and leverage their purpose is one of a leader's greatest tasks. Without purpose we just go through the motions. We're mere shadows of what we could and should be. Our days lack color and zing. This is no way to live—and it certainly doesn't set us up to serve our patients, our coworkers, and our communities.

While we won't dwell too much on the COVID-19 pandemic, I will say the past few years have directed a spotlight on the need for purpose. (I am writing this in early 2022.) When we wake up to the truth that life is fragile and often far too short, we really want our lives to have great meaning. When we're battered and bruised, as so many in healthcare are, we need a sense of purpose just to keep going.

In other words, purpose has always mattered, but it *really* matters now.

On a personal note, purpose is central to how I approach my career, my relationships with other people, and my efforts to create positive outcomes in every aspect of my life. Purpose became a foundational part of my life's philosophy long before I knew that I wanted to go into healthcare, or even before I reached adulthood. In fact, I can tell you exactly where I was when the seeds were planted. I was about six years old, sitting on my family's living room couch, staring at my mother in total bewilderment.

Let me back up and explain. I grew up outside Boston in a very loving household with my parents, my older brother, and my younger sister. We lived in a modest two-bedroom, one-and-a-half-bath home that was partially heated by a wood stove. We had what we needed, but because my father was working his way through graduate school, money was tight.

To help make ends meet, my mother cleaned houses every day while my siblings and I were at school. No matter how busy she was during the day, she always made sure that she was home with us in the afternoons: driving us to and from our various athletic practices, making supper each evening, and instilling values that I have lived by throughout my adult life.

One day, when we got home from school, my mother sat my brother and me down on the couch. This was unusual in and of itself, but what really stood out to us was the intense look on her face. In a voice that trembled with anger, she told us two things: "One, never think that you are more important or better than someone else. Two, *everyone in the world has a special purpose.*"

My brother and I glanced at each other. Where was this coming from?

"Just think about the garbage men," Mom continued. "People look down on them because their job is dirty, but without them, trash would be piled up at the end of the driveway. At the end of everyone's driveway! That's the garbage men's special purpose—to keep our town clean and safe. What they do is very important. *They* are very important. Do you understand?"

My brother and I said that we did. Then we slunk out of the room. What, exactly, had we done to bring on this "special talk"? As it turned out, *we* hadn't done anything. We later learned that during one of Mom's housecleaning jobs that day, she had struck up a conversation with a high school student who had come home early. Mom asked him, "Do you know what you'll be doing in a few years after you graduate?"

His response was, "Well, I'm certainly going to college. I don't want to be stuck with a job like yours!"

Looking back, I can imagine what my mother must have felt at that moment: a mixture of shock, shame, and anger at the teenager who saw her and the service she provided as *less than*. I understand why she felt it was so important to explain to my brother and me that everyone has a special purpose. My mother certainly had a very important purpose, not just to the family of the teenager who so rudely dismissed the hard work she did, but to *our* family as well. The truth is, my mother is a remarkable woman. She taught me many things I've never forgotten and, along with my father, shaped the way I see the world.

A BIG LESSON FROM MY MOTHER

Over 40 years later, I've come a long way from that confused six-year-old sitting on the couch. But what my mother taught me that day has stayed with me ever since. It has directly influenced how I relate to other people and has deeply affected my leadership style. In fact, her lesson connects has directly to this chapter and is one of the foundational principles throughout much of this book: No one is more important or valuable or special than anyone else, and everyone has a unique contribution to offer. This is why I strive to make humility a daily practice. My job isn't "better," my opinions are no more valid, my concerns aren't of greater importance, and my contributions aren't more valuable. With that in mind, I try to treat every person with the respect I wish my mother had gotten that afternoon at her housecleaning job.

This essential lesson on purpose is intertwined with my belief that leaders need to aggressively break down the power gradient that creates a perceived difference in status between various team members, which leads directly to a perceived difference in the value of others' thoughts and opinions. Later in this book we'll explore how a rigid power gradient degrades an organization's culture. We often hear about its impact on safety (as we'll discuss later, in one famous incident it even led to the deadliest aviation accident in history), but the power gradient counteracts everything leaders are trying to do to keep people connected to purpose. It impedes communication, harms engagement and morale, and keeps people from sharing their valuable insights.

Once you embrace the two premises that nobody is more important than anyone else and that everyone has an essential purpose, it becomes natural to break down the power gradient in your organization. You won't do it because it's morally right or because you're a nice person; you'll do it because it has a tremendous positive impact on individual employees and on the organization as a whole. Breaking down the power gradient creates an entire workforce of engaged, energized, mission-driven people who trust leaders enough to tell the truth.

While the importance of breaking down the power gradient cannot be overstated, there are many other benefits that flow from connecting employees to their individual purpose and to that of the organization. They range from improved clinical outcomes to reduced turnover to a workforce that finds joy in their work. We'll take a closer look at those benefits throughout the rest of this chapter.

APPLYING THE "PURPOSE PHILOSOPHY" TO HEALTHCARE

I'm going to share a story from earlier in my career that illustrates my philosophy. Back in 2010, I became president and CEO of a new community hospital in an exceptionally competitive market (there were six healthcare systems within one county). When I accepted the position, this organization—which I will call Hospital

X—was really struggling. In fact, we were losing over $10 million a year.

However, once we became intentional about creating a culture that helped people tap into purpose, things began to turn around. Our financial loss of $10 million a year turned into a profit of over $50 million a year, and our patient satisfaction scores, patient safety results, and employee engagement results moved into the top tenth percentile in the country. Our purpose-based culture was the foundation of the turnaround.

As a healthcare executive, my intention is always to focus on people first and metrics second. I've found that when people believe they are doing important work (i.e., when they feel they have a purpose) and are appreciated for doing that work, they deliver the best outcomes to the patient. From there, the metrics related to achieving organizational goals will naturally start improving.

Thus, when I stepped into the role of president and CEO at Hospital X, my team and I focused on making sure every employee understood their value and purpose, both within their department and within the organization as a whole. We approached this task by keeping several guiding principles in mind as we went about our work.

Define the Organization's Purpose

First, every employee has a role in fulfilling the mission of their organization and their department. That's their professional purpose. As the leader of Hospital X, my goal was to make sure that everyone clearly understood the purpose of their position and how it aligned with and contributed to the purpose of the organization. Therefore, the first task was to define that organizational purpose.

We decided that the hospital's purpose would be "to change the lives of others." This encompassed our mission to deliver care to patients, but it also reminded people that their work affected patients' whole lives, not just their current state of health.

For example, we wanted our employees to remember that a hip replacement surgery didn't just repair an injury after a fall; it gave a grandparent more years of activity and adventure with their grandchildren. Diagnosing a patient with diabetes and developing a plan to manage the condition didn't just aim to keep the patient's glucose level within normal limits; instead, our goal was to end months (or years) of that patient feeling sick. We would also strive to give the patient tools to prevent future complications of uncontrolled diabetes, such as stroke, kidney failure, amputation, or blindness. Essentially, our work at Hospital X was not just about fixing the current medical illness; it was also about improving our patients' ongoing quality of life.

To encourage this mindset of changing lives for the better, we began to refer to patients as "loved ones." Every time they heard this term, employees were reminded that each patient was more than just a chart, a list of symptoms, or an unpaid bill; they were someone's mother, father, sibling, partner, parent, or friend. They led a full life before being admitted to our hospital or being seen in one of our medical clinics, and the care we provided could help them return to that life, or even improve its quality. I often reminded employees that if you picture a patient as someone's loved one and treat them as you would your own loved one, you will always make the right decision and provide the best care.

I'd like to add one more thing about Hospital X's purpose statement "to change the lives of others": When formulating it, we intentionally used the word *others* instead of *patients* or even *loved ones*. That's because my fellow leaders and I wanted our organization's environment and culture to improve the lives of our caregivers (clinical and nonclinical) by providing them with meaningful work, as well as daily satisfaction and joy. Part of this sense of meaning, as we'll discuss a little later, centered on sponsoring community education events and encouraging volunteerism to increase those positive feelings. That brings me to the final group of people whose lives we hoped to change: individuals living in the surrounding community.

Change the Way People See Themselves and How Their Role Contributes to a Larger Purpose

Once the organizational purpose was in place, the leadership team could focus on assisting each employee in aligning their purpose with that of the organization.

It's fairly easy for a nurse or physician to see how their job supports the hospital's purpose "to change the lives of others." However, the connection might not be as obvious to employees in other departments. I realized this when, during a meeting with the organization's leaders, I conducted a "stand up if . . ." exercise.

First, I asked everyone who was a caregiver to stand. Most of the individuals who got to their feet were physicians, nurses, respiratory therapists, and other direct caregivers. Next, I asked everyone who had a caregiver reporting directly to them to stand. "You are caregivers because you assist those who deliver care directly to patients," I pointed out. Then, I asked those who made decisions that could affect the way care is delivered to stand, because they were thus caregivers as well. A few more leaders in Finance and Operations got to their feet.

At this point, most of the leaders who remained seated were in charge of nonclinical departments. I said, "Well, what about Environmental Services? Your work prevents infections. It is directly responsible for keeping staff, physicians, and patients safe. Food and Nutrition is responsible for ensuring that each patient receives the correct meals. If a cardiac or diabetic patient receives the wrong food—or even if a patient has a food allergy—there will be negative patient outcomes. If someone in Registration inserts an incorrect date of birth or the wrong name, that could affect the care that's given."

Heads began to nod. I continued by reminding these leaders of an incident that had recently occurred, and that stood out in everyone's memory.

Our hospital was located on land with a higher elevation than the surrounding region, and it was typically hit by lightning 10 to

12 times per year. After one storm, an alarm sounded because a lightning arrestor had been destroyed after appropriately sacrificing itself to arrest the bolt of lightning. To make the necessary repairs, we would need to shut off the electricity for several hours in one wing of the hospital, which included the operating rooms (ORs). This presented a significant challenge because our hospital was a trauma center.

We decided to conduct the repair in the middle of the night, when emergency room (ER) traffic is at its lowest. Operational teams worked with emergency medical services (EMS) to divert patients to other hospitals, minimizing the chance that any patient who entered the ER during the repair would urgently need to be transferred to the OR. Meanwhile, Plant Operations had to communicate continuously with hospital leadership to coordinate the timing of the repair and work quickly to ensure that our ORs would be available again as soon as possible. I finished the story by pointing out that it was an example of how the Plant Operations team were caregivers.

At the end of the meeting I asked everyone, especially the leaders who had remained seated, to think about how they and their departments affected care. I encouraged them to contact one of the senior leaders if they had difficulty making the connection, and I posted my own mobile phone number in case anyone wanted to speak with me directly.

Over time, we shifted to calling everyone at the hospital *caregivers* (instead of *employees*) to emphasize that we all contributed to the care that was given. Yes, even people who did not interact directly with patients, like inventory control techs and financial analysts, were called caregivers. (From this point forward, I will often use the term *caregiver* instead of *employee* to refer to anyone in a healthcare organization, whether they are clinical or nonclinical.)

The point? When employees shift the way they see themselves and the way they see patients, outcomes and metrics improve. Seeing themselves as caregivers to loved ones helped our hospital's employees find purpose in coming to work each day. Their engagement increased, they put in more discretionary effort, turnover was reduced, and other key performance metrics such as clinical outcomes and customer satisfaction improved.

Keep Leaders Connected to the Frontline Purpose

It's easy for leaders to become so focused on administrative tasks, problem-solving, and planning for the future that they lose sight of what their frontline workers experience, what the organization's purpose looks like on the ground, and how they themselves are connected to the patients through their purpose. When I was CEO, I intentionally spent one day a week treating patients in the Emergency Department as a physician. Working clinically kept me focused on our hospital's purpose: delivering care and changing lives.

I eventually asked my whole executive team to spend one day every other week working with the front lines in the hospital. As you might imagine, there was some pushback. The chief nursing officer (CNO) said, "It's been years since I've put in an IV." I said, "You could help change a bedpan or check a patient's blood pressure." The chief financial officer (CFO) said, "I don't have any medical skills, and I've never touched a patient!" Since the CFO was a big guy, I suggested that he could pitch in by transporting patients.

Eventually, we found a frontline role for each leader. As the weeks rolled by, I heard fewer and fewer complaints. My executive team eventually told me that seeing how their decisions affected employees and patients reconnected them to the organization's purpose. We also discovered that this effort resulted in stronger relationships between the executives and the caregivers (clinical and nonclinical), which contributed to breaking down the power gradient and allowed leaders to receive tremendous feedback and suggestions from the front lines.

Hire for Culture First and Skills Second

The executive team decided to focus on culture from day one. One major change we made was to hire new employees who were excellent cultural fits—not necessarily applicants who had all the right skills. We knew we could teach new recruits how to give a breathing treatment or how to place an IV, but we couldn't forcibly instill in them qualities like work ethic, compassion, humility, teamwork, and empathy. In other words, it was important to hire people who wanted to serve a greater purpose, not *just* collect a paycheck. We also wanted to ensure that all new hires' purpose was in alignment with that of the organization, the department, and their specific role.

Think Big: Shift Your Organization's Purpose to an Even Higher Level

Once you get everyone thinking about their purpose in the normal course of work, you have a foundation in place for making the next big shift. Remember, at Hospital X our purpose was "to change the lives of others." After ensuring that everyone understood the important work they were doing with patients, we were able to broaden the scope of our mission. Now, rather than seeing ourselves as a siloed business dedicated solely to delivering healthcare, we began to broaden our purpose to include responsibility to the community. (Remember, this was one reason we used the broad term *others* in our purpose statement instead of specifying that we would only change the lives of *patients*.)

For example, Hospital X became part of a community program that allowed us to enroll 12 special needs students in a yearlong paid training course. Each day, these students were given simple tasks such as cleaning windows or floors, delivering food, or transporting equipment. Yes, these students learned skills that would help them find work later on, and they earned a paycheck. But perhaps the most valuable thing they gained from the program was a greater sense of purpose for themselves. Most had never been part of any sort of team (whether a sports team, an academic project team, or an employment-related team) and had never seen how their efforts could contribute to a greater good.

Our hospital hired several of these special needs students each year after they completed the training program, but we gained much more than new caregivers. Our existing team found a new way to fulfill their purpose: teaching, helping, and mentoring these students. The students' enthusiastic, excited attitudes infused our whole organization with even more positivity. In addition, our patients and the surrounding community appreciated our training efforts and increasingly viewed the hospital as a community partner and essential asset that they wanted to support.

Another program to consider is Volunteer Days, which encourages caregivers to periodically spend a day volunteering at a location of their choice in the community, with pay from the organization. Whether employees walk dogs at an animal rescue, serve meals at a soup kitchen, or tutor at-risk children, they are making a positive impact outside of their usual roles. For obvious reasons, the Volunteer Days program is a win for the community. It is also a win for all caregivers because it shows them that their employer values what *they* value. Finally, it is a win for the organization because it increases visibility and strengthens relationships with the community.

Understand the Purpose Progression

What I came to realize is that when you commit to purpose, a natural progression is set in motion. When you recognize your own purpose, you change the way you see yourself. Next, you begin to see other people's purposes and shift the way you think of them. Then as you treat them differently, other people change the way they see themselves. Finally, the whole organization realizes that it's not an "island." It has the power to positively influence the whole community.

Purpose creates a ripple effect. When you decide to put it at the center of your work and your life, its positive effects spread outward like the waves from a pebble dropped in a pond. That's the beauty of purpose: As it expands, it improves the lives of everyone it touches. In addition, the organization grows, clinical outcomes improve, and the financial margin increases.

The Results You Want Will Follow

As we had hoped, our hospital's focus on purpose improved outcomes. We eventually earned top ratings in patient safety, patient satisfaction, caregiver engagement, and labor productivity. We even won a few prestigious awards regionally and nationally. It was an exciting time and one that I am truly grateful to have been a part of.

As these results started to roll in, our culture began to shift too. Because they were driven by a sense of purpose, employees took more personal pride in their work. Our turnover rate dropped (eventually becoming one of the lowest in the region), our unplanned absentee numbers went down, our caregiver engagement scores went up, and discretionary effort increased. Employees consistently went the extra mile because they understood that their purpose was to be a caregiver to someone else's loved ones. Ultimately, this mindset shift enabled them to become "owners" instead of "renters" within the healthcare system.

I'd be remiss not to mention burnout here. Back in 2010 when Hospital X was making its turnaround, there wasn't nearly as much attention paid to employees' mental and emotional health as there is now. But I am convinced that if we had tracked such metrics back then we would have found that as purpose went up, burnout rates went down.

As we'll discuss in chapter 12, there's a distinct correlation between burnout and loss of purpose. It's pretty well accepted that the more connected to mission and purpose people feel, the less likely they are to burn out—and the more likely they are to be engaged, energized, and passionate about their jobs.

Isn't this how it should be? If people spend half of their waking hours during the work week at their jobs, don't they deserve to feel pride and purpose? As I alluded to earlier, helping people experience those good feelings is a lot more than the right thing to do. It's also the *profitable* thing to do. It absolutely gets them energized and focused on doing the things that, over time, lead to superb performance—any way you measure it.

There is no doubt in my mind that the ability to help people find and live their sense of purpose is not a soft skill at all. It is a hard business skill and one that every leader needs to develop. In the case of Hospital X, we went from losing over $10 million a year to making more than $50 million a year only five years later.

That's my "purpose" story. When my mother sat my brother and me down for that "special talk," she had no idea that she was dropping such an important pebble into the pond of my life. The ripples of her words are still expanding and touching the lives of many others to this day.

The good news is that you and your organization have a lot to gain from the purpose journey too. In the next section I'm going to sketch out some practical tips that will help you and your organization achieve your goals.

EMBARKING ON THE PURPOSE JOURNEY: HOW TO GET STARTED

Purpose is a buzzword that goes hand in hand with words like *mission*, *vision*, and *values*. Yet it's no empty cliché. We keep circling back to it because it works. We know it's a fundamental part of human psychology and driver of hard results, but what most of us don't know is *how* to create it. If we do know how, then it often feels like such a challenge that we find every reason in the book not to do it.

I understand this. Healthcare leaders are pulled in many different directions. We have so much to do, decide, and oversee—all in a rapidly evolving landscape. It isn't an easy job. But the good news is that once you get serious about connecting yourself and your team to purpose, and start putting in the work, you'll usually find the process rewarding and energizing.

At Hospital X, we got really intentional and granular. I believe this is why we ultimately succeeded. We found practical ways to infuse purpose into our leadership and culture—ways that really moved the needle. You can do the same. To follow are some tips and tactics you can put into practice at your own organization.

Create Your Organizational Purpose Statement

What is the purpose of your organization? Don't assume people know. Many have never even considered it. This exercise is perhaps even more important than identifying your organization's mission or vision, because purpose is the force that gives meaning to the daily ritual of getting out of bed and going into work.

Your organization's purpose should be stated as simply and plainly as possible. Remember, purpose is what fuels engagement, retention, clinical outcomes, and more—so this is not the time to rely on fancy-sounding buzzwords. It is the time to be very clear and succinct. For example, recall that Hospital X's purpose was "to change the lives of others." Another healthcare organization I worked for chose "to advance healing and reduce suffering."

For an academic healthcare system, a purpose statement might include phrases like "educating the next generation" or "revolutionizing the science of medicine," in reference to the system's educational and research missions, respectively. If the academic healthcare system has a strong partnership with a university, its leaders might even consider working with the university's leadership to align and unify the two organizations' purposes through similar language.

How do you go about identifying your organization's purpose?

- First, include all stakeholders from the beginning. You want everyone in the organization to be connected to its purpose. Ask for input from all departments and levels up front. When an organization's purpose is "handed down from on high," so to speak, the power gradient is only reinforced and employees are less likely to engage with it.

  If the purpose statement is for an entire organization, then the stakeholders range from the board of directors to frontline caregivers to the community being served. If the purpose statement is for a department or division within an organization, the stakeholders include the leadership team of the organization, caregivers and leaders from within the department, representatives from other departments that are frequently collaborated with, and patients.

- Once you have gathered a focus group of stakeholders, explain what a purpose is and why the organization is developing a purpose statement. You might say something like "Purpose is the reason why the organization exists. If the organization were to die, its purpose would be the one-phrase eulogy you would want it to be remembered by. If mission is *what* the organization does, vision is *where* the organization wants to go, and values are *how* the organization will behave to get there, then purpose is *why* the organization exists." (Likewise, an individual's personal purpose statement describes why they exist and what drives them to wake up each morning—we'll get to that later!)

- To zero in on your organization's purpose, discuss questions like *Why do we open our doors every day? What do we hope to achieve by coming to work? How does our work have a positive impact?*

- As the purpose statement is being refined, ask yourself and your focus groups if it is what you would like to see featured in a newspaper article describing your hospital, or on a community pamphlet describing your department. Make sure the purpose statement accurately describes your "why" and that it is succinct and easy to understand.

Keep People Connected to Your Purpose, Now and Long-Term

Once your organizational or departmental purpose is written, you'll likely want to do an official rollout. Make a big splash. What you should absolutely *not* do is put the purpose statement on a shelf. It needs to be front and center at all times. People need to be consistently reminded *why* they do what they do. Here are some ideas for keeping purpose top-of-mind and, over time, hardwiring it into your culture:

- If your organization has a standardized meeting agenda template, put the purpose at the top to remind everyone of the purpose at each meeting.
- Place the purpose at the bottom of system-standardized PowerPoint slide formatting.
- Incorporate it into business cards and e-mail signatures.
- Some organizations have an employee of the week or month. How about a "caregiver with a purpose" award? Share the story behind the award with the entire organization, and perhaps even with the public as another connection to the community.
- Ask employees to regularly submit goals that further the organization's purpose.

- Recognize and celebrate milestone achievements that connect to your purpose.

Connect Your People to Their "Work" Purpose

One of a leader's responsibilities is to assist the leadership team and employees in finding their purpose and then aligning it with that of the organization and department. It is likely that many people have never identified their purpose. Others may have entered their careers with a purpose but have lost touch with it or changed paths over time.

As we did at Hospital X, start by determining how many of your leaders see themselves as caregivers. Help those who *don't* see themselves in this way to identify how their department affects the care that patients receive.

Perhaps each leader in the organization should perform the same "stand up" exercise with their respective departments. When they are done, each person in the organization should be able to articulate how their individual role affects care.

Measure Results

As mentioned earlier in this chapter, helping people understand the purpose of their work can lead to tremendous benefits for your organization:

- Reduced turnover
- Reduced burnout
- Reduced unplanned absentee numbers (in other words, fewer people calling out "sick" on sunny days), which results in fewer gaps in staffing
- Numerous shareable stories of caregivers (clinical and nonclinical) going above and beyond to provide excellent service

- Improved caregiver engagement scores
- Increased discretionary effort from caregivers, leading to improved outcomes

It's true that all these changes lead directly to better clinical outcomes and improved finances, but don't just assume the efforts are working. Put measurement tools in place and regularly track these metrics over time. Share the data with the organization. Metrics might be measured weekly (e.g., unplanned absentee numbers), monthly (e.g., turnover), or semiannually (e.g., caregiver engagement). After all, if purpose is essential for the organization's success, then it is essential to share information about how well you're "living" it.

If the results don't trend upward, then the efforts have not been successful in connecting people to purpose. It may be time to audit the processes, leader behaviors, and other aspects of the organization to see where the barriers lie.

ARTICULATE YOUR PERSONAL PURPOSE

Just as your organization or department has a driving purpose, so do you—but you may not have spent much time thinking about it. I recommend working on developing your own personal purpose simultaneously with developing your organization or department's purpose. (This isn't always the case, but often the two intertwine.)

When you articulate your purpose, you'll find that it becomes much easier to make decisions, navigate relationships, and prioritize your various responsibilities. In fact, I believe that achieving happiness, success, health, and overall well-being depends on knowing your own personal purpose. When someone isn't guided by purpose, it's too easy for them to stray from their values, beliefs, and goals. It's too easy to lose focus and momentum. (Remember the connection between burnout and lack of purpose?)

Purpose Is for the Dogs (and Us Too)

Finding and fulfilling your purpose (personally and professionally) is essential to happiness. To see the truth of this statement, just look at man's best friend.

Talk to any veterinarian and they'll tell you that most dog breeds have a purpose that *needs* to be filled. If you have a herding dog like a border collie or Australian shepherd, you need to make sure that your dog has an opportunity to herd (or, in our modern lives, has plenty of exercise and mental stimulation). If you have a hound that was bred to run at high speeds, your fenced-in backyard may not cut it—you better take lots of trips to the wide-open dog park. When I worked with the FBI and SWAT, I observed that the canines had a purpose each day. If a dog "retired" due to age or injury, it lived at home with the canine officer and their family but would often sink into a type of depression because it was no longer fulfilling its sense of purpose.

You get the point. Different dogs were bred to perform different functions. Even though many of those functions are now obsolete, our pets still need to tap into their purpose in order to lead happy and healthy lives. We humans are no different. In fact, studies demonstrate that the death rate increases disproportionately in the first few years after retirement, compared to the years prior to retirement and the later retirement years. It is hypothesized that the cause of this increased death rate is a loss of purpose, which had previously been fulfilled through individuals' professions.

I borrowed from Hospital X when articulating my personal purpose: "to change the lives of others." Looking back on my life, the desire to positively affect others has always been a driving force. (I suspect it's the same for many of us who chose to work in healthcare.) Fortunately, my career as a physician and healthcare executive fulfills my purpose for most of my waking hours.

When I'm not at work, I try to live out my purpose in a variety of ways, just as Hospital X eventually expanded its purpose into the community. For example, I keep small granola bars in my car in case I encounter a person experiencing homelessness. (Yes, my children occasionally raid my stash.) If I encounter a military servicemember at a restaurant, I pay for their meal.

Perhaps like me, you'll find that your personal and professional purpose are one and the same, or that they overlap significantly. Alternatively, you might conclude that your personal purpose is distinct from your professional purpose.

For instance, your personal purpose might be "to raise my children to be respectful individuals with high integrity and passion for whatever they choose to do in life." Your professional purpose might be "to improve the health of those with obesity-related medical complications by leading a bariatric medicine program." Hopefully, these purposes are compatible! If by chance your professional and personal purposes don't align, you may want to spend some time reflecting on your personal and professional purpose statements. Perhaps you can reshape your role at work to make it a better fit. If not, is there a different role that is in better alignment? Fulfilling your purpose is best for you *and* best for your organization—in any industry.

What if you're having trouble putting your finger on what, exactly, your purpose is? I recommend thinking about your eulogy. (Yes, really!) What do you hope people will say about you after you pass away? Are there accomplishments, skills, and talents you want to be remembered for? Or do you want to be remembered as a mentor, teacher, or friend? Are there certain values or characteristics that you hope others associate with you?

Ikigai: An Additional Path to Purpose

If you prefer a more granular, step-by-step process to help you find your purpose, I recommend Ikigai. Originally based on an Okinawan concept that means "a reason for being," Ikigai has been adapted into a visual that asks the following questions:

1. What does the world need?
2. What are you good at?
3. What do you love doing?
4. What can you be paid for?

At the intersection of these questions, you will find a purpose that helps others, utilizes your skill set, fulfills you, and supports you financially. I encourage you to learn more about Ikigai if you would like to supercharge your purpose. I prefer the step-by-step visual by Sebastien Aguilar, founder of Impactivated, shown in exhibit 1.1.

Once you pinpoint what type of legacy you want to leave, you'll be able to work backward and identify what your purpose should be *right now*. Take your time and give this exercise significant thought. When you believe you have articulated your personal purpose to the best of your ability, write it down and keep it close. Your purpose will serve as your life's true north, the direction in which you should always keep traveling through thick and thin. It will keep you from making missteps, and if you *do* veer off track, it will guide you back to your path. Generally, your own personal purpose will not change unless a major life event (the birth of a child, the death of a loved one, a significant illness, etc.) alters your perspective and goals.

Exhibit 1.1: Impact and Life Purpose with Ikigai

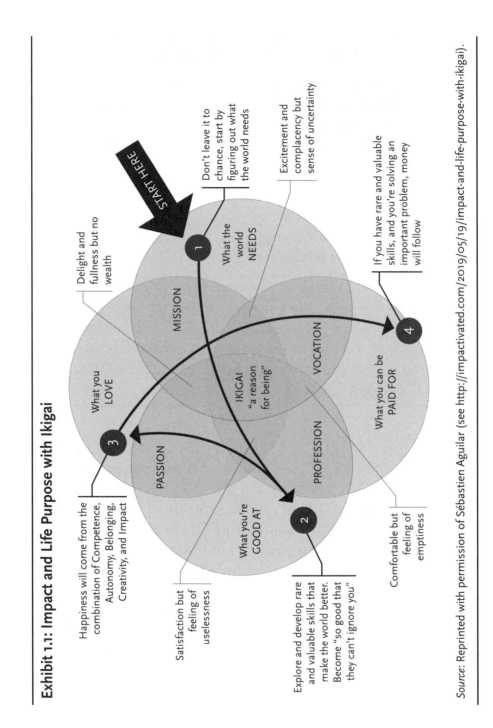

Delight and fullness but no wealth

Don't leave it to chance, start by figuring out what the world needs

Excitement and complacency but sense of uncertainty

START HERE

What the world NEEDS

MISSION

VOCATION

If you have rare and valuable skills, and you're solving an important problem, money will follow

What you LOVE

IKIGAI "a reason for being"

What you can be PAID FOR

PASSION

PROFESSION

Comfortable but feeling of emptiness

Happiness will come from the combination of Competence, Autonomy, Belonging, Creativity, and Impact

Satisfaction but feeling of uselessness

What you're GOOD AT

Explore and develop rare and valuable skills that make the world better. Become "so good that they can't ignore you"

Source: Reprinted with permission of Sébastien Aguilar (see http://impactivated.com/2019/05/19/impact-and-life-purpose-with-ikigai).

CHAPTER 2

Transitioning into Leadership: What Got You Here Will Not Get You There

THREE YEARS AFTER my residency training, I was selected to be the medical director of Hospital X's Emergency Department (ED). Because the hospital was still under construction and wasn't slated to be completed for an additional year, at that point I was the *only* physician associated with the organization. (In fact, when I was hired, Hospital X only had a total of five or six people on its payroll!) Thus, I was responsible for building the ED's culture as well as the physician culture of the entire hospital. That meant deciding what service lines to focus our efforts on, recruiting physicians, creating bylaws, crafting myriad policies and procedures, and so forth. It presented an ongoing challenge that I enjoyed, and I thought I was pretty good at the whole building-and-leading-a-team gig. As it turned out, I knew just enough to be dangerous.

One year after the hospital fully opened, the acting system CEO and dean of the college of medicine called me on a Friday night. He asked my wife and me to join him and his wife for dinner that Sunday. Of course, I accepted. I even thought I knew why we had been invited: *He's going to ask me to be the hospital's chief medical officer (CMO)*. After all, I had been unofficially filling most aspects of that role for two years.

What I was *not* expecting to hear as we finished our meal was "Kevin, I'm going to appoint you as the CEO of the hospital tomorrow morning at 7:00 a.m." To say I was shocked is an understatement! After driving home in a daze, I had about 10 sleepless hours to contemplate what I was getting into—then I was thrust into this new position of authority, ready or not!

During my first three months as CEO, I didn't have a ton of guidance and had to figure out many things on the fly. To familiarize myself with my new role, I read several excellent healthcare leadership books. (If you're curious, a few that stood out are *Leadership and Medicine* by Dr. Floyd Loop, *Straight A Leadership: Alignment, Action, Accountability* by Quint Studer, and *Wooden on Leadership: How to Create a Winning Organization* by John Wooden and Steve Jamison.) While the books helped a lot, I was still struggling. I worried that no amount of reading in my very limited free time could teach me everything a good CEO ought to know.

In truth, I was barely keeping my head above water. I gained significant weight, started taking medication for high blood pressure, and slept horribly. So much of my new job seemed beyond the scope of anything I had accomplished or experienced before. Everywhere I looked, there was a problem to be solved or a fire to be put out. I was expected to give direction and answer questions I felt unqualified to address. It seemed that many of my so-called subordinates knew more about my job than I did. And it quickly became apparent that the leadership tactics I had successfully utilized as a physician didn't always translate well to influencing my fellow organizational leaders. Similar to most healthcare workers, I am resilient with great tenacity. But I do remember thinking, *This problem may be my Goliath* (which is how many feel when they are put into a new position).

Since you're holding this book in your hands, you've probably guessed that my new job didn't lead to my downfall. It's true that my tenure as CEO of Hospital X was ultimately a success, but my journey from overwhelmed rookie to confident leader was extremely rocky. I learned a lot of things the hard way—and I am about to share many of those lessons with you so that you can learn from my struggles and revelations.

Your path to leadership probably looks different than mine. Perhaps you knew your promotion was coming in advance. You may have been actively working toward it for some time. Your previous experience might be nonclinical as opposed to clinical. You probably aren't skipping up multiple rungs in your organization's hierarchy, as I did—for better or worse.

Whatever the case may be, consider this chapter a mini-course on transitioning to a leadership role and between leadership roles. It covers what I wish someone had told me on my first day in the C-suite, and I believe it will help you navigate your first weeks and months in your new role. As you read further in this book, you'll find that I delve more deeply into many of the topics introduced here.

THE BIG TRANSITION: SHOULD I STAY OR SHOULD I GO?

In healthcare, it's common for clinicians to be promoted into leadership roles. For instance, a physician becomes a medical director, or a nurse leader becomes director of nursing. Nonclinical caregivers also move up the organizational hierarchy into roles like marketing manager or vice president of Human Resources. But no matter where you started or what your job title is now, we all have one thing in common: Transitioning into leadership is a major shift. Transitioning between leadership positions can also be a major shift.

You may be working in the same field or industry, but instead of "doing something" (whether that was clinical or nonclinical), you're now leading others so that *they* can do something. Instead of outcomes being based on what you can do yourself, they are based on what you can inspire others to do. Reactions to this transition vary:

- Some like the shift in roles and responsibilities and are good at it.

- Some like the shift but are *not* good at it.
- Some *think* they will like the shift but find out they don't.

Wherever you fall on this list—especially if it's in the second or third category—be assured that there is no shame in changing your mind, changing course, or going back to your old role. Being a great nurse or data analyst doesn't mean you'll be a great manager. Being a fantastic educator doesn't mean you can be the best residency director. Our success, happiness, and purpose are paramount and should be prioritized over following a certain career trajectory. When we are in a role that best allows us to serve patients, their families, and our colleagues, we are doing the most good for ourselves and our organizations.

Case in point: I once worked with a brilliant and well-respected physician. His vertical and horizontal colleagues regularly asked for his insights and advice—not just regarding clinical matters but also on subjects ranging from their career paths to their personal lives. Surely this physician was a natural leader! It was an easy decision to promote him into a formal leadership role.

However, it quickly became clear that although the physician was exceptional at giving advice and greatly enjoyed it, he didn't enjoy managing the performance and behaviors of others. Since he was now responsible for the outcomes of other caregivers, his engagement style evolved from mentor to micromanager. People slowly stopped seeking his advice, which was unfortunate because many of them could have benefited from his wisdom. Over time, the new leader lost a part of what he saw as his purpose: to be a mentor for others. He also lost much of the joy he once had when going to the hospital each morning. After significant consideration, he decided to step down from leadership and return to his previous role.

Just a few months later, this physician was once again a very happy and sought-after leader (just without a formal title). He later admitted that stepping down from leadership was a very difficult decision for him, in part because he mistakenly internalized this move as a failure. Fortunately, he came to see that it was the complete opposite. "Failure would have been refusing to take on the challenge of leadership in the first place," he reflected. "Failure would also have been continuing in a role that didn't lead to my success or happiness." He was confident that he made the right decision, and he was better able to serve others and himself without a formal leadership role.

This physician experienced a silver lining: Contrary to what many people might think, others didn't view him as a failure for stepping down. In fact, he earned their respect as they witnessed the courage it took to initiate this transition. The physician also developed greater wisdom that he was able to share with others through his mentorship.

A Few Words of Encouragement for Clinicians in Leadership

As a physician, I want to say a few words to those who come from a clinical background. The work of a clinician is mostly based on science and relies on proven evidence. The work of a leader is less centered on science and much more of an art (although the science of leadership and the body of evidence-based best practices is rapidly growing). At first, I can guarantee that you'll feel challenged in ways that you probably haven't since you were a student. You'll struggle with not knowing the answers. You'll feel unprepared for the challenges ahead (more on this later). But I also want to remind you that as a clinician, your background can be a big asset as you settle into your leadership role. Consider the following points:

Hospitals with greater clinical leadership have higher quality scores. It was noted several years ago that the top five healthcare systems in the United States were all run by

continued

continued from previous page

physicians. The Mayo Clinic, Johns Hopkins, Cleveland Clinic, Massachusetts General Hospital, and several other internationally acclaimed hospitals and healthcare systems are all physician-run. Articles have been written on the association between clinical leadership and quality. This is not to say that nonclinical leaders are not successful, as that is certainly not true; the point is that having a clinical background *does* provide a perspective that cannot be gained in any way other than having directly cared for patients.

Leaders who have directly treated patients have first-hand understanding of the nonbusiness side of the equation. This experience will influence their future decisions regarding priorities, strategies, budgeting, and much more. For instance, a clinical leader may have better insight into an initiative that won't have a large monetary return on investment in the short term but *will* increase quality—which will lead to better financial metrics in the long run.

Clinical leaders speak and understand frontline caregivers' language. Clinical leaders have had their hands and eyes on the inside of the clock and thus know how the clock is made and how it works—not just what time the clock displays. This is of great value in understanding what patients and clinical caregivers need from their leaders on a daily, and even hourly, basis. As we'll discuss throughout this book, it's essential for leaders to be familiar with frontline caregivers' opinions, observations, and suggestions so that we can effectively support and develop them. When clinical caregivers see us as "one of their own," many will feel more comfortable speaking up transparently with their thoughts and concerns.

This chapter was written for those who believe they are ready for the transition into leadership, who have recently accepted a leadership role, or who are in the midst of a transition into a different leadership role. My goal is to provide useful strategies that will facilitate greater success and enjoyment of the new leadership adventure. The majority of the information I'll share can be utilized by any leader in transition, regardless of their background.

LEADERSHIP IS A TEAM SPORT

When I first stepped into a leadership role, it didn't take me long to realize that I was playing in a completely different ball game. I think most new leaders, whether they come from a clinical or nonclinical background, feel similarly.

When someone, clinical or nonclinical, is working on the front lines, of course they are part of a team—but the "sport" they are playing resembles swimming or track. In swimming, for instance, all the swimmers are working together to win the meet, but the individual swimmer's primary focus is on personal success in her individual race. At the front lines of healthcare, we are concerned about the success of our unit or department, but the nurse's primary focus is his patient. A communication specialist's primary focus is her newsletter.

The minute we step into a leadership role, we begin to play a different sport that more closely resembles baseball or soccer than track or swimming. In this new sport, the team's success is paramount. There are no individual events. (In fact, putting our own success above that of the group can be more harmful than helpful.) We must rely on teammates to move the ball across the field and score goals, or to move our organization closer to its goals. Everyone wins together or loses together.

MOVING UP THE LADDER

My situation—being promoted to hospital CEO when I was a practicing physician and medical director of the ED—is unusual. As I shared at the beginning of this chapter, I was unprepared and struggled tremendously with this huge role shift. When someone first takes on a leadership role, it's much more likely that they will be moving from the front lines to become a manager. Then they will move from manager to director, and from director to vice president. Let's take a brief look at what each of these transitions entails, as they are all different and require very different skill sets. What made someone successful in one position will not necessarily make them successful in their next position, and what got us here will not necessarily get us there.

Front Lines to Manager

As I mentioned earlier, this transition is from "doing something" (e.g., treating patients, programming software, drafting a policy, analyzing data) to coaching others so that *they* can perform those tasks. Yes, there will be a learning curve regarding the new role and its responsibilities, but I've found that things like paperwork, scheduling, and strategizing aren't what tend to trip up most people.

One of your biggest priorities must be developing your people-management skills, which is more of an art than a science. If that phrase makes you nervous, you're not alone; the great majority of new leaders have received zero or minimal leadership training. Later in this chapter I'll share a few tips to help you navigate your relationships with the people you manage, and subsequent chapters delve even more deeply into various aspects of people management.

Manager to Director

At this level you're managing people who are managing other people. You need to give the managers who report to you your direct guidance and support but, in general, resist giving them specific direction. This may be different from your previous role as a manager, in which you were the decision-maker and were expected to give your team clear, concrete instructions. Remember that the managers you oversee need to grow by thinking on their own. Your job is to develop their leadership skills and empower them to take ownership. (We'll talk more about how to do that later in this book.) Another core part of this job is bringing your managers together to form a collaborative team that's moving in the same direction, supporting each other, and working toward broader organizational goals.

Director to Vice President

As a VP (and later, as a member of the C-suite), you're still managing people who are managing other people, but you acutely feel how far away you are from being an expert on many of the disciplines you oversee. It may have been years since you performed the tasks some of your downstream reports are responsible for, while others' jobs are completely outside your realm of experience (e.g., a VP of Nursing may have been a critical care nurse but never an obstetrical nurse, or a VP of Legal Services may have extensive experience in contracting but none in a compliance department). That's okay—your job as a VP is less about the skills you possess and more about your ability to think strategically and take a higher-level view of the organization's goals and priorities. Others (i.e., directors, managers, and other frontline leaders) are responsible for making sure that things get done. You're the one who needs to decide *what* gets done and *why*.

Do Successful Executives Need Recent Relevant Experience?

I once worked with a nurse who had been part of the human resources department for many years. This woman was a fantastic leader with an exceptional track record of developing others. She was committed to strengthening our organization's culture of service and always had the best interests of patients and caregivers (clinical and nonclinical) in mind. Because of her many achievements, she was asked to be the healthcare system's chief nursing executive.

Initially, this promotion was eyed with trepidation by many in the organization (including the nurse herself) because she had not worked in a clinical setting for over 20 years. However, her job was not to teach clinical care; it was to partner with other nursing leaders to create strategy, to develop and strengthen the culture within nursing, and to assist in prioritizing the efforts of nursing departments across the system. She was also expected to work with the system's executive team to drive the organization toward success and ensure that exceptional care was delivered to patients. In all of these areas, the nurse excelled—and she remains one of the most successful nursing executives beside whom I have been fortunate to work.

In the same vein, I have promoted an operational-minded pharmacist to be the executive over the operations of all ambulatory clinics and tapped a director of security to lead the staff productivity program. Both individuals were exceptionally successful and experienced tremendous professional growth.

TIPS TO MANAGE THE TRANSITION INTO LEADERSHIP

Whether someone is a new leader or assuming a new leadership role, it is often easy to rely on the strategies, actions, and philosophies that led them to success in their previous role. However, what made someone successful in the past will not necessarily make them successful in the future. It is always beneficial to go back to the basics of leadership when in transition. Especially when adjusting to a new role, it is easy to become overwhelmed, lose sight of the bigger picture, and move away from the fundamentals.

Don't Go at It Alone

You are far from the first person to move from clinical or nonclinical work to a leadership position, or to transition from one leadership role to another. Many others have walked in your shoes and have faced the challenges you are facing. Here are a few ways to learn from them:

- **Find a mentor.** Is there a trusted colleague who has been in a similar role for longer than you have? If you respect this person and would follow her yourself, ask her to mentor you through your leadership transition. It may help to assure your prospective mentor (who is undoubtedly as busy as you are) that this won't be a big demand on her time. Tell her that you'd like to have breakfast or lunch every few weeks so that you can talk about how things are going, hear her input, and ask any questions that may have come up. Since this mentor has been in your shoes in the fairly recent past, she'll have relevant advice about the challenges you're facing and the skills you need to develop.

One caveat: I don't recommend seeking out a mentor who has been promoted three or more levels above your new position, or someone who has not been in your role in the last 10 years. While these mentors' intentions may be great, their relevant experience is distant.

- **Mine your own past for lessons.** Consider bosses, teachers, and other supervisory figures with whom you've worked in the past. Make a list of those you most admired, and just as importantly, make a list of those who struggled with leadership. Figure out *why* you felt that way about each. What qualities would you like to emulate? Whose leadership style was particularly inspiring? What would you like to avoid with your own team? What have your experiences with rewards and recognition been like, and which tactics were most effective? What have past leaders done to inspire your trust and hard work, or to break down trust and demotivate their teams? What did they do that made you feel energized and happy versus stressed and unhappy?

  Your answers to questions like these can help you set out on your management journey with intention instead of reactivity. Adapt the "dos" to your own role and situation. Keep the "don'ts" top-of-mind too. They are valuable because they can keep you from making the same mistakes that compromised the leadership of others.

- **Educate yourself.** As I mentioned, leaders in healthcare are often thrust into their roles with little to no leadership training. If you find yourself in this position, seek out as much education as you can. I know this it is easier said than done because you're beyond busy and may not have much mental bandwidth left at the end of the day. But every hour you spend strengthening your leadership skills will make your job more manageable. Here are some avenues to explore:

- **Books and scholarly articles:** There is a growing body of research and literature about leadership. Don't focus only on healthcare; learn what you can from other industries and adapt that information to your organization's needs. You can also zero in on specific topics such as emotional intelligence, managing behavior, strategy, or burnout. Throughout this book, I'll share some resources that I have found to be particularly helpful.

- **ACHE (American College of Healthcare Executives) and AAPL (American Association for Physician Leaders):** ACHE and AAPL both offer online and in-person leadership courses. They also publish books, journals, and newsletters focusing on different aspects of healthcare leadership. And don't forget the value of networking at conferences and during online events. If you haven't been successful in finding a mentor or getting an answer to a particular question within your own organization, chances are good that *someone* in the wider world of healthcare leadership can help.

- **Online resources:** On social media you'll find experts and organizations to follow, leadership development groups, bite-sized pieces of wisdom, and links to more in-depth resources. (On LinkedIn, I recommend following "Leadership First" and "Let Us Lead." LinkedIn also offers leadership courses.) There are also a plethora of quality podcasts and videos focused on leadership. Personally, I have found content from Simon Sinek and Quint Studer to be eye-opening, practical, and actionable.

Be Ready for Established Relationships to Change

If you have been vertically promoted within your own department, one of the most challenging things you'll have to adjust to is the way your relationship with coworkers changes. Those who were your trusted teammates, and even your good friends, are now reporting to you.

You'll probably find that some of them treat you more formally than before and perhaps no longer include you in social activities like break room chats or after-work happy hour. Other team members might not change the way they interact with you, and it will be up to you to make them understand you are now in a position of authority. Unfortunately, you'll probably have to deal with hurt feelings and frustration when your former peers realize their friendship with you does *not* entitle them to special privileges.

When your professional relationships change after a promotion, it can feel like a loss—but it's a necessary one. If you don't separate good friendship from good leadership, you probably won't be a leader for long. As your professional relationships evolve, approach your team with as much patience and humility as possible. Remember that they are learning how to navigate a new normal with a new manager and are trying to adjust to the change in relationship, just as you are. I suggest having a conversation, whether it's with an individual or the whole team, to discuss the changes your new role will spark. It's a good idea to bring this issue into the open, as it will certainly cross the minds of your colleagues at some point. They'll appreciate the reassurance and clarification only you can offer.

At one point in my career, I was promoted to a position that made me the hierarchical equal of my previous boss. Knowing that this promotion had the potential to cause confusion, frustration, and awkwardness, I asked my former boss to have dinner with me so we could talk through our updated expectations of one another. The conversation was not the most comfortable, but I am certain it helped us avoid much greater discomfort over the longer term, and also made us both more successful moving forward.

Expect Emotional Challenges

Many people will quickly go from feeling excitement about a new promotion to experiencing anxiety, stress, and perhaps a fear of failure. This emotional roller coaster isn't surprising. Your performance in your previous role was outstanding, which is one of the reasons you were promoted. But now you may be feeling like a minor league all-star playing in a major league division. You were used to being the person others came to for advice and instructions; now you're the one who has all the questions. You're back to being a beginner, and for the first time in a while, you're comparing yourself unfavorably to your peers.

I once worked with a fantastic charge nurse who was promoted to stroke director of a hospital. She'd always earned stellar reviews in her previous role and was very upset when her first review as stroke director was mediocre. She was visibly stressed and questioned whether she was in the right role. "Do I not have the skills needed to serve my team and our patients?" she asked. "They deserve a fantastic stroke director, not someone who is barely earning average ratings."

I knew what this nurse leader was likely feeling. Her emotional distress was probably affecting her confidence, making her second-guess herself, causing her to lose sleep at night, and even affecting her relationships outside of work. Along with the rest of my leadership team, I assured her that her performance was just as we expected and that we had zero regrets about placing her in this important position. "You have gone from knowing everything about your job to knowing only 10 to 20 percent," I said. "You have a lot to learn. No one is great at leadership right out of the gate." Even with this reassurance, it took our new stroke director several months to gain the confidence she needed to truly thrive in her new role—but I'm pleased to report that thrive she did. She's now every bit as much of an all-star stroke director as she was an all-star charge nurse.

When you're feeling discouraged or stressed, it may help to remind yourself that those who chose you for your new role made that decision because they believe you have what it takes to do the job—not because they believe you already know everything about the job. The people who put you in this role also want you to do well and have a vested interest in your success, so lean on them for advice. Ask a *lot* of questions, and don't be afraid to say that you don't know the answers. Humility will get you much farther than pride and bravado!

Don't Bow Out Too Soon

I'll say it once more: Even if you go on to become an outstanding leader, the transition to this role *is* going to be hard at first. In fact, you can probably expect things to get worse before they get better. That's because you're moving from unconscious incompetence (where you don't know what you don't know) to conscious incompetence (where you're painfully aware of everything you don't know). In my experience, most new leaders are tempted to leave their new roles when the full weight of conscious incompetence hits them. However, knowing that this learning process and the challenge of conscious incompetence is normal, don't give up.

As an analogy, consider a marathon. If runners didn't know to expect feelings of exhaustion, negativity, and the urge to slow down (or stop) around mile 20, many would quit at this point. But knowing what to expect helps marathoners manage their expectations and keep running those last six or so miles.* Similarly, knowing what to expect as a new leader can reassure you and prepare you for the anxiety and uncertainty you'll feel. Hence why I wrote this chapter—to help you stay the course!

*At least that's what I've been told. I only run only when I'm being chased, and nobody has chased me for 26.2 miles yet!

Understand the Importance of Emotional Intelligence (EQ)—and Commit to Boosting Yours if Necessary

When caregivers are starting their careers, most employers they encounter focus their hiring decisions based on applicants' IQ and ability. This is especially true in healthcare, where knowledge and technical skill are paramount in providing the best care. However, as a caregiver moves into leadership and progresses into higher positions of authority, EQ slowly becomes more important. It's not that healthcare organizations don't expect their leaders to have high IQs—far from it. But if leaders don't also possess skills like self-awareness, empathy, and the ability to connect with others, they will struggle to manage their own emotions and to motivate their team. I've heard it said that at all levels, IQ gets you the job and EQ loses you the job. I agree.

The good news is that nobody is stuck with their current EQ. Unlike IQ, which we are born with, EQ can be developed. Even if we consider ourselves to be emotionally intelligent people, there is always room for improvement. Many of the strategies I'll share in this book involve person-to-person connection with peers and caregivers, and they depend on EQ to be effective. It can be a positively reinforced cycle: The more you use EQ to connect with others, the more robust your EQ becomes.

There is a growing body of literature on EQ: what it is, how it affects leadership success, and how to increase it. If you'd like a brief but very effective introduction to EQ, I recommend *Emotional Intelligence 2.0* by Travis Bradberry and Jean Greaves.

Refuse to Be a Mushroom

We can all probably think of a leader or management team that treats their employees like mushrooms: They keep their people in the dark and feed them BS. (Perhaps this describes a former leader on the "do not emulate" list I encouraged you to create earlier in this chapter.) Of course, treating others like mushrooms is the opposite of what great leaders do.

The inverse is also true. As someone moves up the leadership ladder, they may hear some BS from the ones they lead—or, as is more often the case, a lot of silence. There are a number of reasons we might find ourselves being treated like a portobello:

- Our team doesn't feel that we are connected to them or that we care about them, so they don't trust us with their concerns.
- The power gradient makes caregivers reluctant to approach us and give us their honest feedback.
- We isolate ourselves in our offices and rarely spend time with caregivers on the front lines.
- We haven't provided employees with clear, timely, and actionable direction and feedback—which means that they, in turn, don't know what information we need to support them.
- Our team is afraid of the consequences if they tell us something we don't want to hear. (Maybe we have reacted poorly to bad news in the past?)
- We micromanage and rush to fix problems ourselves instead of trusting and empowering people to find their own solutions. (This leadership style quickly becomes suffocating.)
- We are focused only on metrics, which sends a message to others that nonmeasurable areas (like culture) are of less significance. This can have negative downstream effects. For instance, if employees perceive that we don't prioritize culture, they will hesitate to raise behavioral concerns or point out areas with a large power gradient.

I'll address all these leadership stumbling blocks in detail throughout this book. For now, know that you can avoid being left in the dark through good communication, being accessible, putting caregivers and their needs first, and humbly admitting when you are wrong. It all boils down to treating caregivers the way you would like to be treated by your own leaders—and refusing to allow dysfunctional dynamics to persist within your team.

Learn to Find Gratification in New Places

Finding gratification is important for everyone transitioning into a leadership role, but this shift is often especially challenging for clinicians of all disciplines. That's because clinicians are used to getting frequent and immediate gratification from external sources. Whether you're a physician, RN, respiratory therapist, or other type of practitioner, you interact with patients every day. Often, they'll thank you directly: "I really appreciate you taking the time to answer my questions." "I feel so much better after starting my new medication." "You've put my mind at ease about my upcoming procedure." Even when patients can't or don't verbalize their appreciation, you can see the positive impact your work is having on their lives many times per day, and often in real time. Nonclinical caregivers tell me that they've had similar experiences as they serve patients and fellow caregivers from different departments.

However, when someone becomes a leader, that changes. For example, a former caregiver is no longer directly caring for patients, and thus his gratification from external sources decreases dramatically. Additionally, the front line might not connect streamlined new processes to the leader's efforts. It may take weeks or months for metrics to rise or for new equipment to be purchased and installed. In other words, the gratification you receive changes from frequent and external to infrequent and internal.

This lack of immediate and frequent external gratification is often compounded by the fact that leaders naturally focus on what's wrong. We're trained to look for things that are broken or that need to improve. We are often hyper-focused on solving problems and avoiding future obstacles. This damage-control mindset is often necessary for leadership success, but it can keep us from recognizing the many things that we and our teams are doing right.

In your new role, you'll need to rely on internal gratification to stay motivated and fulfilled. Remind yourself that you put in great effort that resulted in great improvements. Train yourself to look for the bright spots. Did you run an efficient, productive meeting? Did you secure the funding to upgrade your department's imaging equipment? Is your feedback helping a caregiver grow and develop? Did you spend time listening to your team's concerns and challenges? Sometimes you may need to be proactive and reach out for feedback. Ask your superiors, peers, and direct reports, "How was that performance review?" "What do you think about the direction our unit is going?" "What should I change?" "What is going well?"

Everyone wants to make a difference. Nobody wants their time and effort to *not* have a positive effect. We all need to find gratification, fulfillment, and recognition in various dimensions of our lives—both personal and professional. When this does not happen, our joy decreases and our burnout increases. For the sake of your personal health *and* so that you can fulfill your potential as a leader, strive to be aware of how full your "gratification account" is so that you can address any deficits before burnout hits.

Always Remember That You Are "Onstage"

When I was an ED physician, despite the stressful nature of the job, I had a lot of fun. I genuinely enjoyed the company of my coworkers. We would laugh, tell jokes, talk about our lives outside the hospital, and shoot the breeze with one another when we were not caring for patients. Nurses and techs would sign up to work on my shift because we had so much fun.

When I became medical director of the ED, things began to change. Cognizant that my leadership role made me more visible throughout the organization, I knew I had to mind my p's and q's.

I stopped cracking so many jokes and sharing so many personal stories. I noticed that my colleagues weren't making as much of an effort to work on my shift.

When I became CEO of the hospital, I spent more time than ever thinking about my image: *What kind of example am I setting? Is this something people should see their boss doing? Is it appropriate to joke this way with a subordinate?* This new self-consciousness didn't evaporate outside of work hours, either. More than once I recognized a caregiver when I was out in public and did a quick assessment to make sure that my appearance and behavior were appropriate.

I also noticed that as CEO, I almost always had to take the initiative to seek out my former teammates. I don't believe my company was *that* unpleasant; rather, the perceived power gradient that came with my new position made people reluctant to approach me. It's also true that while I strove to be friendly and humble, I just wasn't "fun" in the way I had been before becoming a leader.

Most leaders experience something similar. A successful leader needs to understand that they are always "onstage." They are constantly being watched and emulated. Their team, peers, and even their own leaders are always taking note of how they handle various situations, their emotional reactions, and how they treat others. For instance, if we tend to become frazzled and grouchy when we have a lot on our plates, that will negatively affect our image. Our irritability might also rub off on other people, adversely affecting their own interactions.

Leaders are onstage even when they're not at work. If we are rude to a cashier, cut someone off in traffic, or have one drink too many at a bar, caregivers from our organizations might notice, remember, and share the story. Sadly, some people are always looking for ways to discredit others and will use any excuse to tarnish your image—and social media makes it *very* easy for them to do maximum damage. It's not always fair, but that's the reality. While everyone in the organization represents the organization, a leader's behavior is an especially strong endorsement (or contradiction) of their organization's values and priorities.

Know That Your Decisions Won't Always Be Popular

When I first became a chief resident during my residency, the residency director told me he would be asking me to make a lot of decisions. "I *could* make these decisions on my own, but you won't grow as a leader if I tell you what to do," he explained. "I'll help and support you whenever you need, but you're in charge." Then the residency director told me something about decision-making that has stuck with me ever since. "When you make a decision and everyone is upset, you probably made the wrong choice. When you make a decision and everyone is happy, there's a good chance you still made the wrong choice. But if 90 percent are happy or ambivalent, and 10 percent are upset, you're probably in the right ballpark."

In the years since, I've found that the residency director's observation was accurate. Whether you're updating a policy, changing behavioral expectations, buying new equipment, or adjusting the timing of a shift change, you'll never make everyone happy. Some of the people in that 10 percent just don't like change, and any adjustment to the status quo is upsetting to them. Others might be pushing back to test your authority, especially if you're a new leader. Some may genuinely think you're moving in the wrong direction and have a detailed list of reasons why. Make sure to genuinely listen to their thoughts and concerns.

I remember leading a meeting of my organization's physician leaders. I was excited because I had called the meeting to share some excellent news . . . or so I thought. "Our organization is starting a financial incentive plan," I announced. "You'll all be eligible to earn a bonus based on the quality of certain patient outcomes. The higher the quality level, the higher the bonus." Even then, one of the physicians complained because he thought it was insulting to receive additional compensation based on advancement of clinical outcomes.

Despite opposition, don't fall into the trap of delaying a decision or failing to move forward because you don't want to upset others.

Just make sure that you're communicating with your team in a clear, timely manner. Listen to their concerns, explain why the decision was made, and discuss why the other options weren't chosen. As with so many facets of leadership, if you give people the *why*, you're much more likely to earn their respect and cooperation.

What Happens If You Try to Please Everyone?

Since we've been discussing the many challenges you'll face as a new leader, I'd like to insert a little levity into this chapter. The following parable should make you smile—and it also makes an important point about trying to please everyone with your decisions.

A man and his son were going on a long journey. They walked from town to town leading their donkey. In one town the people said, "Isn't that a perfectly healthy donkey? Why isn't someone riding it?" So the boy climbed onto the donkey, and the man and son continued down the road. In the next village, an old woman said, "What a selfish boy! Why is he riding the donkey? He should have more respect for his father." So the boy climbed down and let his father ride. But soon, a group of men in the marketplace said, "Why is this man making the boy with the smaller legs walk? He has to take two steps for every one his father would take." So the man reached down and pulled his son onto the donkey with him. Before long, people were jeering, "You are lazy and cruel! What a heavy burden this donkey has to carry! It will collapse in the heat. You should be ashamed."

At their wits' end, the man and his son decided that the only option left was to carry the donkey. At the next town no one criticized them, but they did receive plenty of strange

continued

continued from previous page

looks as they carried the donkey. As they exited the town, they came upon a bridge. When they got to the middle of the bridge, it began to sway. They lost their balance and dropped the donkey, which fell to its death. Here's the moral of the story: If you try to please everyone, you may as well kiss your ass goodbye!

Be Intentional About When You Are "On" and "Off"

People working on the front lines as clinical or nonclinical caregivers usually have specific hours during which they are expected to be at work. Sure, from time to time they may need to stay after their shift to finish a task, or bring some paperwork home. Clinical caregivers may be on call once in a while. But by and large, work and personal time are separate. That changes when someone become a leader.

In some senses, leaders are always working. Thoughts about work are always in the back of their mind and may intrude on personal time. Their to-do lists are never-ending, and there's a temptation to spend evenings and days off chipping away at the most urgent projects. Most leaders are always on call (albeit unofficially) because an emergency issue requiring their immediate attention might arise in their unit, shift, or department. For all of these reasons, it's a challenge to turn off the leadership part of the brain.

However, we leaders *must* learn to focus our minds away from work or we will suffer the consequences. As I shared at the beginning of this chapter, during my first few months as CEO of Hospital X, I gained weight, lost sleep, and began taking blood pressure medication. My relationships with family and friends suffered. And the worst part is, much of the time I spent worrying about work wasn't even productive. I wasn't making progress on solving problems or learning a skill that would help me lead—I was just ruminating on how I'd messed up and stressing about what *might* go wrong in the future.

Had I not learned to turn off my thinking about the job (well, the unhelpful thoughts, anyway), I have no doubt that my health, marriage, and career would have suffered irreparable damage. In addition, I certainly wasn't fulfilling my leadership potential because all of that anxious rumination was causing mental fatigue.

Your transition into leadership or between different leadership positions doesn't have to eat you alive the way my first few months of leadership did. There are tactics that can help you hit the "off" switch, avoid burnout, and maintain balance in your personal life. I'll share a lot of them in the next section, which focuses on prioritization, and you'll glean more throughout the rest of the book.

For now, I encourage you to think of leadership as an essay. First, think back to your algebra homework. You solve the equations, and you're done for the day. Now contrast those math problems with writing an essay. Even after you achieve the word count, you can edit endlessly. You never reach a clear finish line, because—in theory—the essay can always be polished a little bit more. But at some point, you need to declare that you're done and turn in the assignment.

Leadership is the same. You'll never check everything off your to-do list. You'll never achieve perfect metrics. There will always be issues to deal with, improvements to make, and caregivers to counsel. The best thing you can do for yourself, your health, and your relationships is to become confident in saying, "This is a good essay. I've put forth my best effort, and I'm turning it in now." As the saying goes, the enemy of greatness is perfection.

Become a Pro at Prioritizing

When a frontline caregiver doesn't have time to complete a task during his shift, in many instances the following shift will handle it. After all, the blood test needs to be run. The medication needs to be administered. The equipment needs to be sanitized. The patient's call needs to be returned.

There usually isn't another person to whom you, as a leader, can hand off your responsibilities. There are a lot of decisions only you can make, conversations only you can have, and tasks only you can complete. And if you aren't careful, you can fall victim to analysis paralysis. You can't decide what to focus on, you spin your wheels, and nothing gets done. Meanwhile, your confidence in your own ability takes a big hit and your anxiety ratchets up several notches as deadlines loom closer.

That's why learning to prioritize is a must. Here are some tactics that have worked for me:

- **Keep a written (or digital) to-do list and look at it every day.** It's incredibly helpful to see at a glance everything that needs to happen. I recommend looking at your to-do list first thing each morning and right before leaving work. Add or remove items as necessary. Ask yourself if priorities have changed. Determine whether there is anything you can delegate, or anything that isn't necessary anymore.

   I also suggest asking your direct reports to keep a similar list. Have them share it with you regularly so you can stay abreast of what they're working on. This will also enable you to help them prioritize and ensure that they are working toward strategic goals.

- **Put each task in a parking lot.** Imagine that you have a "today" lot, a "this week" lot, and a "this month" lot. Sort each task into the appropriate lot and park it there until you can give it your complete focus. You might even draw these lots on a whiteboard that you update each day. Parking tasks in the appropriate spot sounds simple, and it is. However, it has tremendous value in helping you determine where to focus your efforts so that you can increase your success and reduce your stress.

- **Determine what's emergent and what's not.** Imagine a graph. The y-axis goes from "urgent" to "emergency."

The x-axis goes from "easy" to "hard." Every task falls somewhere on this graph (see exhibit 2.1).

Exhibit 2.1: Prioritizing Tasks

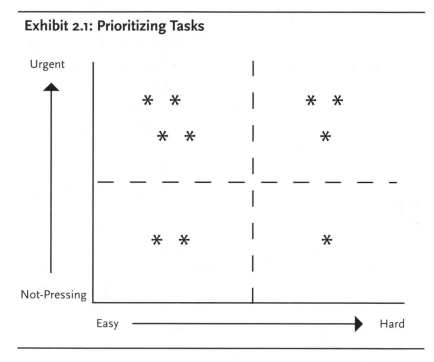

Many people tend to do the easy things first—often subconsciously. The problem is that easy items are not always as critical or do not add as much value as the difficult items. They keep leaders busy but do not accomplish much. I've heard this referred to as "confusing activity for progress." Instead, leaders need to focus on tasks that are emergencies or strategic. This requires a lot of intentionality: We have to categorize each task, decide which lot to park it in, *and* discipline ourselves to stick to the plan. But the payoff is big: We won't be left scrambling to complete a task at the last minute—or worse, be responsible for something that didn't get done.

• **Decide what *not* to do.** Sometimes a leader's most difficult decision isn't what to do, but what *not* to do.

Often, we are faced with several options or opportunities, all of which make sense—but we can't do all of them at once. So what are you *not* going to do? It may help to remind yourself that if you try to juggle too many balls, you'll drop them all. It's better to do fewer things well and make them sustainable, rather than stretch your attention and resources among too many tasks.

For example, imagine that you are considering three excellent strategic plans. They cost $100,000 each, but you only have a total of $150,000 to spend. Obviously, you'll need to identify two projects to put on the back burner— even though they have the potential to greatly improve your organization.

Here's a scenario that many leaders might find more challenging. Let's say that the root cause analysis of a patient injury determines there are five major processes that need to be revised to prevent similar incidents from reoccurring. The problem is that your organization doesn't have the resources to adequately address all five areas simultaneously. If you *do* tackle all five at once, the necessary changes will be slow to launch, and the pace of forward progress will be similarly sluggish. It is also likely that somewhere along the line a solution will be rushed, which could lead to continued patient injuries. Or perhaps the creation of a new process is effective in achieving its goal, but because time wasn't taken to hardwire it into operations or culture, it isn't sustainable and your organization's efforts need to be repeated at a later time.

However, if you determine that your organization's efforts will be focused on only two of the five processes, you'll be able to revise them much sooner. You'll also be able to spend more time and energy hardwiring those processes into your organization's operations and culture. Ultimately, this strategy enables you to make more sustainable progress toward achieving your goal: to reduce patient harm. Exhibit 2.2 shows an example of a spreadsheet used to help determine an optimal strategy.

Still, it's not an easy decision to make. I know that as a leader you want to do everything you possibly can, as quickly as you can, to improve performance—especially if the goal is to prevent another patient from being harmed. However, it truly is better to put focused effort toward solving fewer problems. The solutions will be reliable and sustainable, and you won't have to repeat your efforts in the future. Sometimes less is actually more.

- **Learn to delegate effectively using the three-column approach.** I learned about this strategy after reading a column by Quint Studer (2019) and have found it to be very useful. First, write down the actions and responsibilities associated with your job. Then draw three columns to the right of this list. Put a check in Column 1 beside every task only you can do. Column 2 is for tasks that could be passed on to others, as long as that person is trained. And Column 3 is for tasks that could be passed on right away (perhaps with minimal training or instruction).

  Column 1 is where the majority of your time and efforts should be concentrated. But to focus on Column 1 priorities, you must effectively manage Columns 2 and 3. Fortunately, Column 3 is relatively straightforward to handle: Commit to reassigning these tasks to others as soon as possible.

  Column 2 is trickier. When you look at these tasks, you're probably thinking, *While I'd like to hand this off to someone else, I don't have time to train them. It's easier just to handle it on my own.* Trust me, I get it. But if you invest a little time now, you'll thank yourself later—and so will the caregiver you're training.

  To start, choose just one Column 2 task, give it to a subordinate, and put a timeline on both the training and the task's completion. Remember that part of your job

Exhibit 2.2: Prioritization Spreadsheet

	1 week	2 weeks	3 weeks	4 weeks	5 weeks	6 weeks	7 weeks	8 weeks	9 weeks	10 weeks	11 weeks
All 5											
Change #1		Process Design					Process Implement				Process in Effect
Change #2											
Change #3											
Change #4											
Change #5											
2 at a Time											
Change #1											
Change #2											
Change #3											
Change #4											
Change #5											

Assumption: Each change takes 1 week of effort to design.

Each change takes 1 week to implement.

Rate of process failure of "All 5" is twice that of "2 at a Time."

Failure rate of "All 5" is 1 failure after every 10 weeks that a change is implemented.

Failure rate of "2 at a Time" is 1 failure after every 20 weeks that a change is implemented.

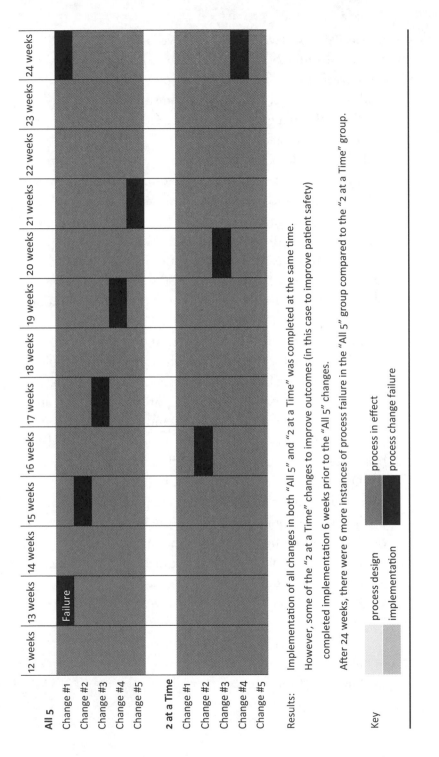

All 5

	12 weeks	13 weeks	14 weeks	15 weeks	16 weeks	17 weeks	18 weeks	19 weeks	20 weeks	21 weeks	22 weeks	23 weeks	24 weeks
Change #1													
Change #2		Failure											
Change #3													
Change #4													
Change #5													

2 at a Time

Change #1													
Change #2													
Change #3													
Change #4													
Change #5													

Results: Implementation of all changes in both "All 5" and "2 at a Time" was completed at the same time.

However, some of the "2 at a Time" changes to improve outcomes (in this case to improve patient safety) completed implementation 6 weeks prior to the "All 5" changes.

After 24 weeks, there were 6 more instances of process failure in the "All 5" group compared to the "2 at a Time" group.

Key   process design   process in effect

         implementation   process change failure

as a leader is to develop and grow your employees, and this is one of the best ways to do that. Plus, training your employees to a higher level of competency takes part of the load off your plate, so it's a win-win situation.

When I was a new leader, I worried that training subordinates to take on some of "my" tasks might make them feel like they were being dumped on—but I soon found that the opposite tended to be true. When delegation is framed correctly, most people see it as a form of flattery rather than as a source of resentment. Imagine that your boss approaches you and says, "I have several important projects that need to get done soon. I really need your help to complete one of these critical tasks because I don't have the time." You'd probably feel proud that you were trusted with this crucial task!

- **Stay on top of your inbox.** As I'm sure you're aware, e-mails can quickly become overwhelming. Before you know it, you have hundreds of messages in your inbox and can't tell at a glance which ones require action, which are associated with particular projects, and which are junk. When this happens it's all too easy to miss deadlines, drop balls, and waste time on low-payoff tasks.

  Developing an e-mail organization system doesn't have to be complicated, but it does require you to be disciplined. At regular intervals throughout the day, categorize your e-mails and file them in appropriate folders. For example, a system of folders might include:
  - Do now or today
  - Do later (*Make sure you assign a time frame to each of these e-mails. You can create subfolders for each work week; e.g., April 4–8, April 11–15, etc.*)
  - Delegate
  - File away for reference

If there are several active projects or goals, you can create these as subfolders under the project heading.

As you tackle the challenging days of early leadership, whether you are a first-time leader or an experienced leader transitioning into a new position, the most helpful thing to remember is that you don't need to know it all right out of the gate—nor are you expected to. I think a lot of new leaders throw in the towel not because they don't have the potential to succeed in their new role, but because they simply had no idea what to expect, falsely believe that they are failing, and aren't sure what development tools are available to them. But when you know what to expect and where to turn for help, you can summon up the gumption to keep moving onward and upward.

REFERENCE

Studer, Q. 2019. "Why We Hesitate to Delegate (and Why We Need to Overcome That)." *Pensacola News Journal*. Published June 15. https://www.pnj.com/story/money/business/2019/06/15/why-we-hesitate-delegate-and-why-we-need-overcome-tendency/1427336001/.

CHAPTER 3

Pursuing the Right Priorities

WHEN YOU THINK of quickly evolving industries, sectors like tech and energy probably come to mind. If healthcare also made the list, you're correct! To say that our industry is advancing rapidly is almost an understatement. Consider the following:

- The FDA approves around 50 new medications each year. That's approximately one per week!
- In 1953, James Watson and Francis Crick discovered that the structure of DNA is a double helix. Now just 70 years later (a blink of an eye over the course of human history), we are targeting medical therapy based on a patient's unique DNA.
- In 1967, surgeons performed the first human-to-human heart transplant. In 2022, a heart was successfully transplanted from a pig to a human.
- At the beginning of my career as a physician, I would never have imagined that surgeons would have the capability to provide someone with a new heart valve through a catheter instead of by opening the chest cavity and heart. Yet here we are!

How Quickly Is Medical Knowledge Advancing?

I read an article published in 2011 that stuck with me because of its bold predictions regarding how quickly medical knowledge was expected to advance (Densen 2011). A little over 10 years later, I would say that the authors' predictions were accurate. Allow me to share a brief passage here:

> It is estimated that the doubling time of medical knowledge in 1950 was 50 years; in 1980, 7 years; and in 2010, 3.5 years. In 2020 it is projected to be 0.2 years—just 73 days. Students who began medical school in the autumn of 2010 will experience approximately three doublings in knowledge by the time they complete the minimum length of training (7 years) needed to practice medicine. Students who graduate in 2020 will experience four doublings in knowledge. What was learned in the first 3 years of medical school will be just 6% of what is known at the end of the decade from 2010 to 2020.

Technological advancements, business practices, and consumer trends are also evolving rapidly, and they can have an even bigger impact on leaders than advancements in clinical care. You are probably familiar with some of the following changes that are overhauling the way we lead healthcare organizations:

- **Technology:** Telemedicine and predictive analytics
- **Policy:** Health Insurance Portability and Accountability Act (HIPAA) and Emergency Medical Treatment and Active Labor Act (EMTALA)

- **Insurance:** High-deductible health plans and value-based contracts instead of low-deductible plans and volume-based contracts
- **Location:** Clinics located in supermarkets, big-box stores, and pharmacies; telehealth (or virtual video) consultations

PRIORITIES KEEP YOU ON COURSE

With healthcare moving this fast, there is too much for one leader to focus on. There are too many "essential tasks" to do. Too many "crucial topics" to stay abreast of. Too many competing recommendations and best practices to implement. Too many people, departments, and shifts asking for a finite number of resources. Managing all of this can feel like drinking from a fire hose, and it's all too easy for the unrelenting flow of tasks and information to sweep you (and therefore, your organization) off course. That's why a major part of leadership involves the following:

- Knowing how to prioritize the organization's resources, energy, personnel, budget, and so on.
- Knowing what patients' priorities are in order to provide great service. (Patients' priorities may not always align with the priorities of a department, unit, or individual caregiver.)
- Having the ability to communicate priorities to your team and to help them prioritize their own efforts (e.g., "Do this project first, keep that one on the back burner, and make sure that our goal to reduce infections by 10 percent is always top of mind").
- Having the ability to keep focused on the identified priorities despite distractions.

If leaders are challenged on any of these points, their department or organization will suffer. The leader's team will have difficulty moving in the same direction. The team members' focus will be divided among too many objectives. There will also be a struggle to adapt to the rapid pace of change in healthcare.

The good news is that some things about healthcare never change. There are prioritization best practices that will *always* serve you, your organization, and your patients well—no matter how quickly healthcare is evolving or what's occurring in the external environment. Several of them are discussed in this chapter.

PRIORITIES IN HEALTHCARE: WHO COMES FIRST?

One challenge leaders often agonize over is the prioritization of stakeholders. If multiple parties will be affected by a decision, whose interests should come first? What if one party will benefit greatly but another might be negatively affected? Is there a priority system to assist in making these difficult decisions? Yes!

Your First Priority Should *Always* Be the Patient

Imagine that a family member is taken to the Emergency Department (ED) at 11:00 p.m. with chest pain that *might* be a heart attack—the diagnosis isn't certain. A cardiologist who puts himself before the patient might think, *I'm at a dinner party, and it doesn't seem like the patient is going to die in the next few hours. I'll evaluate the patient in the morning.* Admittedly this is a very simple example, but we can all agree that the physician did not make the right decision.

Changing patients' lives for the better is why healthcare organizations exist, and it is our moral obligation to do what is best for patients. (See chapter 7 for ideas about how your organization can put patients first.) You may recall that at Hospital X we referred to patients as "loved ones." In large part this was to remind us that each individual under our care was more than just a procedure, an injury, an appointment, a protocol, or a chart—they were someone's loved one. Our constant aim was to treat each loved one as if they were our own mother, brother, child, or friend—in other words, as our top priority.

Wait . . . Who *Actually* Comes First?

I have a confession: There's a caveat to "patients always come first." Years ago, I came across a book called *Patients Come Second* by Paul Spiegelman and Britt Berrett (more on this book in chapter 8.) The book's inflammatory title had the desired effect because, filled with indignation, I picked it up and read it. I soon realized the authors are absolutely correct. To give patients the best care, we have to make caregivers our top priority.

But didn't we just say *patients* are the top priority? Well, yes. And I know it's a little confusing. But it may help to think of caregivers as a "hidden" tier in the priority hierarchy. If caregivers don't feel safe, supported, and purposeful in their jobs, it will ultimately be a challenge for them to deliver the very best care to a patient. Really, patient care and caregiver care are a package deal. It is impossible to separate them. We'll devote several chapters later in this book to supporting, developing, and empowering caregivers.

The Healthcare Organization (or System) Is the Second Priority

If the organization doesn't thrive—whether that's due to strained finances, poor culture, or something else—caregivers won't be equipped to give patients the best possible care.

An organization I once worked for identified a particular service line that was consistently losing money. There were not enough patients to raise the revenue needed to cover the service line's substantial fixed costs, and the financial loss was causing significant strain on the healthcare system. If the organization closed the service line in question, the money saved could be used to provide better patient care in other service lines.

Understandably, caregivers who worked in the unsustainable service line did not want it to be closed. (If you've ever been part of a similar situation, you know that the voices of people whose jobs are on the line can be poignant and persuasive!) However, if the system maintained the financial loss, it would suffer, that service line would suffer, and ultimately the patients would suffer. Leadership knew that the system and the patients had to be prioritized.

Prior to closing the service line, leaders did perform an analysis to ascertain that other healthcare systems in the area had ample capacity and capability to provide care to the patients who would be affected. (Remember, patients are our *first* priority!)

The Department (or Division) Is the Third Priority

This is where the priority system gets tricky for many leaders. Obviously, you want each department to be successful. (This is especially true for department leaders.) But if a department is utilizing too many resources, the organization will eventually suffer—and that will compromise your ability to deliver optimal care to a greater number of patients.

I think it's natural and understandable for department leaders to make decisions that benefit their teams, even at the expense of the overall organization. These leaders don't have nefarious intentions; they simply care about their teams and want to give them the maximum amount of support. But imagine that leaders in multiple departments consistently do what is best for their departments at the expense of the organization. Each time the organization is not prioritized, the chinks in its armor increase. Over time, it could face significant struggles.

Here's the irony: When the whole organization struggles, downstream effects will inevitably hurt the departments that prioritized themselves. Perhaps the cost of a new magnetic resonance imaging (MRI) machine with better resolution isn't in the budget. Or a breakdown in culture causes employees to leave the organization, putting a strain on the remaining frontline caregivers. No matter what the specifics are, patients will ultimately receive a lower quality of care if the departments are prioritized over the system.

Prioritizing the organization over a particular department— while still making sure the department has what it needs to deliver care—often feels like a tense balancing act. However, it's one that leaders *must* learn to succeed at.

We Are a Priority Too

As an ED physician, I missed a few of my children's soccer games when the ED became very busy during shift changes. When I was CEO of Hospital X, some of our executives and public relations employees were needed on Thanksgiving because of an important community event. These stories are hardly unique. All caregivers— clinical and nonclinical, from the front line to senior executives—are asked to put in extra effort from time to time. And assuming that our purpose is to improve the lives of others, we understand why it's necessary to sometimes put patients and the organization ahead of ourselves.

Although it is true that healthcare workers can't always put ourselves first, we cannot think of ourselves as being the *last* priority, either. It is imperative for a leader to prioritize the welfare of their team; not only because it is the right thing to do for each individual, but also because it is necessary for the team to achieve the best results possible. We need to take care of ourselves and look after each other. Remember that no one can pour from an empty vessel. All of us, whether we are leaders or not, need to regularly replenish our passion and energy so that we can continue to deliver the best outcomes for patients and the organization (and for our own families and loved ones). If we don't, then we are at a greater risk for burnout. Since burnout is such a critical and timely topic, we'll devote chapter 12 to examining it in greater detail.

Ultimately, in order for us (leaders) and all caregivers (clinical and nonclinical) to thrive, our department or unit needs to thrive first. In order for the department or unit to thrive, the organization or system needs to thrive. And for the system to thrive, we need to focus on the patients. Hence, the priority order we've just established:

1. Patients
2. Organization/System
3. Department/Division
4. Ourselves and all other caregivers, clinical and nonclinical

When patients get exceptional care that is safe, high-quality, and marked by great service, the organization will grow and strengthen. That being the case, let's look at what leaders and organizations can do to prioritize patients so that everything else falls into place.

What's on the Front of Your Jersey?

Even if you aren't a sports fan, you've probably heard of the semifinal men's hockey match from the 1980 Olympic Games. It was the height of the Cold War, and Team USA was up against the Team USSR: high stakes indeed. Team USSR consisted of professional hockey players who had trained and played together on the international stage for years. Team USA consisted primarily of college boys who had never competed together and who were

continued

continued from previous page

not professional players. Together, they comprised the youngest hockey team to ever play in the Olympics.

In the movie *Miracle on Ice*, which follows Team USA's journey, Coach Herb Brooks had his players continuously skating sprints. Some players became so exhausted that they vomited. But Coach wouldn't allow them to stop. At regular intervals, he would ask the young men, "Who do you play for?" The players had various answers—but apparently not the right one. So they'd do another sprint.

After what must have seemed like hours, Coach asked the question again: "Who do you play for?"

One player gasped out, "I play for the United States of America!" That is when the sprints stopped.

Coach stated, "When you pull on that jersey . . . the name on the front is a hell of a lot more important than the one on the back," meaning representing the USA is more important than old personal rivalries or being a superstar on the ice.

This scene exemplifies the "one team, one mission" motto that guides those of us in healthcare. After all, no matter where you work or what your role is, no matter what your personal goals are, your overriding mission is to deliver the best care possible to patients. Never forget that the name of your organization, system, department, or unit is on the front of your jersey.

TO PRIORITIZE PATIENTS, UNDERSTAND WHAT *THEIR* PRIORITIES ARE

As we'll discuss at length in chapter 7, healthcare is a service industry. Within that framework, patients are our ultimate customer. As is the case for any organization in any industry, we in healthcare must put our customers first in order for our organizations to survive, much less grow and thrive.

To best serve our customers (i.e., patients or loved ones), we need to understand what *their* priorities are when they are seeking healthcare. Note that a patient's priorities might not align with a caregiver's priorities. For instance, a nurse might be focused on getting a patient up and walking while preventing a fall. Meanwhile, the patient's top concern is alleviating their fatigue and pain. As much as possible, it's our job to ensure that we provide for the patient's medical needs while also giving them the things that are most important to them.

Patient surveys are critical. They allow us to capture the customer's perspective and thoughts so that we can improve our systems, processes, and culture to provide a better experience. You'll probably find that most patients value service highly. (In fact, as we'll discuss later in this book, for many people service is a surrogate marker for quality of care.) Therefore, I strongly recommend paying close attention to direct feedback, indirect feedback, and the various Consumer Assessment of Healthcare Providers and Systems (CAHPS) surveys.

Be Proactive About Capturing Patient Feedback

Patient feedback is vital if we are to provide high-quality care and service that focuses on patients' priorities. Thus, we *cannot* be passive in waiting for it. We need to be proactive in seeking it out. In addition to the traditional e-mail and paper mail surveys that are widely used in healthcare, here are some strategies to capture what patients think:

- Set up a table at the building's entrance and/or exit and staff it with someone who can ask arriving and departing patients for their feedback. In addition to

continued

continued from previous page

asking global questions such as "How was your visit to the clinic?" and "What can we do to make your experience better?", ask specific questions such as "Were you able to find a parking space easily?" "Did you have any trouble locating our clinic within the hospital?" "How long was your wait time?" "Did you feel that all of your questions were answered by the provider?"

One big benefit of this strategy is that you catch the patient while their thoughts and opinions are fresh in their mind. You also have a chance to provide service recovery *before* they go back into the community with unheard complaints. In addition, you'll have better compliance with providing feedback. Many people don't like to fill out surveys but are willing to speak with a "real live person" about their experiences.

- Designate someone to round on patients during their visit with the sole goal of receiving feedback. Doing so opens an opportunity to improve the patient's stay at that moment, prior to them leaving the facility. One important note: Don't ask a generic question like "Do you have any feedback?" Instead, say something like "Our hospital [or clinic, practice, etc.] is always trying to improve the experience and outcomes of our patients and their family members. We would like to know how you think we can make things better. Is there anything we can do for you right now?"
- Ensure that patients receive post-visit follow-up calls. Sometimes people find it easier to discuss

continued

continued from previous page

a concern when they aren't face-to-face with a caregiver. This phone call can also be used to ask the patient if they are feeling better, if they need anything, if they understand their discharge instructions, and so on. This type of call demonstrates that their healthcare provider cares, and it has been shown to increase patient satisfaction and improve patient outcomes.

If your organization has volunteers, it's possible to utilize all these feedback-gathering strategies at no added cost. As a bonus, patients usually find volunteers to be less intimidating than providers, and because volunteers are seen as a third party, many patients are more willing to be transparent with them. Of course, if the patient has clinical questions, the volunteer will need to involve the appropriate caregiver. I have found that volunteers really enjoy interacting with patients in this capacity because most of them decided to donate their time to healthcare in order to help others. Volunteers can directly connect this type of effort to their purpose.

It's also important to directly ask patients what their priorities are. When I see patients in my capacity as a leader *or* as a physician, one of the first things I do after entering the room is ask the patient and their guests, "What are your goals or concerns for today?" Asking this simple question is meaningful to the patient and their loved ones. And you will be surprised by some of the answers you'll get.

A patient might respond that she wants to return home by the time her children get off the school bus. Another patient might share that he's worried about what will happen to his pets if he is admitted into the hospital. Both of these answers provide information that is outside the bounds of what a caregiver would have otherwise focused on. Addressing patients' goals strengthens their confidence in the organization and is the foundation for patient loyalty.

Occasionally, it isn't possible to address a patient's needs because of complex logistics, medical impossibilities, or other compelling reasons. When this is the case, don't dismiss or ignore their requests or goals. Acknowledge the patient's concerns and make certain to provide the "why" behind your answer. Then, if possible, work with the patient to achieve a different, but hopefully satisfactory, resolution.

While each person is different, I've found that overall, patient priorities tend to line up in the following order:

1. Don't hurt me.
2. Heal me.
3. Be nice to me.
4. Don't waste my time.
5. Keep me healthy going forward.

Make Sure *All* Caregivers Understand Patient Priorities

Everyone in your organization, clinical and nonclinical, needs to have a good understanding of what is important to patients. Even if someone isn't on the front lines, their work affects patients' care, service, and overall experience. Try to keep patient priorities front and center for each employee so that patients (i.e., the organization's customers) aren't eclipsed by other concerns. To help you get started, here are a few suggestions for how you can hardwire Patient Priority #1 ("Don't hurt me") into your organization's operations:

continued

continued from previous page

- Begin all meetings with a safety or "good catch" story. For corporate departments like legal, marketing, and finance, you can discuss a reliability story. (Safety is the end product of reliability at the site of care.)
- Ask the board of directors to put safety as the first item on their agenda.
- Give a monthly or quarterly award that is linked to safety. (But don't stop there—you can give an award linked to each one of the five priorities!)

Let's look at why each of these priorities is important to patients—and by extension, why it's important for your organization to prioritize these things as well.

Don't Hurt Me

Above all, patients want to receive safe, high-quality care. A caregiver's actions should not cause them to leave a medical facility in a worse state of health than when they entered. Nor should their treatment cause them to experience pain that is not a necessary part of their care. This priority is why all physicians take the Hippocratic oath, which often includes the vow to "first do no harm" or some variant thereof.

It's also why the government, insurance companies, and healthcare rating agencies use surgical site infections after joint replacements as a marker in evaluating the organization's performance. It is always horrible when a patient goes into the hospital for an elective procedure and becomes sicker or less healthy.

> ## "Mom, Will I Have to Get a Shot?"
>
> I would venture to say that for most of us, "don't hurt me" has been our first patient priority since we were toddlers. I know that when I was a child, before every pediatric appointment I asked my mother whether I would be getting a shot. My own children asked me the same question. As we grow, we realize that pain is sometimes necessary to maintain and improve our health, but the desire to have a caregiver "not hurt me" never completely dissipates . . . and most of us never learn to love shots, either!

Heal Me

This is the primary reason why people seek healthcare. In other words, they go to your organization because they have an acute illness, a broken bone, concerning symptoms, a chronic illness, or another issue that needs medical attention. Although they might not say so explicitly, we understand that all patients want accurate and complete diagnoses with appropriate, timely, and quality care to resolve their concerns. As leaders, we must support providers so they can reliably deliver exceptional care.

Be Nice to Me

I can't think of anyone who prefers to be around people who are not nice. Patients certainly don't visit physicians, nurses, and other caregivers to be belittled, ignored, mocked, or patronized. In fact, a bad experience with an unfriendly caregiver can cause a patient to avoid future treatment.

As I mentioned earlier, healthcare is almost exclusively a service industry. Arguably, most patients are not able to effectively judge the safety or quality of their care unless it is very poor. (And when this is the case, the caregiver has probably also failed to uphold priority #1 and/or #2.) Even as a physician, I am usually not able to accurately judge the finer details of safety or the quality of a specialist's performance because I am trained as an ED physician, not as a cardiologist, podiatrist, orthopedic surgeon, or another specialist.

Here's the point: Most patients use service as a surrogate marker for safety and quality. If they received excellent service—if their caregivers are thoughtful, empathetic, kind, and attentive—patients extrapolate that their overall care was also high in quality.

Don't Waste My Time

This priority is a measure of efficiency, and for many patients, it's where healthcare organizations tend to drop the ball. It is unfortunate that inefficiencies in healthcare are now an expectation. I have spoken with so many patients who say that when they go to see a physician, they assume they will not be seen by the provider at the scheduled time. They expect to still be sitting in a waiting room chair (or maybe alone in the exam room) for a half hour after the appointment should have begun. Odds are, you've had this frustrating experience yourself!

I will never forget an oncologist I worked with named Dr. Ed Crane. One day during a medical executive committee meeting, we were discussing physicians being late for patients' appointments. Dr. Crane has always been one of the most professional, caring, and kind individuals I have ever met. However, when he spoke in this meeting, his passion and frustration at physician tardiness were evident.

He said, "I don't know why physicians think that they can be late to an appointment. Nobody's time is more valuable than someone else's. A physician's time is not more valuable than a patient's time. We physicians need to keep in mind that while we are at work doing our jobs, our patients have often taken time off from their own jobs to seek our care. So not only are tardy physicians wasting the patient's time; they could be affecting the patient's income or wasting their valuable personal time."

Dr. Crane then went on to say that he viewed his patients' time as being *more* valuable than his own. "As an oncologist I see patients who do not know their own life expectancy. Often the only thing they *do* know for certain is that their time on earth with their family is limited. It would be a shame for me to waste any of that time." Suffice it to say, Dr. Crane "gets it."

Before moving on, I think it's important to underscore the fact that patients are increasingly less willing to put up with so-called inconveniences like long wait times. If they are unhappy, they'll go to another place to receive healthcare. They might also post a negative online review of your organization.

Keep Me Healthy

After the previous four priorities have been observed, patients want their caregivers to keep them healthy going forward. Historically this has usually consisted of an annual appointment with a primary care doctor, gynecologist, and/or other specialists. Perhaps patients also schedule some interval blood work or screening procedures such as a mammogram or endoscopy. Now, though, the "keep me healthy" priority is expanding and is often referred to as "population health."

Many healthcare systems have made population health their primary strategic initiative. They invest tens of millions of dollars each year to transform the system from an acute injury health system (where organizations are the passive recipients of patients who are ill or injured) to a healthcare system that is proactive about keeping patients healthy. These systems strive to minimize acute and chronic illness to keep patients out of the hospital—and ultimately to support them in living a longer, higher-quality life.

Here are two simple examples of how the healthcare industry is supporting patient health:

- **Practitioners are more proactive about keeping patients healthy.** Especially for primary care physicians and specialists who perform screening procedures, it has been common to only see patients outside of annual appointments when the patient initiates contact. But more and more often, physicians and other caregivers are tracking their patients' health so they can proactively contact and support them.

  When speaking about this topic, I often share the example of a primary care physician who developed a program in his electronic medical record system to alert him if there was anything unusual with a patient's care. One day, this physician received an alert about a pediatric patient who was suddenly visiting the ED every couple of weeks for breathing difficulties.

  The physician proactively contacted the patient's mother and asked her to bring her son into his office for an appointment. After a thorough conversation with the family, he soon discovered that the patient's window air conditioning unit had not been working for the last couple months, which exacerbated the boy's asthma. The physician quickly went to a home improvement store and purchased a window unit for the patient. The patient no longer had any ED visits.

- **Technology is relaying information from patients' homes to the physician.** Here's a good example: Patients with heart failure often accumulate water in their legs and lungs if the treatment is not sufficient, or if other factors affecting the patient have changed (e.g., diet). A simple and effective way to measure the effectiveness of a patient's treatment or the status of their heart failure is to monitor their weight. Rapid increase in weight is often due to water retention from worsening heart failure.

Technology now allows the patient's home scale to send their weight to their primary care physician's medical record system each day. The physician can then call the patient into the office for further evaluation if the numbers are concerning. Early detection and early treatment will prevent the patient from getting significantly worse, which might necessitate a hospital admission or more aggressive treatment.

Of course, this is not the absolute order of all patients' priorities. Some people may be more concerned with time efficiency than politeness, for example. However, I do believe that when these five priorities are met, most patients will feel that they and their concerns have been put first. They will be satisfied with their service experience and will be more likely to become loyal "customers."

As leaders, it is our responsibility to familiarize our teams with these patient priorities. We then need to build systems, design processes, provide tools, and create a culture that collectively enable the organization to deliver exceptional care and service. It is our grand purpose as leaders to serve our teams so that they can best serve our patients.

One final thought: As leaders, we must hold our teams accountable to the priorities we set for the organization. (We'll look much more closely at accountability in chapter 11.) When someone puts their department's best interest above that of the system, there needs to be accountability. If someone starts to row in a different direction, they need to be guided back on track. And if any organizational initiatives or goal changes cause you to place less attention on any one of these priorities, you need to rethink your direction! Remember, no matter how quickly the healthcare industry evolves, our priorities shouldn't.

But What About the Budget?

Many leaders in healthcare measure the success of an organization by its financial performance. Without question, keeping your balance sheet in the black is essential to the long-term success of any organization. I know that it can also feel unsettling to place any of the priorities we have discussed in this chapter above "the numbers," especially when efforts to support those priorities cut into your budget.

However, if you make patients your first priority and successfully focus on delivering care that achieves exceptional outcomes in safety, quality, service, efficiency, and your patients' ongoing health, then your organization *will* grow. I have seen this firsthand at Hospital X, and colleagues around the country have shared similar experiences. In fact, we agree that financial growth is a trailing indicator for the delivery of exceptional, high-quality care with great service.

REFERENCE

Densen, P. 2011. "Challenges and Opportunities Facing Medical Education." *Transactions of the American Clinical and Climatological Association* 122: 48–58. https://www.ncbi.nlm.nih.gov/pmc/articles/PMC3116346/.

CHAPTER 4

Assembling Your Leadership Team of Experts

WHEN YOU'RE BUILDING an organization centered on helping people live their purpose, few decisions matter as much as the leaders you hire to serve alongside you. These are the people who will speak the words and carry out the actions that make or break your culture. It is vital to choose the right people. You can have a firm grip on your purpose and values, you can have wonderful processes and procedures, you can have an army of top-notch caregivers, and you can be the world's smartest CEO—but if you have the wrong leaders in place, none of it matters.

In chapter 2, I shared the story of how I became CEO of Hospital X. To recap, I did not expect the promotion and was unprepared to step into the C-suite. Calling my experience a "steep learning curve" would be an understatement. Most days, I felt like I was climbing a sheer cliff face without a safety harness! As you might recall, in my first few months as CEO I gained significant weight, was prescribed medication for hypertension, and almost forgot what a good night's sleep felt like. The stresses of my new job and the fear of failure were eating me alive.

One of my biggest sources of anxiety was my lack of knowledge about so many of the disciplines I was now expected to oversee. For instance, how was I supposed to lead the chief of Human Resources

(HR) when he had so much more expertise in that field than I did? And yes, while I *am* a physician, I am *not* a nurse, so how was I going to lead a chief nursing officer? At that point I didn't have my MBA, so what did I know about marketing or finance? Leading a chief nursing officer (CNO), a chief marketing officer (CMO), or a chief financial officer (CFO) seemed impossible.

YOU DON'T HAVE TO BE THE EXPERT (THAT'S WHAT YOUR TEAM IS FOR!)

Looking back, I can see where I went wrong: I thought that leading the hospital would be similar to being a physician leader in the Emergency Department (ED). In that role, I had to know the acute treatment and stabilization of every person who entrusted my team with their care, whether they had been in a severe car accident, suffered a stroke, were about to deliver a baby, or simply had a sore throat. When I worked clinically seeing patients, I was expected to be the most knowledgeable person in the ED regarding all ailments and injuries that presented, while efficiently and effectively coordinating all of our patients' care—and I was good at my job.

As a newly minted CEO, I quickly learned that I was far from the most knowledgeable person in most of the areas I was expected to oversee: HR, finance, marketing, nursing, and many more. Trying to cram a career's worth of knowledge about these disciplines into my brain while feeling inadequate in all of them was easily one of the most stressful and unrealistic things I have ever attempted to do.

Thankfully, I eventually realized that knowing more than everyone else about every subject is *not* leadership. In fact, it is the complete opposite of good leadership. One day it simply dawned on me that if I *were* the smartest person in the room in every discipline I oversaw, then I had actually failed as a leader because I had not hired the right people. As CEO, my job was to recruit people who were experts in their fields, and then coordinate those bright minds so our team could establish the desired culture, strategies, and organizational direction. In a very real way, I realized that I worked *for* my team because my role was to remove obstacles, bridge gaps, and provide resources so the rest of the organization could successfully deliver exceptional care.

After that epiphany, things changed. Take finance, for instance. I realized that I did *not* have to be a financial expert. I *did* have to be able to speak about the topic fluently and proficiently. I needed to be able to think strategically about the hospital's finances and prioritize financial decisions. But most importantly, I needed to make sure I hired and gave my full support to a financial expert. Our hospital's success depended on how capable our CFO was, so this person had better know more than I did about finances!

Similarly, I didn't have to know everything about nursing. But because nursing is a critical aspect of a hospital's operations, I had to be able to facilitate exceptional working relationships between nurses, physicians, therapists, and other care providers. I also needed to hire an exceptional, experienced CNO who knew much more about nursing than I did.

The same was true for marketing, human resources, legal, information technology, and so forth. As CEO, I needed foundational knowledge about each discipline—and I had to be able to identify and hire the true experts in each. Letting go of my need to know everything freed me to channel my energy where it would do the most good: focusing on areas such as strategy, culture, and community engagement, and coordinating the expertise of my carefully selected leadership team.

Recognizing that I didn't have to be the expert greatly eased my burden of stress too. I lost weight, got off of hypertension medications, and was even able to fit in a few much-needed cycles of REM sleep.

Although I was a hospital CEO when I learned the importance of hiring experts, this principle applies to all leadership roles. For example, a director of plant operations will probably not have experience in all the disciplines she will be managing. The director's job is to find and hire the person who knows the most about HVAC, the most about plumbing, the most about electricity, the most about building design, and so on—and then coordinate all those experts to deliver the best care.

The Consequences of "Know-It-All" Leadership

Before we move on, let's briefly look at the consequences of leaders who believe they *must* be an expert on all facets of the organization or department.

Like me, you'll probably suffer from the deterioration of your physical and mental health. You'll also experience the deterioration of your leadership capabilities. That's right: Trying to become a "super leader" by knowing and controlling everything in your purview almost always has the opposite effect. It's a very short step from needing to know everything to micromanaging everything. As you are no doubt aware, micromanaging prevents leaders from focusing on their own roles and responsibilities. It also leaves leaders with little time and energy to develop their own leadership skills, much less the leadership skills of others.

"Know-it-all" leadership also causes people to disengage from and resent you. Whether you intend to or not, you'll be perceived as dogmatic and inflexible. An "I'm *the* expert" attitude stifles feedback and thus inhibits organizational potential. Downstream effects include a widening of the power gradient, which (as we'll discuss in a later chapter) has significant negative consequences on culture, productivity, delivery of care, and more.

CREATING YOUR LEADERSHIP TEAM

I once heard a fantastic quote from Tom Ricketts, the executive chairman of the Chicago Cubs: "Hire good people who hire good people, and let them do their job" (Ellefsen 2016). In the same vein, Steve Jobs once stated, "It doesn't make sense to hire smart people and tell them what to do; we hire smart people so they can tell us what to do" (Lipman 2018).

I would add a few things to those quotes: Support your people, give them the resources they need to be successful, and remove any barriers holding them back. Continuously train your team, provide mentorship, give feedback, and hold everyone accountable—including yourself! (We'll look at each of these topics in more detail throughout the book.)

For now, let's focus on step one: hiring good people for your leadership team. Here are some things to keep in mind whether you are starting from scratch or trying to fill a specific need.

Look for Experts Who Are a Good Cultural Fit

As I've explained, any leader you hire should know much more about their discipline than you do. Although hiring an "expert in their field" is essential, it's not the only qualification you should be looking for. In fact, it can easily be argued that being an "expert" should take a back seat to being a cultural fit for the organization and for the team with whom the newly hired leader will be working.

As a CEO, I made sure to hire leaders who displayed compassion, empathy, a strong work ethic, and a commitment to changing the lives of our patients (which, as you might remember, Hospital X referred to as "loved ones"). It's especially important to make sure that your leaders' purpose and values align with those of the organization, because leaders set the example for everyone else in their department and the organization. (Of course, we should always ensure that *all* new hires throughout the organization are cultural fits, not just leaders.)

How do you determine which candidates align with your organization's culture? Well, if cultural fit takes precedence over expertise, then the interview takes precedence over the resume. Granted, candidates for any position still need to be qualified and have the aptitude, enthusiasm, and humility to learn. When interviewing potential new leaders, a large portion of the conversation should be devoted to asking behavioral interview questions.

Behavioral Interview Questions for Potential Leaders

Here are some sample behavioral interview questions for consideration:

- *Tell me about a time when you were wrong and the error had a negative effect on someone else. How did you respond?*
  - The goal of this question is to expose the leader's comfort level in making a mistake, admitting it, and recovering from it. Does she hide or admit errors? Does she blame others or herself for errors? The candidate's answer to this question will reveal her level of humility.
- *How do you approach a tense situation when members of a group have differing opinions? What if their opinions don't align with your thoughts?*
  - Conflicts and differing opinions are inevitable, and how leaders navigate this situation will shine a light on their style of leadership. As we will discuss later in this chapter, when different viewpoints are discussed with civility, they are actually very

continued

---

continued from previous page

beneficial in helping a team achieve success. We need to encourage diversity of thought and constructive conflict.

- *Describe a time when someone on your team was not performing to your standards. How did you address the situation?*
  - To be successful, a leader must be able to give constructive feedback and mentor others with compassion—while still holding them accountable. The goal of this question is to understand how the leader manages performance. How does he treat members of his team: as partners or as subordinate tools to get a job done? Does the leader provide mentoring and education, or does he quickly remove the individual? Is his style of accountability condescending or respectful?
- *What gets you out of bed and excited to start a day?*
  - This question is intended to gain insight into the candidate's personal purpose, which, as discussed throughout this book, essential. Does the candidate's purpose align with that of the organization?
- *Healthcare is changing rapidly. Highlight a time when you had to implement a difficult and unpopular change.*
  - This question will hopefully enlighten the interview team regarding the leader's experience and tactics in change management. Does the leader dictate the change, or does she explain the "why" behind it? Does she prescribe what the change is going to look like, or does she engage others in conversation on how to meet the challenge and

continued

continued from previous page

> empower her team to be key leaders in the change?
> When the candidate asks for feedback, does the
> leader genuinely listen and seriously consider what
> she hears, or is the input of others a formality?
> A good follow-up is *Tell me about a time when*
> *you thought you knew the answer or direction but*
> *changed your mind because of feedback from others.*

The consequences of favoring expertise over cultural fit are real and significant. If you hire a leader who is not a cultural fit, *at best* that individual will leave your organization quickly. You will then have to spend more time, effort, and expense to replace that person. This situation is a true lose-lose-lose for all parties: the new leader, the organization, and the loved ones we care for. At worst the leader will become disengaged with your organization, provide poor care, and disrupt the culture that you have developed within your area(s) of oversight.

Putting a significant amount of work into hiring the right person for a position will lead to significantly *less* work in having to manage that person later. Although there is often pressure to fill a vacant position, settling for a candidate who brings less to the table than desired is almost always regretted. Take the time and effort to hire the person who not only has the right expertise but is also aligned with your culture, purpose, and values.

Hire People Who Think Differently than You—and Are Willing to Challenge You

President Abraham Lincoln famously assembled a cabinet known as his "team of rivals" (Chervinsky 2020). Each of these men had strong opinions, and some frankly disliked the president, at least initially. Their perspectives often clashed with those of their fellow department secretaries—or with those of Lincoln himself. This was purposeful on Lincoln's part. He knew that it was important to surround himself with people who held different viewpoints and who would not be afraid to challenge him, because this would lead him to the best solution.

Like Lincoln, it's important for today's leaders to surround themselves with diverse thoughts, perspectives, and opinions. Teams aren't successful if everyone thinks the same way, or if people only tell the leader what she wants to hear. I personally don't recommend hiring people who actively dislike you or whose viewpoints and ideas are irrevocably opposed to yours, because this dynamic will likely breed more conflict than cooperation. Rather, try to hire independent thinkers with varying experiences and viewpoints who are not afraid to voice their convictions.

As author Jeffrey Baumgartner (2010) once wrote, "Diversity is the key to creativity. Not just diversity in your workforce, but in your personal life."

Search for Innovators

Jack Welch, former CEO of General Electric, once said, "If the rate of change on the outside exceeds the rate of change on the inside, the end is near" (McCullen 2018). He's correct. Like many industries, healthcare is evolving exceptionally quickly. Having expertise in how things were done five years ago, or one year ago, or even in how they're done *right now*, isn't good enough.

For your organization to stay relevant and competitive, the members of your leadership team should be forward-thinking innovators who constantly survey the healthcare landscape and question the strategy. They should expect disruption. They should never be so focused on or confident in what their organization is doing *today* that they fail to consider what might happen tomorrow.

We're all familiar with the cautionary tale of Blockbuster, which was an extremely popular and successful organization for decades. Initially, emerging competitors like Redbox and Netflix didn't seem significant. In fact, Blockbuster's CEO even turned down the opportunity to acquire Netflix (Chong 2015). However, to use Jack Welch's language, Blockbuster failed to take into account the rate of change on the outside. It paid the ultimate price: failure, and in this case, bankruptcy. Making sure this *doesn't* happen to your organization is a prime responsibility for your team, whether it's made up of a group of executives or your department's frontline caregivers (clinical and nonclinical).

Now, for example, one of the big external changes we're dealing with in healthcare is the rise of telemedicine. Out of necessity, telemedicine has grown tremendously as a result of the COVID-19 pandemic, and it is already having a significant impact on care. If healthcare systems and provider groups are not moving aggressively into telemedicine, then they will fall behind because consumers clearly desire greater and easier access to care.

Patient consumerization is growing quickly. Consider that younger generations have grown up with immediate delivery of service in all areas of their lives. For example, they aren't familiar with sending a written message to a friend and waiting days for the postal service to deliver a reply. They most likely have never called an airline or used a travel agent to book their vacation. And relying on the Yellow Pages to look up a phone number is a foreign concept.

The point is, healthcare needs to be more immediate and convenient than it has been in the past, and video visits provide that convenience (not to mention representing an opportunity to deliver care in a more cost-effective manner). Patients are starting to expect online scheduling of appointments. Some practices and providers are even using remote technology (think smart watches and smart scales) to assist in telecare.

But many hospitals and healthcare systems are struggling to keep up. If processes are not put in place to help us adapt to the rapidly evolving external environment, just like Blockbuster, we'll eventually pay the price. As leaders, we need to assemble a team that is innovative, nimble, and eager to change at a pace even faster than healthcare itself is moving. Change is one of the few things in healthcare that is constant.

Consider Leveraging Expertise from Other Industries

In healthcare, our focus is primarily on providing quality care to patients. But there are many other aspects of running a healthcare system, ranging from safety to service to marketing. In my opinion, healthcare tends to lag behind many other industries in these areas. We cling to systems that can be inefficient, ineffective, inconvenient, and off-putting to patients.

To maximize organizational effectiveness and productivity, those of us in healthcare must focus on improving the packaging and delivery of the patient experience. What better way than by hiring experts from other industries? A background in healthcare is not always a prerequisite when hiring in healthcare. Consider taking job descriptions, which often begin with requirements like, "X years of experience in healthcare" and flipping them upside down.

For example, let's say you'd like to improve patient experience. Why not hire a leader from the hotel and hospitality industry who is an expert in delivering consistently exceptional customer service? You'll be able to train this person in the culture and language of healthcare. However, it would be much more difficult to teach a healthcare provider the expertise of customer service.

At a previous healthcare system, I created an Institute for Reliability, Safety, and Performance Improvement. The vice president I hired to run it is an engineer whose expertise is in designing effective, efficient, reliable, and sustainable processes. Yes, I provided some assistance to this person in regard to the nuances of the healthcare industry, but the return on investment was exceptional.

How Do You Compare with These Leaders in Their Fields?

Consider the following list in which I've paired companies or industries with something they excel at. How does your organization compare in each category?

- **Disney = Culture:** Companies send representatives to Disney theme parks to learn how Disney has developed and maintained its culture. It's impressive that in an organization with attractions all over the world, each character acts the same way at each location. There are even different behavioral expectations for so-called cast members depending on whether they're in front of guests or "backstage."
- **Ritz-Carlton = Service:** There is little argument about the exceptional service provided at all Ritz-Carlton locations, which is why the organization can command and receive such a premium rate in nightly accommodations.
- **Apple and Tesla = Innovation:** Unless you've been living under a rock, you know how much these companies have done to revolutionize the tech and transportation industries—and all of our lives. Enough said!
- **Airlines = Safety:** With lives on the line, the aviation industry is laser-focused on standardizing communication, breaking down the cockpit power gradient, developing technologies to assist pilots, and more.

This VP was able to review processes with a fresh set of eyes and approach solving problems from a different angle than what is usual in healthcare. Frankly, his lack of clinical experience was a benefit because he didn't have preconceived notions of how things should be done. Instead, he had to ask healthcare providers many probing and provocative questions in order to develop lean, reliable, effective, and sustainable processes. In doing so, he also exposed many faults and weak points in our current practices.

One more "bonus" of hiring outside the healthcare industry is that you'll be adding *many* more diverse thoughts and experiences to your team—which also enhances the delivery of exceptional healthcare. Remember, to arrive at the best solutions you want leaders on your team who think differently than you do!

Utilize 360-Degree Interviews for Hiring and Promotions

When someone applies for a position on your leadership team, it's a given that they'll have interviews with you and other leaders. After you have vetted a candidate, ask them to interview with their future peers, direct reports, and others with whom they'd work closely (often in different departments) before deciding whether to extend a job offer.

For example, let's say a hospital was hiring a nurse leader for the critical care unit. In addition to the candidate interviewing with his future boss, he might interview with some of the unit's physicians, respiratory therapists, critical care pharmacists, and other staff. He would also interview with several of the nurses who would be reporting up to him.

Cross-interviewing up, down, and horizontally ensures that you focus not just on the applicant's expertise and personal qualities, but also on how she might fit into your team as a whole. A potential hire's direct reports will almost certainly bring different priorities and concerns to the interview than you will. Once a hiring decision has been made, the people working most closely with the new hire will have a vested interest in helping her succeed, because they had a voice in selecting her.

Finally, Make Sure You *and* Your Team Know What Your Focus Is

Once your team has been built, explicitly tell them, "I'm here to do these things (focusing on strategy, setting the direction of the culture, etc.). The rest is up to you. I trust you to oversee your area of expertise and do what's best for the organization." Knowing where your purview ends and theirs begins will empower your team to take full ownership of the job you hired them to do—so that you'll be free to do yours. Make sure to reiterate that a major part of *your* job is to support *them* (which we will discuss in much more detail in chapter 5).

This conversation also helps break down the power gradient. As we've already mentioned, and will discuss in more detail later on, the flatter the power gradient the better collaboration, teamwork, innovation, communication, and everything else will be. In healthcare in particular, we think of addressing power gradients in terms of safety, but focusing on this issue has many other benefits as well.

FINAL THOUGHTS

Co-founder of LinkedIn Reid Hoffman (2012) once observed, "No matter how brilliant your mind or strategy, if you're playing a solo game, you'll always lose out to a team." I agree. Taking the burden of leadership solely on yourself is a challenge you're bound to fail, no matter how smart or experienced you are.

Whether you are a CEO or other leader at any level, creating a leadership team will be one of the most important tasks you take on. The right team will enable you to maximize your own performance while capably managing and growing their respective departments. So let go of the notion that leadership means *being* the smartest person in the room. Start searching for the smartest people you can find, and then put them in the room with you. Just make sure they are a good cultural fit with aligned purpose and values.

REFERENCES

Baumgartner, J. 2010. "Why Diversity Is the Mother of Creativity." Innovation Management. Published November 24. https://innovationmanagement.se/2010/11/24/why-diversity-is-the-mother-of-creativity/.

Chervinsky, L. M. 2020. "Abraham Lincoln's Cabinet." White House Historical Association. Published May 29. https://www.whitehousehistory.org/abraham-lincolns-cabinet.

Chong, C. 2015. "Blockbuster's CEO Once Passed Up a Chance to Buy Netflix for Only $50 Million." Insider. Published July 17. https://www.businessinsider.com/blockbuster-ceo-passed-up-chance-to-buy-netflix-for-50-million-2015-7.

Ellefsen, E. 2016. "Building an Engaged School: Management Matters." CACE: The Center for the Advancement of Christian Education. Published November 28. https://cace.org/building-an-engaged-school-management-matters/.

Hoffman, R. 2012. "Why Relationships Matter: I-to-the-We." LinkedIn. Published November 6. https://www.linkedin.com/pulse/20121106193412-1213-why-relationships-matter-i-to-the-we.

Lipman, V. 2018. "The Best Sentence I Ever Read About Managing Talent." *Forbes*, September 25. https://www.forbes.com/sites/victorlipman/2018/09/25/the-best-sentence-i-ever-read-about-managing-talent/?sh=2c80cb5bcdfb.

McCullen, A. 2018. "If the Rate of Change on the Outside Exceeds the Rate of Change on the Inside, the End Is Near." Medium. Published February 2. https://medium.com/thethursdaythought/if-the-rate-of-change-on-the-outside-exceeds-the-rate-of-change-on-the-inside-the-end-is-near-3145f65c9c61.

CHAPTER 5

Serving and Supporting Your Team with the 15-70-15 Service Model

WHAT HAPPENS WHEN you hear the words *servant leadership*? If you're yawning or even rolling your eyes right now, it's okay. I understand. The phrase has unfortunately become a bit of a cliché. Most people have heard it because it's thrown around all the time—but the truth is, not all can explain what it really means. Even fewer have seen it in action.

Servant leadership is based on the idea that when employees are empowered, supported, engaged, and fulfilled, they'll do the type of work that leads to organizational growth and success. A servant leader understands that frontline workers are ultimately responsible for delivering the product or service that customers experience. Thus, the primary job of a servant leader is to make sure that their team is successful in delivering the best product or service to the customers. As we'll discuss in this chapter, leaders do this by removing obstacles, providing resources, breaking down barriers, and more. The leader serves others; others don't serve the leader.

Another of a servant leader's main responsibilities is to build and support organizational culture. In my career, I have seen that a strong culture and purpose-driven employees are leading indicators of financial success. (That's why servant leadership is an essential tenet of the style of leadership explored throughout this book.)

Most discussions about servant leadership revolve around the characteristics of servant leaders (they're empathetic and inspiring), the results of their leadership (empowerment and teamwork), how they lead (with humility and respect), and why this leadership model is successful (it is efficient and self-sustaining). This (and more) is all true, and you've probably heard most of it before.

Where I've found information about servant leadership to be lacking is the *how*. How do you put the servant leadership model into action? What does it look like across an entire organization at all levels? And what is it that leaders do when they are not "serving"? Those are the questions I want to answer in this chapter.

But first, let's change our terminology and stop calling this model *servant leadership*. *Servant leadership* has many different interpretations, and as I mentioned earlier, it's used so often that it has become a cliché instead of a call to action. I try not to use it because I don't want my point to go in one ear and out the other. Instead, I use the term *15-70-15 service*.

THE 15-70-15 SERVICE MODEL

As I navigated my way through the early years of leadership, I sometimes found myself thinking, *I've hired people who know more about their areas of expertise than I do, and I've empowered them to hire more good people. I'm learning to get out of their way and let them do their jobs. So with all of these capable, experienced people on my team, what's left for me? What, exactly, is my job as a leader?*

As I briefly shared in chapter 4, I eventually realized that one of my main roles as CEO of Hospital X was to develop, guide, support, and empower my executive team—in other words, to serve them. When I started to break down that role even further, the 15-70-15 service model was born. The numbers refer to how you spend your time. Here's how it works:

First 15 Percent of Your Time: Set the Direction

As a leader, you must set the culture, chart the direction, coordinate your team's activities, develop strategy, monitor performance, and so on. Then you must communicate these things to your team and (here's the hard part!) step back and allow them to decide how to proceed. Parameters do need to be set, but by and large it's up to your team to decide how to achieve each objective. Remember, you hired your team because they, not you, are the experts.

You may have to cultivate your ability to release control. Especially at first, it can feel uncomfortable, stressful, or downright frightening to see that everything isn't being done exactly as you would choose, or on the precise timetable that you would want.

Don't Be *That* (Micro)manager

Some leaders struggle with the first 15 percent because they believe it's a leader's job to tell others what to do and how to do it. Not true! If you tell your team exactly what to do and how to do it, that's micromanagement—and nobody likes a micromanager! That's because micromanagement does the following:

- Disenfranchises and stifles others.
- Does not develop new leaders.
- Takes away valuable time from the micromanager. Tasks only they can do might be neglected.
- Takes away ownership from those doing the work.
- Leads to suboptimal results. (In most cases, those on the ground level have better ideas and more accurate perspectives than leadership does.)
- Contributes to disengagement, low morale, burnout, and high employee turnover.

Middle 70 Percent of Your Time: Work for Others

As your team works toward the goals you've set, they will bump into obstacles they can't remove, require resources they do not have, and be stalled by barriers they can't find a way around. That's where you come in. You are essentially working for your team by doing what is necessary to ensure their success. This likely requires a mindset shift for many leaders. After all, the very term *leader* implies that others are working for and following you. In the 15-70-15 service model, the leader is working for her team. In addition, humility and a desire to flatten the power gradient are both essential for the leader and her team to be successful.

When I share this service model with others, I often hear feedback along the following lines: "I agree that leaders need to serve and support their teams, but devoting 70 percent of your time to this task seems like too much. When will I get my own work done?" Remember, serving and supporting your team is *the* work of a leader. In the end, you will accomplish more because you have empowered an entire shift, department, or organization to strategize, find solutions, and drive toward goals.

Many leaders don't initially realize that the bulk of their routine tasks fall into the 70 percent. Here's a short (and certainly not exhaustive) list of things that can be categorized as supporting employees:

- Rounding on/connecting with caregivers
- Leading new employee orientations
- Providing feedback
- Mentorship
- Helping caregivers fix a problem (this is especially true if the leader doesn't solve the problem outright but instead provides resources, advice, and support as caregivers work through it themselves)
- Empowering others

- Building a culture and environment that creates an exceptional place to work
- Recruiting and re-recruiting others
- Essentially, everything in this book

That said, there might be some growing pains as you work toward living out the 15-70-15 service model. Usually, leaders have trouble achieving 70 percent because they are spending time on work that others *should* be doing. To begin carving out more time, look back at the three-column strategy in chapter 2.

Do You Want to Be a Level 5 Leader?

If you're going to lead with the 15-70-15 service model, keep in mind the following quote from Jim Collins (2001). Collins is talking about what he calls a "Level 5 Leader," or someone who has the capacity to take a company from good to great:

> On the one hand . . . Looks in the mirror, not out the window, to apportion responsibility for poor results, never blaming other people, external factors, or bad luck. Yet on the other hand . . . Looks out the window, not in the mirror, to apportion credit for the success of the company—to other people, external factors, and good luck.

Someone who takes responsibility for shortfalls but who credits the hard work of others for successes—isn't that a great definition of a leader who spends the majority of his time working for his employees and not for his own gratification?

Last 15 Percent of Your Time: Evaluate and Adjust

At regular intervals (often after a milestone has been reached or a project has been completed), you must evaluate both the results of the initiative and each person's performance in order to make course corrections. If you use the Plan-Do-Study-Act cycle (or the Plan-Do-Check-Act cycle) to continuously strategize, improve, and enact change, this last 15 percent is the "S&A" or "C&A."

Of course, these percentages (15-70-15) are approximate. At any given time, a leader may need to focus more or less on one of the three components. I chose the numbers I did because I wanted to demonstrate that, overall, leaders should spend more than two-thirds of their time supporting the rest of the organization. If the members of your team are successful, you will be successful.

Not coincidentally, the benefits of 15-70-15 leadership inversely mirror the drawbacks of micromanagement that I listed earlier. The 15-70-15 leadership model accomplishes the following:

- Empowers good leaders
- Develops new leaders
- Gives you more time to devote to tasks only you can do
- Gives caregivers a greater sense of ownership in their work because they are making decisions and actively shaping the end result
- Leads to better results because those "on the ground" are closest to the issue and usually have the best solutions
- Contributes to an engaged, empowered, and committed workforce

THE 15-70-15 SERVICE MODEL IN ACTION

Let's take a real-life look at how the 15-70-15 service model differs from a traditional leadership approach. This story takes place when I worked as the chief medical officer (CMO) for a hospital system that I'll refer to as System A. Two regional CMOs (RCMOs), each of whom was in charge of several hospitals within their region, reported to me. My direct reports also included 18 physician system chiefs who were in charge of the 18 different specialty service lines within System A. And across the system, there were over 1,500 physicians who ultimately reported to the Office of the Chief Medical Officer.

After the first COVID-19 surge, a significant percentage of the clinical and nonclinical caregivers at System A were exhausted and demoralized—and there was no end to the pandemic in sight. Like many healthcare leaders around the country, my fellow executives and I were concerned about the looming possibility of widespread burnout. I wanted to do everything I could to help the over 1,500 physicians in the system.

Under a Traditional Leadership Model, Here's What Might Have Happened

The system CMO (me) would have told the two RCMOs and 18 system chiefs what the system was going to do to combat burnout. It's possible that a few questions or surveys might have been sent out across the system first. But chances are, many of the solutions would be standardized, and because they weren't developed with input from the front lines, they wouldn't get to the heart of the issues that were contributing to physician burnout.

In my experience, standardized solutions *do* address aspects of the problem but often benefit some groups more than others (and some not at all). Because of their uneven benefits, implementation is rarely as thorough or effective as leaders would like. It's difficult to get buy-in from physicians who were not involved in developing the solution and who don't believe it will help them. Unfortunately, it's also common for standardized solutions to die on the vine, so to speak, because of practical barriers that can't be removed or necessary resources that frontline caregivers don't have.

Under Our 15-70-15 Service Model, Here's What *Did* Happen

15: Set the direction. I worked with the two RCMOs and 18 system chiefs to identify objectives and set up the basic parameters of our strategy. Since we couldn't change the realities of the pandemic, we decided to target other inefficiencies and frustrations that were contributing to bad days. (I believe that for most people, burnout is not caused by a big, cataclysmic event—it develops slowly over the course of many bad days that chip away at caregivers' outlook, morale, and engagement. I'll delve more deeply into the "bad day theory" in chapter 12.)

The RCMOs worked with leadership at all levels of their hospitals to create a list of things that were causing bad days. The 18 system chiefs worked with their service line leaders and physicians to develop similar lists.

70: Work for others. It became apparent that many "bad day issues" could be solved by the physicians themselves—but only if they had assistance in removing obstacles and acquiring resources. That was the job of their leaders. If the RCMOs or system chiefs didn't have the capability or resources to make a needed change, I stepped in. And if I couldn't remove barriers or provide resources, I contacted System A's CEO and asked for his assistance. Here are a few examples:

- Some physicians were frustrated because they felt that their units' newly hired support staff hadn't been adequately trained and didn't have enough experience. These physicians shared that they would be willing to set up a program to educate already-hired nurses, technicians, and other staff on critical items. But going forward, the physicians wanted to be a part of the interview process in order to assess whether job candidates had the desired training and experience. This was something they couldn't do on their own, so the system chiefs worked with nursing leadership to include the physicians in updating job postings and evaluating applicants.

- There were several cellular "dead spots" in our hospitals' operating rooms (ORs) where physicians, nurses, and vendors' cell phone calls would break up or drop. Obviously, this was not something our caregivers could fix. It wasn't something that service line, hospital, or system leaders could directly fix, either. Ultimately, I contacted the chief informatics officer (CIO), who was one of my executive colleagues. She was able to get the Information Services Department to beef up the repeater system in the ORs.

15: Evaluate and adjust. I met monthly with the RCMOs and service line leaders to review their plans. We discussed questions like: How are your initiatives going? What has been accomplished? What do you need additional assistance with? What plans need to be adjusted? Are there other items that we need to add to the list of things to work on?

THE 15-70-15 SERVICE MODEL WORKS AT ALL LEVELS

I have shared a few examples of how leaders in System A utilized the 15-70-15 service model to help and support physicians. But this model is of limited efficacy if it's practiced *only* by senior leaders. When 15-70-15 is cascaded down throughout the organizational chart, all leaders at all levels are working for each other and, ultimately, for the frontline caregivers. As you'll see, even frontline caregivers them-selves can practice 15-70-15 service when caring for patients! After the 15-70-15 service model has been successfully cascaded through your entire organization, your organization's culture will truly begin to flourish, and employees at all levels will be empowered and motivated to provide the highest level of care.

To hardwire 15-70-15 into how caregivers do their jobs at all levels, each leader needs to fully understand the model, practice it, and then educate the individuals reporting to them. Then, those individuals do the same.

What If My Own Leader Is Resistant?

What should you do if you're practicing the 15-70-15 service model, but your own leader is skeptical or downright critical of leadership styles that don't adhere to traditional ideas? First, I advise having a conversation to describe the "why" behind 15-70-15. Your leader may be operating based on common "servant leadership" misconceptions. Explain that this model will drive improved engagement scores, create better service and outcome metrics, decrease turnover, and result in other improvements. As much as possible, gather data and use evidence to demonstrate that this model is successful. Get specific about what tasks fall into the 70 percent to reassure your leader that you will be performing your expected role.

If a conversation alone isn't effective, adhere to the 15-70-15 model as closely as you can without violating your leader's policies and expectations. Sometimes seeing is believing. Your leader's opinion might change after seeing how successful this model is in action. As in any position, if your values, beliefs, or style run against the grain of the organization or your leader, you should reflect on whether your role is a good fit.

I am a believer in auditing all processes (hence the last 15 percent: evaluate and adjust). I also believe most audits of cascading processes should occur one and two levels down. This ensures that you have appropriately trained your direct reports and that they are putting the process into action. It also ensures that your direct reports have appropriately trained *their* direct reports and that they are putting the process into action as well. When practiced throughout the organization, auditing two levels down provides several layers of evaluation and accountability for nearly every leader.

When cascading a process like the 15-70-15 service model, use data, stories, and examples to illustrate what the process should look like and why it works. As much as possible, directly relate these things to the leader's or caregiver's role so that the information feels relevant. A nonclinical leader (e.g., director of finance) might not absorb much applicable information from a story about how the director of nursing cascades 15-70-15 throughout her department.

Once your staff has been educated on the 15-70-15 service model, you can utilize it to cascade various goals and initiatives throughout the organization. Here's one example. When I was CEO of Hospital X, as part the first 15 percent of my job, I identified customer service as one of the strategic directions I wanted our organization to focus on.

- First, I made sure that the chief nursing officer (CNO) understood this strategic direction. Then, he worked with his leadership team to craft their strategy for improving customer service within nursing. As their plans unfolded, I provided the resources they needed and broke down barriers that were holding them back (my 70 percent). For example, the CNO thought it would be great to provide patients with free copies of each day's newspaper. After reviewing the goals, anticipated benefits, and options for putting this newspaper service into practice, we decided to have volunteers deliver newspapers to interested patients. My role was securing the budget to purchase the newspapers.

- The CNO then worked with the directors of nursing to share how he hoped to achieve the strategic goal of customer service (this was the first 15 percent of his job). He then spent 70 percent of his time providing resources and removing obstacles for the directors. For example, he partnered with the chief experience officer to provide the directors with a volunteer workforce.
- This process was repeated, with the directors setting strategy for their teams and then supporting the managers. The managers then worked to develop the strategy in their departments (Emergency Department, Obstetrical Department, etc.) and then supported their supervisors. In this way, Hospital X's focus on customer service cascaded all the way to the frontline caregivers.

You might think that the 15-70-15 service model stops with front-line caregivers, but it doesn't! They are leaders as well, because they are leading the care of each patient. Here's an example of how a nurse can utilize 15-70-15:

- **15: Set the direction.** A nurse enters a patient's room in the morning and sets the strategic direction for the day: "Good morning, Mrs. Achebe! Today we are going to get you up out of bed to walk the halls four times. We are going to advance your diet from liquids to solids. We are going to get you a follow-up CT scan for postsurgical evaluation. And if you'd like, we will provide you with an opportunity to meet with a chaplain."
- **70: Work for others.** Now it's the nurse's responsibility to make sure that all of these things happen—to serve and support the patient and to remove any barriers the patient may be facing. This might look like ensuring that Mrs. Achebe is ambulated by the medical assistant or personal care assistant encouraging her to focus on her recovery instead of her fatigue, changing her diet orders, making

sure she gets to her CT scan on time, answering her questions, and so on.

- **15: Evaluate and adjust.** At the end of his shift, the nurse should think back on the day. *Did Mrs. Achebe get out of bed and walk the halls four times? Did she get to see the chaplain, if desired?* This is the time to think through course corrections that might need to be made. For instance, perhaps Mrs. Achebe couldn't tolerate her solid food diet and needs to return to liquids.

15-70-15 INVERTS THE ORGANIZATIONAL CHART

Since 70 percent of a leader's job is to serve others, I have sometimes drawn organizational charts upside down. Patients are at the top and frontline caregivers occupy the next level down. Then come other tiers of leaders, with the CEO at the bottom. You can interpret this visual in several different ways, and they all adhere to the spirit of 15-70-15 leadership.

Leaders Support Everyone Else

I think this inverted pyramid of leadership makes a lot of sense because it sends a strong visual message that a leader's job is to support everyone else in the organization instead of resting on the efforts and achievements of others.

Leaders Sustain a Tough Balancing Act

If you think balancing the entire pyramid on its point seems difficult and precarious, I agree! The most challenging tasks *should* be left up to the CEO and other senior executives. When there are faults in the system or when an initiative fails, it's highly likely that the senior executives did not design the right processes, create a strong culture, or set the best direction (which is the first 15 percent of their jobs).

Leaders Are Often the Recipients When You-Know-What Rolls Downhill

The inverted organizational chart makes it easy to see how "sh*t rolls downhill." If someone above you has a problem they can't solve, a complaint to air, or a task they can't do, that all has a tendency to keep rolling downhill until it hits the leader's desk. Sometimes the dungball rolls down several levels, gathering more mass and smelling riper and riper, until someone (often a service-oriented leader) finally takes responsibility and adds it to their 70 percent.

Those at the "Summit" Deserve to Be Recognized

Think of the inverted organizational chart as a mountain. Mountain climbing is very difficult, and those who reach the summit deserve credit for their achievement. Similarly, those at the top of the inverted chart—clinical and nonclinical frontline caregivers—should also be recognized and celebrated for their hard work.

Before you protest, yes, I agree that we leaders have immense amounts of responsibility. You'd have to be out of your mind to say that our jobs are "easy"—and that's not what I'm trying to imply. Some of the tasks only we can do (like deciding whom to promote, how to allocate resources, and when to terminate someone's employment) are extremely difficult. My point is that we should never lose sight of the fact that those on the front lines are doing the challenging, relentless, and sometimes thankless work of setting bones, delivering babies, treating diseases, cleaning rooms, comforting families, negotiating payment plans, handling legal cases, implementing new electronic systems, and more.

Let's never forget that the frontline people are the "face" of the hospital to patients. Like all customers in all organizations, patients' experience depends on how well the leaders behind the scenes enable caregivers to provide outstanding service.

Case Study: Cruising into Service

Several years ago, my family and I booked a Disney cruise. After the excitement of boarding the ship and casting off, it was time for us to find our cabin. We took the elevator to our deck and were immediately faced with a choice: go left or right, depending on whether our room was on the ship's port or starboard side. Soon after, we faced another left or right choice, depending on whether we were staying toward the ship's bow or stern. We must have looked a little lost because one of our deck's hostesses approached us, said hello, and introduced herself. The she said, "Follow me. Your cabin is this way."

I stopped, confused. How did this hostess know where we were supposed to go? We hadn't told her who we were or what our cabin number was.

"You're the Joseph family, right?" she asked. I nodded and began to follow her again. On the way to our cabin, the hostess told us about several events that would be taking place on the ship that night. When we reached our cabin, she added, "Oh, and the family you're traveling with—the Sheffers—are staying right over here. I'll leave you all to get settled."

I thanked the hostess, still a bit confused. Was this the famous Disney magic at work? I had spoken with the hostess for less than three minutes, and I was already in awe of her. In hindsight, I've decided that our hostess's

continued

continued from previous page

omniscience was probably due to the presence of service-focused systems, not magic.

Before boarding the cruise ship, our family's photo was taken and we were issued wristbands that could be used to charge food, drinks, and other purchases to our cabin. For security reasons, cashiers could view our family photo whenever a purchase was made via wristband. I believe that other crew members, including our deck's hostess, had access to that photo as well. And since we'd booked our vacation with family friends, we must have been linked together in the ship's system.

Whether my guesses are right or wrong, one thing is for sure: This was an outstanding service experience. Disney Cruise Line's leadership put systems and processes in place that set up our deck hostess for success. The leadership team essentially worked for her by supporting her mission to help guests have a magical cruise. And that deeply impressed the Joseph family before we had even set foot in our cabin. (Yes, first impressions really are critical!)

As a longtime leader myself, I know that Disney's leaders must have put in considerable thought, planning, and work behind the scenes. Leaders probably set a direction for the cruise line to provide an exceptional experience for every passenger. Then, those leaders cascaded the direction downstream and trusted their teams to identify and implement unexpected ways to provide great service. This was their first 15 percent.

Next, they provided the tools for their employees, including our deck hostess, to be successful (their 70 percent). In this case, Disney's leaders had to greenlight the development of technology and provide the resources

continued

continued from previous page

for implementing it. Finally, I'm sure that by the time my family took our cruise, the photo-sharing technology had undergone multiple updates, improvements, and repairs (the final 15 percent).

Sure, these systems might have been costly for Disney Cruise Line to put into place and train its crew members to use. But the return on investment continues to be tremendous. When I remember my family's cruise, I always think of the exceptional service we experienced—and I know it would not have been possible without leaders who were committed to making their employees successful.

TAKE THE INITIATIVE FOR YOUR 70 PERCENT

James Conway, an Institute for Healthcare Improvement Senior Fellow, once said, "Our systems are too complex to expect merely extraordinary people to perform perfectly 100% of the time. We as leaders have a responsibility to put in place systems to support safe practice" (Costa 2008).

In other words, it is our responsibility to develop systems and processes to make others successful. Don't wait for caregivers to come to you when they could use help, when they encounter a barrier, or when they need resources only you can provide. As much as possible, you should proactively look for ways to support your employees and make it easier for them to successfully do their jobs.

For example, let's say senior leaders want to implement systems to support reliable, effective, efficient, and sustainable practices. They decide to focus on a nonclinical area: human resources. They might ask—and act on—questions such as the following:

- Is the application process for job candidates simple and easy to navigate?

- After a candidate has applied, is the application sent to reviewers who are able to rapidly review it so that the organization does not miss out on an opportunity to hire a high performer?
- Is the onboarding process effective and reliable?
- Do new caregivers (clinical and nonclinical) get the same orientation experience and receive standardized information?
- During orientation, are new hires given information that is useful, accurate, and memorable?
- Is there a fair and just disciplinary process that is used equitably throughout the organization?

If leaders design and implement systems to improve even a few of these areas (after seeking caregivers' input, of course), it's easy to see how 70 percent of their time could be filled. Now, let's move down the organizational chart (or *up* the chart, depending on how you look at it). The following paragraphs illustrate what developing support systems might look like for a nurse—that is, a leader on the front lines.

Think of how complex healthcare can be for someone who is being discharged from the hospital. That individual might receive instructions like, "Follow up with your PCP in two days. Get this lab work and imaging study in five days. See a cardiologist some-time in the next two weeks. Don't forget to stop taking these two medications and start taking this additional one. We also changed the dosage of your blood pressure medication. Increase your walk-ing 10 minutes every few days until you get to 60 minutes per day." It is the job of the frontline leader—the nurse—to put a system in place that enables the patient to navigate these complex needs. For instance, the nurse could do the following:

- Ensure that the patient's discharge instructions are as clear and concise as possible.

- Help the patient make follow-up appointments before leaving the hospital.
- Ensure that the patient knows who to contact if there are any questions.
- Discuss the patient's ongoing care needs with the patient's family members or other support people.
- Connect with the patient's pharmacy to change the patient's medications.
- Call the patient a few days after discharge to see how things are going.

Ultimately, the 15-70-15 service model is closely tied to two other concepts that are woven throughout this book: purpose and empowerment. When caregivers at all levels are connected to their purpose and feel empowered to do everything necessary to provide great care, they will naturally be driven to focus the majority of their time (their 70 percent) on serving and supporting others. Your culture, your patients, and—yes—even your bottom line will all benefit.

REFERENCES

Collins, J. 2001. "The Misguided Mix-up of Celebrity and Leadership." Published September/October 2021. https://www.jimcollins.com/article_topics/articles/the-misguided-mixup.html#:~:text=On%20the%20one%20hand%E2%80%A6%20Looks,external%20factors%2C%20and%20good%20luck.

Costa, D. 2008. "Human Error: Is It an Inevitable Part of Health Care, or Is There a Better Future?" RT Magazine. Published March 11. https://rtmagazine.com/department-management/clinical/human-error-is-it-an-inevitable-part-of-health-care-or-is-there-a-better-future/.

CHAPTER 6

Breaking Down the Power Gradient

ON MARCH 27, 1977, the largest air travel disaster in history occurred on Tenerife, one of the Canary Islands off the coasts of Spain and Morocco. Two Boeing 747s collided on a runway blanketed in dense fog, killing 583 people. You might be thinking, *That's horrible, but what does an aviation accident have to do with healthcare?* My answer is that the tragedy teaches a vital lesson about power dynamics and communication that we should *all* take to heart.

Here's what happened that day in 1977: Los Rodeos Airport on Tenerife was severely congested. As a Pan Am 747 slowly taxied the airport's single runway, a Dutch KLM 747 began to take off from the opposite end. The two 747s could not see each other due to the thick fog—and the air traffic controller couldn't see *either* jumbo jet.

Shortly before the crash, Pam Am had radioed to the tower that it was still on the runway, but the communication was inaudible to KLM because of radio interference. In a radio exchange confirming flight instructions, KLM's first officer was told by the tower, "Stand by for takeoff. I will call you." That sparked a fateful miscommunication: Apparently, KLM's Dutch captain focused on the word *takeoff.* (It's worth noting that in 1977, as now, the word *takeoff* would not have been used in the United States until actual permission had been given. This accident prompted international communication guidelines to be standardized.)

"Is Pan Am still on the runway?" asked KLM's second officer, who had correctly heard the tower's message to stand by.

"What did you say?" asked the highly tenured captain.

"Is he not clear [of the runway], that Pan American?"

"Oh yes!" replied the captain. In the wake of that emphatic statement, the second officer was apparently hesitant to challenge his captain again. The aircraft continued to pick up speed. Soon thereafter the Pan Am 747 became visible on the runway through the fog, but it was too late. Despite attempts by both pilots to get clear, the jets collided. Everyone on board the KLM flight was killed. Only 61 individuals on the Pan Am flight (including the captain, first officer, and flight engineer) survived.

Disaster might have been averted had any number of variables been different: no fog, clearer radio transmissions, and standardized terminology among them. But what stands out to me and to many others who've studied this tragedy is the KLM captain's dismissal of his second officer's doubts, and the second officer's unwillingness to speak up again. The power gradient (or amount of authority) between these two men turned out to have deadly consequences.

Tenerife's Legacy

The Tenerife disaster led to a widespread restructuring of cockpit procedures. Instead of emphasizing hierarchy, a team-based approach to decision-making called *crew resource management* (CRM) was developed. Now, more junior crew members are encouraged to question, challenge, and contradict senior pilots if they believe something is amiss. Senior crew members are required to listen to any concerns and reevaluate their decision accordingly. CRM has proven very effective in improving communication, reducing human error, and increasing safety in the cockpit.

KLM's Captain Veldhuyzen van Zanten was one of the airline's most senior pilots. He was also chief of flight training for the entire airline. In other words, Captain van Zanten was a highly respected leader with a great deal of authority. Although we will never know for sure, it is speculated that the second officer was reluctant to continue challenging an esteemed captain who stood well above him in the cockpit hierarchy.

What can we learn from the Tenerife incident? Plenty. We may never sit at the controls of a massive aircraft, but we hold lives in our hands each day. Those we lead should never be afraid to challenge us—and we should never hesitate to listen to their voices of experience and wisdom.

Why *Power Gradient*? A Word About My Terminology

Google the Tenerife disaster and you'll see the phrase *authority gradient* pop up over and over. You may also see the phrase *power distance*. These two phrases are used to describe the difference in perceived superiority between two individuals. Whichever term you use to describe that difference—in terms of how comfortable people are in voicing their thoughts or concerns—the smaller it is, the better it is. This is true for the organization, all of its employees (caregivers), and ultimately the customers (loved ones). As this difference decreases, all metrics will improve: safety, strategy, culture, service, empowerment, engagement, and more.

That said, you may have noticed I use the term *power gradient* throughout this book. It's a hybrid of the two aforementioned terms. In the context of this book, I prefer the word *power* to *authority*. Why? Because *authority* differences

continued

---

continued from previous page

(or gradients) between levels of leadership *are* valid—not all decisions can be solved by consensus, and someone has to make the final call. That's just reality, and we're not trying to remove anyone's authority.

What we do want to remove is the perception of *superiority*, which, to me at least, the word *power* suggests. If Person A is superior, then person B must be inferior, right? If person B feels inferior, they may keep their mouth shut at times when it would be far better for everyone if they spoke up. So, whichever terminology you prefer, let's work to eliminate the superiority difference between the levels of leadership.

THE POWER GRADIENT IN HEALTHCARE

Historically, healthcare has tended to have a hierarchical culture. In other words, nurses, more junior physicians, and other employees have been reluctant to speak up to senior physicians and leaders due to fear of punishment or other repercussions.

Perception Is Reality

Even among supposed peers, a *perceived* power gradient has long existed in healthcare settings. Here are a few examples of relationships where this might be the case:

- Two team members have the same role or "rank," but one team member has several more years' experience than the other.

continued

continued from previous page

- An employee has experience and qualifications but is new to the organization and thus hasn't "proven" himself to the team.
- One person on a team is more "popular" than another and has more social capital.

Even when someone actively tries to flatten the power gradient, *perception* of that person's authority can still affect her working relationships. For instance, a physician might say, "I am not a medical director (or in another position of authority). Therefore, I am simply a caregiver and would like my team to view me as such." However, because this person *is* a physician on whom others rely for expertise, she is in a position of power and thus part of a power gradient. (This situation can happen with nurses and other caregivers too.)

It is also common for patients to perceive their physicians and other caregivers as being in positions of authority and control, even as we strive to live out our purpose of providing respectful, compassionate service. Too often, patients feel reluctant to speak up, ask for clarification, or disagree with their providers because of the perception that "the doctor knows best."

The point is that power gradients are everywhere. Even when they are only *perceived* as opposed to hierarchical, they can have negative, or even disastrous, consequences—and we should be driven by the same urgency to correct them. Don't just look up and down the organizational chart for perceived power gradients; look horizontally at relationships between peers, and even outside the chart at caregiver–patient dynamics. As the saying goes, "Perception is reality."

The good news is that the power gradient in healthcare (both real and perceived) is gradually being flattened as its negative effects on patient care and organizational culture are more clearly understood. Especially as we move toward a value-based, patient-centric care model, more and more leaders realize it is our responsibility to directly confront this issue. However, despite these efforts the power gradient still exists and still affects performance and patient care from time to time. We are doing better—but there's significant work yet to be done.

In healthcare, as in aviation, the power gradient can directly or indirectly cause any number of adverse outcomes—up to and including loss of life. And in fact, when we talk about the power gradient in healthcare, it's often in the context of safety. We are all aware that tiered levels of power between caregivers (or between providers and patients) can directly contribute to human error, just as in the Tenerife crash.

I also want to be clear that a rigid power gradient sends many other negative ripples throughout the organization. It adversely affects culture, communication, innovation, engagement, morale, and more. It prevents caregivers from aligning with the purpose of their role, their department, and the organization. It drives turnover and contributes to burnout.

First, let's review some of the negative effects the power gradient can have within healthcare systems:

- Junior staff do not speak up when they have safety concerns or do not fully understand confusing information. This can lead to a poor patient outcome or poor project performance. (Note that I use the term *junior* very broadly here. For example, a departmental director, who is very high in the overall organizational hierarchy, is still "junior" in relation to the CEO.)
- Junior staff feel that their voices are not heard and that they are not contributing members of the team, which directly contributes to burnout.

- Leaders do not receive valuable ideas and information from frontline employees. Thus, potential gains in efficiency, productivity, safety, or other areas are never realized.
- Teams are afflicted by a lack of trust, cooperation, engagement, and collaboration.
- Employees feel intimidated, stifled, or suppressed and are much less likely to be aligned with the organization's purpose.
- Patients do not feel that they are valued partners in their own care or that their opinions are respected. This type of disengaged patient may seek care elsewhere. Worse, they may not share a critical piece of information that could affect their clinical outcome.

EVALUATING THE POWER GRADIENT IN YOUR ORGANIZATION

Evaluating the power gradient in your organization isn't always easy. Although policies and procedures related to voicing concerns, shared decision-making, and advocating for patient care may be in place, staff may still feel that they will face consequences for challenging a "superior." Longtime caregivers may find it difficult to break away from old patterns of behavior and power dynamics. Here are some diagnostic questions to ask yourself:

- Do nurses feel comfortable raising concerns with a prominent surgeon? Would they stop a procedure to say, "We've lost a needle" or "We're missing a sponge"?
- Do physicians willingly accept feedback and their team's opinions with gratitude? Or do they feel disrespected and believe they have lost face? Think about relationships between physicians and all other roles: respiratory therapists, pharmacists, radiology

technicians, environmental services personnel, medical students, and so on.

- Does everyone in the organization feel comfortable voicing concerns to the CEO? Would they point out potential flaws in the organization's strategy or say, "I have an issue with the new policy"?
- Does one person within a team, shift, or department tend to make all decisions? Or are decisions reached collaboratively?
- Is the entire leadership team (at all levels) supportive of employees speaking up? Are they willing to have a discussion with anyone in the organization? Do they genuinely listen to others with the intent of understanding?
- Do patients feel comfortable bringing forth concerns about their care, or do they act subordinate to providers?

This list of questions is not exhaustive, but it should get you thinking about the power gradient within your organization. Chances are you will identify several areas in which the power gradient creates a barrier to providing the best care, strengthening teamwork, receiving caregiver input on how to improve the organization, and building a strong culture. Throughout the rest of this chapter, we will look at ways to break down the power gradient.

Use the "Introduce Me" Litmus Test

I once heard another leader say that a quick way to evaluate an ambulatory medical clinic's culture and power gradient is to ask some of the physicians to introduce you to the front desk staff. Afterward, in private, ask the physicians to tell you more about those people: Are they married? Do they have children? What are their hobbies?

continued

continued from previous page

If the physicians don't know the names of front desk caregivers, that is a big issue. It implies a dangerous level of disconnection and disinterest on the physicians' part and indicates a rigid power gradient. If the physicians *can* introduce you to their coworkers at the front desk but don't know much about them, a power gradient that prevents communication is probably still at play. Perhaps the clinic's culture simply doesn't revolve around people talking about their personal lives, but most tight working groups do know these fairly basic details about one other. Higher level staff not knowing personal information about coworkers is a sign that you should keep evaluating the culture.

The same litmus test can be used in a tight unit of a hospital (e.g., Emergency Department, Obstetrical Department, Intensive Care Unit, Cardiac Unit, Operating Room). Do the nurses in the ICU know about the respiratory therapists? Do the respiratory therapists know about the physicians? Do the physicians know about the pharmacists?

You can even use this test to assess the leadership within the same specialty of a certain department. Does the manager of Plant Operations know about his team members? Does the general counsel know about the leaders of Compliance, Risk Management, and Contracting? Do the leaders of Compliance, Risk Management, and Contracting know about their own team members?

BREAKING DOWN THE POWER GRADIENT STARTS WITH YOU

As I've stated before, one of my guiding principles as a healthcare executive has always been to put people first with the knowledge that this will shift the culture and result in improved patient outcomes and metrics. A big part of my strategy to put people first is breaking down the power gradient. I've learned that leaders *must* be deliberate about this. Good intentions alone won't move the needle.

Leaders must realize that flattening the power gradient needs to start at the top. We must demonstrate through our own behavior what we expect to see from others. Culture isn't changed by telling people how to behave but rather by modeling behaviors to emulate.

With that in mind, the following sections discuss some tactics we can use.

Be More Accessible

The power gradient can be broken down significantly by developing relationships and increasing communication with individuals from all levels, departments, and roles within your organization. Here are some strategies I used when I was president and CEO of Hospital X:

- Throughout my career, I asked everyone in the organization to call me Kevin. I didn't want to be known formally as Dr. Joseph, because a perceived power gradient can easily originate from something as subtle and innocuous as a title. While the name I went by didn't affect how available I was from a "presence" standpoint, it made me *seem* more accessible because it helped caregivers view me as an approachable colleague instead of a person with greater power, simply because of a title.

  Being addressed more informally also conveyed that I didn't consider myself to be "better than" or to have special privileges because of my position. When it comes to carrying out an organization's purpose, I believe that everyone is "in it" together—we just have different roles. (You might recall the story of how my mother taught me this vital lesson, which I shared at the beginning of chapter 1.)

In a similar vein, I know several surgeons who all but demand that the entire operating room team calls them by their first name, and not by "Doctor Smith." The atmosphere in these operating rooms is very collegial. There is great communication, and no one is hesitant to voice concerns if they should arise.

- When I visited a hospital or site within the system, my laptop was my office. If I had free time, I didn't go to an empty office or other private space. Instead, I set up in the cafeteria, break room, or caregiver lounge—wherever people ate or took breaks. I wanted to be visible and approachable. If you adopt this strategy, don't plan on sending many e-mails or getting much project work done, but *do* plan on getting great value for your time. Through the conversations you have, you will learn a tremendous amount about the organization and where to focus your efforts. Opportunities for improvement, small and large, about all aspects of the organization, will be conveyed to you. As I will explain in the next chapter, healthcare is in the service business—and the quality of service we provide depends on the quality of our relationships.

- When Hospital X was under construction, the leadership team asked that there not be a physician dining room. We wanted everyone to eat together in the cafeteria. This broke down the notion that physicians were special and entitled to privileges that the rest of the staff didn't get. However, all departments did have a break room or lounge available—physicians, nurses, and other caregivers simply used the same space. Everyone needs to (and should) take breaks away from frontline activity throughout the day.

- My cell phone number was public knowledge within the organization because I wanted *everyone* to know that I was accessible. If caregivers didn't see me in person during the course of the day, or if seeking me out was difficult because of time constraints or scheduling conflicts, they could call or text. Over the course of my career as a leader, I have provided thousands of caregivers with my mobile number. It has never been used without good reason. But the impact this action continues to have in breaking down the power gradient is tremendous.

Being accessible is not just about being physically available for a conversation, it is also about being mentally available for a conversation. In other words, an accessible leader takes care to be fully present in the moment. Trust me, I know that when you have a lot of things on your mind, that's easier said than done. Here are a few successful strategies I use:

- When speaking with anyone in the organization, I try to be fully present. That means I not only stop typing or put down my phone; I move away from those devices so that they are not a distraction to the conversation. I try to actively listen instead of thinking about something else. I do not want people to feel like they are bothering me; I want them to walk away from our interactions knowing that I genuinely wanted to hear and understand what they had to say.

    If I'm finishing up an e-mail, a text message, or a conversation, I'll say something like, "Give me two minutes to finish up this e-mail so that I can provide you with all of my attention." Invariably, the person understands why I asked them to wait and is appreciative of my undivided attention once we are able to converse.

- One thing that is helpful for me, and that also demonstrates that I am paying attention, is taking notes during the conversation. I carry around a small notebook and a pen (I have seen other colleagues use note cards). When someone is providing input, I bullet point their thoughts. This helps me remember the items I need to address (which are all too easy to forget during the course of a busy day), and it also sends a strong message to the other individual that I am taking their concerns seriously. I then use this same list as a reminder to circle back to that person once I have found the answer to their question, resolved their concern, or otherwise addressed their thoughts.

- Being mentally present is important in all interactions, despite how brief or innocuous they may seem. For example, when you are passing someone in the hallway, extend a greeting. Not saying "hello" because you are "on a mission" to get somewhere or do something sends a message that (at best) you have something on your mind that is more important than the person you just passed, or (at worst) the other person is not good enough for you to bother greeting them.

Get Out on the Front Lines

In chapter 1, I first told the story of how I asked the C-suite at Hospital X to work on the front lines. To briefly recap: As CEO, I worked one day a week as a physician in the Emergency Department (ED), and I asked all of my executives to work on the hospital's front lines one day every other week. For instance, the chief nursing officer assisted the nursing staff by taking vital signs and answering call lights. The vice president of Operations worked as a respiratory therapist, as that was his previous occupation and he was still licensed. And the chief financial officer, who didn't have past clinical experience, jumped in by transporting patients and cleaning rooms.

As I had hoped, immersing themselves in the day-to-day, patient-facing work of the hospital helped these

continued

continued from previous page

leaders understand their purpose as well as how their decisions affected the care we delivered. To my delight, another by-product of working on the front lines was a flattening of the power gradient. As frontline caregivers began to develop relationships with the departmental directors and executives, their respect for and trust in these leaders grew. Many times, I heard one of the leaders say, "I am learning so much from the caregivers in my department. I didn't realize how many ideas and concerns I *wasn't* hearing before I spent time on the front lines."

When You Make a Mistake or Bad Decision, Admit It Humbly

When I became CEO of Hospital X, it was struggling in many ways, including financially. One of the calculated changes we made to become more productive was to take a close look at staffing. The hospital had 12-hour nursing shifts, and staffing was the same overnight as it was during the day. After talking to nursing managers and directors, my leadership team and I agreed that since the volume of work at night was less than during the day, we could reduce staffing on that shift.

Just a few weeks later, one of the night nurses approached me directly. (Incidentally, the fact that a nurse felt comfortable coming to the CEO proved that my other efforts to break down the power gradient were working!) This nurse told me that the staffing changes were not sustainable.

"The other nurses and I understand the rationale for having less staff at night, but at the 7 p.m. shift change, work doesn't slow down," she explained. "At that time, patients are still getting imaging studies like X-rays, MRIs, and CT scans. Food trays are still being provided. Admissions in the ED are at a high volume. Work doesn't really slow down until around 10 p.m., so for the first three hours of the shift, we are really struggling to keep up."

"You're right," I told her. "Thank you for telling me about this." Shortly thereafter, I admitted my error to the entire organization, and we adjusted shifts so that staffing decreased around 10:00 p.m. Although the original decision to reduce staffing at 7:00 p.m. was made by the entire leadership team, I believed that as CEO the proverbial buck stopped with me, and that any mistakes made throughout the organization were ultimately my responsibility.

By making myself vulnerable and publicly admitting fault, I didn't weaken my position or lose the respect of caregivers. Far from it! Instead, I gained their trust and further flattened the power gradient. They now had proof that their CEO would make time for them, listen to their concerns, and make changes when warranted.

Get Input from All Stakeholders Before Making a Decision

Another important lesson I learned from the night shift staffing incident was to always consult with those who will be directly affected. As I mentioned, I *did* consult with the nursing managers and directors, but none of them worked in a frontline setting, and none of them foresaw how staffing reductions would affect nurses' ability to deliver care in the first hours of the night shift.

As I've noted previously, despite having good intentions, leaders may not know what's best or what's needed at the front line. We need to *ask* the front line what they need, prefer, and think in order to end up with the best outcomes. In this case, I failed to do so up front. I'm very grateful to the nurse who helped me learn the lesson that frontline stakeholders need to be engaged before a decision affecting them is made, even if their leadership team is also engaged in the conversation.

The point is, if a decision affects people other than yourself, you should seek their input before moving forward. (This is especially true if systems or procedures for an entire unit, department, shift, or organization will be changing.) When leaders make unilateral decisions and expect all those affected to obediently fall into line, the power gradient is reinforced. But when you involve stakeholders from all levels in the decision-making process, you show that you are committed to flattening the power gradient *and* to achieving the best outcomes for patients and their caregivers.

Bear in mind that as leaders, we sometimes lose sight of how difficult it can be for frontline employees to approach individuals who may be many levels above them in the organization's hierarchy. Thus, we need to be proactive about seeking out caregivers' opinions and suggestions. Leadership can't be everywhere at all times, but collectively, our employees are. Too often the power gradient (real or perceived) ensures that those employees keep their observations to themselves. Remember that we can't fix something that is broken or improve on something that could be made better if we aren't aware that there is an issue.

What If Input Is Hard to Gather?

Knowing that all plans have flaws, risks, and unintended consequences, I always ask for feedback from others. However, there have been times when the room is fairly silent and no feedback is forthcoming. In these situations, I remind myself that despite ongoing efforts to reduce the perceived power gradient, it will never be completely eliminated. (This helps me not take the lack of feedback personally.) Then, I go around the room asking everyone to punch a hole in my plan.

continued

continued from previous page

This strategy not only provides me with valuable feedback on the plan, but it also helps others become more confident in speaking up and demonstrates my own vulnerability and humility. However, know that this tactic can backfire if your inquiry isn't authentic. If you don't genuinely listen to everyone, if you interrupt, if you don't show respect, or if you quickly shut down their thoughts, you will have taken a step backwards—and you may find it doubly difficult to regain the lost ground.

Always Respond to Feedback

Throughout this chapter, I've talked a lot about the importance of leaders listening to employees' concerns, ideas, and observations. Well, here's the second part of that piece of advice: Always, *always* respond. Whether the feedback is valuable, accurate, actionable, or not, thank the other person for sharing and emphasize how much their contribution matters. During your efforts to break down the power gradient, all eyes will be on leadership. Any slip-up will set your progress back, so you do not want to send the message that people who come forward will be ignored.

When you are having a face-to-face conversation with a team member, it's easy to respond. It may not be as easy in other situations. Here are a few things to be mindful of:

- Don't let voicemails, e-mails, or texts fall into a black hole. Send a reply.
- If you provide comment cards or suggestion boxes for employees to utilize, then acknowledge contributions. Even if responses are anonymous, you can still say, "I

understand from submissions to our suggestion box that many of you are concerned about XYZ." I know of some leaders who dedicate a section of their weekly or monthly newsletters to addressing suggestion box comments. They'll share what the solution to the issue was or, just as important, explain why it can't be done.

- If an employee's feedback leads to change, let that person know what action you are taking, and consider celebrating that person for the suggestion or concern that was raised. This will reinforce the importance of speaking up. Plus, others will want to be similarly recognized and will be more willing to come forward.
- If you can't go through with a suggestion, or if you find that a concern is unfounded, provide an explanation. You should always give people the *why*, but it's especially important when your response could be construed as ignoring their feedback or dismissing their concerns.
- Whether the communication is in person or via e-mail or text, restate the person's concerns, suggestions, or message in your own words. This demonstrates that you are listening and striving to understand their message. It also gives them a chance to set the record straight if you *have* misunderstood something.

Remember That the "Little Things" Can Be Very Powerful

Most of the advice in this chapter is focused on "big" things you can do to break down the power gradient, both real and perceived. But even seemingly small behaviors can have a big impact on helping the caregivers in your organization see you and other senior staff as approachable partners (as opposed to high-and-mighty bosses). Here are six subtle tactics to consider:

- **Say goodbye to the power suit.** Who says leaders *have* to dress formally? Consider letting them know that suits, ties, and more formal dresses are not necessary. Formal business attire can set up a subconscious social barrier for many people. They associate it with authority and power. Remember, a *perceived* power gradient can be just as stifling as an actual one.

- **Let seating arrangements work in your favor.** If you call a meeting with someone and choose to sit behind your desk, you have laid the foundation for the conversation to be governed by a traditional power gradient: The person behind the desk is on their "turf" and has the authority; the person sitting across from them is a subordinate. Contrast this to *both* of you sitting together at a small table, or in a pair of armchairs adjacent to one another— perhaps in a neutral, communal location. In these scenarios, your guest is much more likely to feel like an equal partner in the meeting.

  Perhaps don't even sit—have a walking meeting. During nice weather, who doesn't want to be outside? This format is only conducive to more informal and conversational update meetings but is certainly a welcomed change of pace.

- **Be aware of body language.** We all know that what we *don't* say speaks just as loudly as the words that leave our mouths. In fact, research by Dr. Albert Mehrabian suggests that 55 percent of communication is based on body language and facial expressions, 38 percent is via intonation, and just 7 percent is accomplished through spoken words (World of Work Project 2022)! That being the case, avoid using postures that can be off-putting or dismissive, such as crossing your arms or angling your body away from the other person. Make eye contact and try to relax.

Those of us in healthcare should be particularly mindful of how we converse with patients. Assuming the patient is sitting or lying on a bed or exam table, take a seat so that you are at their eye level. Standing above someone is a quick way to subtly establish that you are in a position of power. (Be sure to share this insight with physicians and nurses, who might regularly spend five or ten minutes in discussion with a patient.)

- **Prioritize promptness.** When leaders are late to a meeting or other type of appointment, they can send the message that their time (and therefore their position) is more important than their staff's. This is especially true if tardiness is habitual. Being prompt shows that you respect the other person's presence and time, and that you don't consider your to-do list more important than theirs.

- **Remember that words matter.** The words you use can either reinforce or break down the power gradient. Take, for example, "I have to be at this event" versus "I get to be at this event." The first sentence indicates that you view spending time at the event as a chore; the second makes other attendees feel valued. Here are a few other examples of phrases that either reinforce or break down the power gradient:
  - "What were you thinking?" versus "Help me understand why you made that decision."
  - "As director of this department, I want you do it this way" versus "Let's consider this option too."
  - "That's not going to work" versus "I'm concerned that this is beyond our capabilities. Let's discuss how we might make this option work."
  - "All employees need to make this change" versus "We are all going to work on making this change together."

- **Proactively define medical terminology.** Healthcare has a giant lexicon of obscure words and medical jargon that can unknowingly create a gradient between colleagues or between caregivers and patients. Many people don't feel comfortable asking caregivers for an explanation of unknown terminology, which can lead to dangerous situations. I have found it helpful to proactively define terminology as it is spoken, with a preference toward using the "technical" word *after* I explain the content of the conversation. For example, compare the following:
  - "Your heart condition is idiopathic cardiomyopathy."
  - "Your heart condition is idiopathic cardiomyopathy. *Idiopathic* means that we don't know what is causing it, and *cardiomyopathy* means that your heart isn't pumping as strongly as it should."
  - "We are not sure what is causing your heart condition, but we do know that it is not pumping as strongly as normal. We call this *idiopathic cardiomyopathy*. *Idiopathic* means that we don't know the cause, and *cardiomyopathy* means that your heart isn't pumping as strongly as it should."

  The third option is easiest for the patient to understand and does not set up as much of a power gradient. Explaining the diagnosis prior to using the technical terminology is a subtle but powerful tactic. I have noticed that when patients hear a complex term or medical jargon first, they often get "stuck" trying to figure out what it means instead of focusing on the rest of the caregiver's explanation.

  This same approach can be used in discussions with colleagues when out-of-the-ordinary terms are introduced. The important thing is to never assume that the other person knows the definition of unusual words.

CASCADING YOUR POWER GRADIENT PHILOSOPHY THROUGHOUT THE ORGANIZATION

As we've discussed, breaking down the power gradient in any organization is a top-down process. Clinical and nonclinical caregivers must see their leaders modeling desired behaviors in order for their own habits and behaviors to change. Successfully combating the power gradient requires the buy-in and participation of the whole organization.

You might recall that in chapter 1, I described why the leadership team at Hospital X decided to refer to patients as "loved ones": because each patient *is* someone's loved one. If we treat every patient as if they were our own beloved parent, spouse, child, or friend, then we will make the correct decisions regarding their care and service experience. With that said, I have a question: Would you want your loved one to be treated by a provider who negates input from others? Who sees themselves as "better than" other caregivers—and potentially patients? If the answer is no, then it is your responsibility as a leader to make sure that doesn't happen in your department or organization. Here are a few strategies.

Hire Caregivers Who Share Your Commitment to Flattening the Power Gradient

I once conducted an interview with a gastroenterologist. About ten minutes into the conversation, I asked why he was leaving his current organization. He said, "The nurses have a tendency to pause procedures when they think something isn't right. It's so frustrating! They slow me down with their objections, and it's not their place to speak up."

Yes, this physician actually told me he didn't think it was a nurse's "place" to speak up when something might be amiss. I then said,

"I don't think this organization is the right fit for you. Thank you for your time!" and shook the physician's hand. It was the shortest interview of my life.

Admittedly, this is a pretty extreme example. The physician in question voluntarily made it clear that he was what I call a power gradient enforcer. Most of the time, people won't be that up front in conveying they support and expect tiered levels of power in healthcare. But you should always be on the lookout for these power gradient enforcers, and you should never tolerate their harmful attitudes in your organization.

When hiring new employees, you can ask interview questions designed to uncover how a candidate feels about the power gradient. For instance, if you're interviewing a physician, ask, "Tell me about a time when someone slowed you down while you were doing a procedure because they had a concern. What was your response to the person and situation?"

If you're interviewing a departmental leader, ask, "How do you go about formulating new policies and procedures? Whose opinions do you seek out?" "When is the last time you spoke with someone on the front lines?" "What was your reaction to an incident when you witnessed or learned of someone 'talking down' to someone else? How did you address the situation?" You could even throw out a more open-ended prompt such as, "Describe your thoughts on the relationship between an organizational chart and culture." The candidate's answer to this broad prompt should spark follow-up questions and informative conversation regarding their views on the power gradient.

Ensure That New Hires Are Entering a Culture Where *Everyone* Is Well-Versed on Power Gradients

Once you have identified a candidate who seems to be a good cultural fit for the organization and who is driven to lower the power gradient, it is time to onboard the new caregiver. At this point, it's important to remember that real and perceived power gradients can span a full 360 degrees, reaching up to the new hire's boss, down to her subordinates, and horizontally to her peers. Therefore, everyone at all levels (not *just* new hires) needs to be trained in the organization's philosophy on flattening the power gradient. I recommend setting a goal for all caregivers to be able to do the following:

- Describe what a power gradient (and *perceived* power gradient) is in healthcare
- Provide examples of superior, subordinate, and peer power gradients
- Detail the consequences of power gradients
- Discuss tactics and methods for breaking down the perceived power gradient
- Describe the organization's philosophy regarding power gradients, and shared standards of behavior that the entire

Flattening the Power Gradient and Pleasing Others Are Not Always the Same Thing

A leader who has broken down the power gradient genuinely seeks out the opinions of others, demonstrates respect for caregivers and their opinions, and builds relationships based on trust, communication, and integrity. This *does not* translate into relinquishing the authority to make final decisions, some of which your organization may not fully support. It is important to contrast authority to superiority. Breaking down the power gradient doesn't break down authority—it breaks down superiority.

It is critical to understand that breaking down the power gradient does not mean that your decisions will always be popular or that they must align with the opinion of

continued

continued from previous page

someone whose input you sought out. As a leader, you will always have to make difficult decisions. And inevitably, some people won't like what you choose. However, if you have genuinely listened to the stakeholders of the final decision and provided the rationale for why your decision is not in alignment with their desires, you have succeeded in lowering the power gradient as much as possible.

organization stands behind. Behavioral standards might include the following:

- "I will treat all colleagues with respect."
- "I will not 'talk down' to anyone."
- "I will not interrupt or silence someone who is sharing a concern."
- "I will provide the 'why' behind my thought process when making a decision."

Give Leaders the Tools to Support and Empower Their Teams

Caregivers need to know that leadership throughout the organization has a zero-tolerance attitude toward power gradients. Leaders can ensure this happens by (1) helping caregivers understand how to escalate a concern or event that enforced a power gradient, and (2) knowing how to address individuals who are power gradient enforcers.

For many caregivers, confronting someone of perceived authority can be an intimidating challenge. It is often helpful to provide suggestions on how the caregiver might approach the situation. For example, I was once approached by a nurse who was concerned that a surgeon was not always washing his hands prior to approaching the patient. The nurse told me that she didn't feel comfortable bringing up this issue with the surgeon and wasn't sure what to say if she did initiate the conversation.

I suggested that she phrase her feedback in the context of concern for the patient and physician, for example, "Dr. Jones, I don't want one of your patients to get an infection, so please don't forget to wash your hands prior to seeing the patient." In general, I've found that caregivers are most comfortable—and those above them in the organizational hierarchy are more receptive—when feedback is given out of concern for the patient or the caregiver in question, not from a policy standpoint (if possible).

Hold Power Gradient Enforcers Accountable

In large organizations, it is inevitable that there will be individuals who are supportive of a power gradient and who do not agree with breaking it down. These individuals need to be held accountable for their actions. If their actions are not addressed, then the team's efforts to break down the perceived power gradient will quickly fall apart.

You don't want consequences for power gradient enforcement to come out of the blue. Ensure that all caregivers, regardless of their role, know what to expect if they violate standards of behavior. Perhaps a first violation would prompt a verbal warning from the caregiver's supervisor, along with a constructive conversation about how the caregiver's behavior needs to change. A second violation might warrant a written warning. A third might earn the caregiver a suspension, performance improvement plan, and/or probation. And a fourth violation of power gradient standards would mean termination. (This is just an example. Chances are, your organization already has a progressive discipline plan in place that could be applied to power gradient violations.)

Bear in mind that everyone in the organization will be closely watching how power gradient enforcers are addressed, and how far their behavior will be tolerated (if at all). It's essential for executive leadership to be comfortable providing feedback to these individuals, disciplining them, or perhaps even terminating the relationship between the individual and the organization.

In all of my leadership roles, I have provided my mobile number to the entire organization with a strong emphasis that caregivers should not hesitate to call or text me with any concerns. If the concern was in regard to power gradient–enforcing behavior, I wanted to know about it immediately! The sooner it was addressed, the more effective the feedback and coaching would be.

FINAL THOUGHTS

I'd like to refer to an observation I made in the first chapter in this book: Everyone has a unique contribution to offer. In the daily effort to fulfill your organization's purpose, no one is more important or valuable or special than anyone else. Yes, we will always need hierarchy to provide structure and leadership within our organizations. Some people will always have more seniority, expertise, and experience than others. Some will always be responsible for making a final decision. However, those distinctions should not create barriers to communication and collaboration, and they do not give us permission to treat anyone with less respect.

Instead, we should always remember that it *is* those very differences in our roles and perspectives that combine to create a full, robust healthcare ecosystem. Ego and the traditional power gradient have no place in providing high-quality care or in creating a positive, purpose-driven culture.

The bottom line is this: Breaking down the power gradient—real *or* perceived—requires trust, humility, authentic respect for others, genuine communication, accountability, and diligent relationship-building. Know that even as you make progress, a hierarchy of power is always present. If left unchecked, it is detrimental to patient outcomes and organizational success. Counteracting the power gradient takes continuous attention. Keep this effort at the forefront of your work every day.

REFERENCE

World of Work Project. 2022. "Mehrabian's 7-38-55 Communication Model: It's More Than Words." Accessed August 11. https://worldofwork.io/2019/07/mehrabians-7-38-55-communication-model/.

CHAPTER 7

Incorporating Exceptional and Distinguished Service

IMAGINE FOR A moment that you are a patient in the hospital. You are at your most vulnerable. You are stressed out, disoriented, maybe in pain, perhaps in emotional turmoil, and almost certainly in the grips of fear and anxiety—worried about your prognosis, about missing work, about the impact this will have your finances, about your pets at home . . . about everything.

Or maybe you're a family member of the patient. You're worried sick about your loved one. At the same time, you're dealing with many of the same practical concerns that are preying on the mind of your loved one.

Either way, this is an incredibly tough time in your life. You want excellent medical treatment. That's a given. But what you also want is *care*. You want to feel that the doctors and nurses and technicians and housekeepers truly care about your needs, your situation, and your overall well-being. Providing great service is how we demonstrate that care. As President Theodore Roosevelt reportedly said, "Nobody cares how much you know until they know how much you care" (Theodore Roosevelt Center 2022).

However, so many things can fall under the "service" umbrella that, frankly, this chapter was difficult to write. Sometimes I had trouble knowing where to draw the line! But you'll find I've made an effort to include the main reasons great service is important as well as some practical tips for providing it consistently.

First, let's look at why service is such a vital part of healthcare delivery.

THE PRODUCT-TO-SERVICE SPECTRUM

People spend their money on only two things: a product and a service. All industries fall into one of three categories: (1) those that primarily deliver a product, (2) those that primarily deliver a service, and (3) those that deliver both. Let's look at a few simple examples.

First is an electronics company that makes products like laptops and TVs. The vast majority of this organization's work is focused on innovating, designing, manufacturing, distributing, and advertising its products. Consumers then spend their money on these cutting-edge products. An electronics company doesn't deliver much of a service; perhaps a relatively minor amount of effort is channeled toward providing customer support.

On the other hand, a hair salon is focused on providing a service to its customers. The consumer judges the salon based on the friendliness of the stylist, the timeliness of the appointment, the cleanliness of the environment, and the visual outcome of the stylists' efforts. The salon might choose to offer a selection of hairstyling products for sale, but those account for a small share of the salon's income, and they probably aren't the reason clients book appointments.

In between these two extremes is a spectrum of organizations that provide both products and services. Consider an upscale restaurant, for example. Its business model is built on offering nearly equal amounts of product and service. The product is the restaurant's food and beverage selection. Factors such as variety, flavor, quality, quantity, presentation, and temperature all contribute to the product's value.

But no matter how delicious a restaurant's food is, the service its customers receive is often of equal or greater importance. Being seated promptly by a host and being served by friendly, attentive, and thoughtful waitstaff are essential to the customer's experience. If service is lacking, customers will leave with a bad taste in their mouths (pun intended) no matter how delicious their food tasted.

So, where does healthcare fall on the product-to-service spectrum? *Healthcare is almost entirely a service industry.* Let's look at a few common objections to that assertion.

"We provide plenty of products, like cardiac stents and brain aneurysm coiling."

Although this statement is true, many patients don't know what a stent looks like or understand the intricacies of how the aneurysm coiling works. Even as an emergency medicine physician with extensive medical training, I have to admit that *I* have never seen a stent or a coil. I wouldn't be able to judge those products if they sat in front of me, and if I needed them myself, I wouldn't know if the correct type had been used. Neither would most patients.

What I (and all patients) *can* judge is service. For patients who don't have a medical background, the only thing they can accurately judge is service: Ease of making an appointment. Timeliness of caregivers. Whether a physician listened fully to their concerns. Whether nurses displayed empathy. Whether staff was respectful and responsive. Cleanliness of the facility. The efficiency and effectiveness of care. How billing issues were handled. How continuation of care was handled. And so much more.

"Safety and quality are the only things that matter."

Over the course of my career, I've encountered my fair share of providers whose motto might as well have been "I'm not here to kiss your butt; I'm here to save it." It's no coincidence that these providers tend to have poor experience scores from their patients (e.g., Consumer Assessment of Healthcare Providers and Systems, or CAHPS, scores such as HCAHPS, CGCAHPS, etc.). Here, I deliberately used the term *patients* and not *loved ones*. I strongly believe that if the caregiver thought of her patients as loved ones, then that caregiver's attitude and delivery of service would be different (and so would her scores).

Just like the restaurant customer who recalls a server's rudeness over the meal's quality, patients give low ratings to caregivers they perceive as being insensitive, arrogant, patronizing, or callous—even if their health outcomes were ideal. Again, service is what we in healthcare are judged by. Patients (or loved ones) and their families use it as a surrogate marker for overall care, including safety and quality.

Just as most travelers cannot judge whether a pilot or plane flies safely unless there is a negative incident, most patients cannot judge how safe a caregiver or hospital is unless there is a negative outcome. In addition, safe care is an absolute expectation. Nobody would book an appointment with a healthcare provider they felt was unsafe, just as they would not book tickets for their family to fly on an unsafe airline.

"Okay, I'll admit that service affects ratings—but I still don't see it as a big part of a healthcare ecosystem."

The way patients perceive their care is connected to how they rate us, which affects reimbursement, which influences the likelihood that they will return in the future and refer their friends and family. And beyond this factor, poor service may be a symptom of bigger problems inside the organization. Good service usually means good processes and systems are in place everywhere. Likewise, poor service means that your processes, systems, culture, or even recruiting and onboarding are inadequate—which can have negative implications for all sorts of other areas that affect quality and cost.

People *Expect* Safety and Quality—So Service Can't Take a Backseat

Yes, you can make the (legitimate) argument that safe, high-quality care is more important to a patient's health than service. But as I alluded to earlier, unless there is a complication or negative outcome, patients tend not to evaluate safety and quality because they assume those things will be present in their care. It's the same in many other industries. When I hire a contractor to renovate my home, I expect the work to be safe and of high quality. Ditto when I take my car to a garage for repairs.

Let's look at an example with which we can all identify: air travel. When you fly, you expect safety. You expect to land at the correct destination without incident. You also expect quality: The plane should be clean. The flight should leave on time. Your luggage should arrive at your destination without damage. Assuming those things happen (I know, not always a given!), you evaluate your flying experience based on the service you receive. Was check-in easy? Were the flight attendants courteous? Did you receive a snack or beverage? Were you satisfied with the in-flight entertainment options? Without you consciously thinking of it, your brain combines all of these factors to determine your overall opinion of the airline.

The service an airline provides can create loyal customers or vehement critics. And especially in today's connected world, customers don't keep those opinions to themselves. With the tap of a finger, they can share their thoughts and experiences with thousands of other people, not just their immediate circle of family and friends. Healthcare isn't that much different. Since the way patients perceive us is at stake, service really can't take a backseat to safety and quality.

Let's not forget that service is definitely linked to patient outcomes and safety. A customer who receives poor service from a hospital may be inclined to "write off" the whole experience. That customer might disregard discharge instructions, fail to take medication properly, and ignore other recommendations. Having a good experience sets up consumers to trust us, which sets them up for good compliance and therefore good outcomes.

All of this factors into organizational performance!

IMPROVING SERVICE IN HEALTHCARE

Service is the cornerstone of the patient experience. As leaders we must pay close attention to customer service scores and focus on delivering and improving service across all fronts. That task can feel monumental. Throughout the rest of this chapter, I'll share methods I've successfully employed to improve service in the organizations I've led.

Great Service Requires Great Employees

Service is almost always provided to customers (patients in healthcare) by individual people. Products, meanwhile, are primarily produced in manufacturing facilities. The customer never has a direct human-to-human experience with the manufacturer of the product. Thus, in all service industries including healthcare, every employee—or caregiver, as I like to refer to healthcare workers—is essential in ensuring that your organization provides great service.

It's vital to hire employees who understand that they are providing a service. You must also provide training on service delivery and hold caregivers accountable for meeting organizational service standards. If the ball is dropped on any of these fronts, your employees have the potential to transform from your greatest asset to your heaviest anchor. Chapter 8 provides more details on these topics.

Incorporate Good Service Protocols into Every Aspect of the Patient Experience

These protocols should be part of the patient experience from before admission to the facility to after discharge. This should be the case whether you're leading a hospital, a clinic, or any other healthcare setting. At Hospital X, we worked to ensure that meaningful service was provided to every patient at every point of contact, from prior to admission (e.g., scheduling of a planned procedure) to post-discharge care management. Here are a few examples of processes that made a difference:

- Any surgical procedure is anxiety-provoking for patients. At Hospital X, we had a joint replacement surgeon and a spine surgeon who each called all of their patients the night before the surgery. The patients were able to ask any last-minute questions, and they were reminded of the period of time during which they shouldn't eat or drink prior to the surgery (their NPO status), time of arrival to the surgical center, and other details. Although one of the goals of the call was to reassure the patient that they were in good hands, that message was conveyed without the surgeon needing to say a word. The very act of the surgeon calling the patient sent a strong message of compassion, empathy, and genuine care.

    It's worth noting that I heard about these phone calls from patients, not from the physicians themselves. Several patients wrote me letters about their care and specifically mentioned the phone call, and I regularly met people in public who talked about how the phone call eased their anxiety about their joint replacement or spine surgery. Certainly, these patients told their friends and family about the physician and the care they received.
- In between hospital room occupants, each room was not only cleaned by hand but was also disinfected with

ultraviolet (UV) light. Environmental Services left a preprinted card on the bed stating this so that upon admission, each patient would be reassured that their room was as safe and clean as possible. Often, a big part of providing great service is narrating the process so that patients know what is being done for them. If we hadn't left a note telling patients that their rooms had been disinfected with UV light, they would never have known—and Hospital X would have missed out on a big opportunity to score service points.

- Shortly after admission, each patient received a phone call from the hospital unit coordinator, who said something like, "Good morning, Mr. Brown. Thank you for entrusting our hospital with your care. Now that you have had a few minutes to settle in, is there anything you need for your stay, like a toothbrush and toothpaste? What else can we do to make you more comfortable? Is there anyone you would like us to call?"

  If this reminds you of checking into an upscale hotel, it should! As you might recall from chapter 4, I am a big believer in learning from other industries. The same tactics that make people feel welcomed and valued during hotel stays will make them feel welcomed and valued at hospitals too. You might even consider hiring an expert from the hospitality industry as your next chief experience officer, or as a part-time consultant. Remember, you can teach this person the high-level operations and culture of healthcare. However, it's very difficult to transform a healthcare worker into an expert on hospitality and customer service.

- Before leaving a patient's room, caregivers from Environmental Services were trained to ask, "Is there anything else we can do for you today?" They asked this question even if they had only entered the room to change out the liner in a trash can. Most of the time the response was "No, thanks," but when a patient responded with a request like "Could I get an extra blanket?" or "Could you ask a nurse to check in?", Environmental Services passed on the request to the appropriate party.

Asking "Is there anything else we can do for you today?" only took a few seconds, but because the question was unexpected, the positive impression left on the patient was tremendous. People remember interactions they feel are out of the ordinary and above and beyond. Over the course of a hospital stay, these interactions combine to give patients the sense that they've received consistent, thoughtful service.

- A day or so after discharge, a nurse would call each patient to ask how they were feeling, if they understood their ongoing care instructions, if they needed anything, if they had any feedback on their hospitalization, and so on. Often the responses were significant, for instance, that a patient was feeling weaker or was having trouble getting his medication. During one very memorable call, a nurse noticed that the patient's speech was slurred, correctly inferred that he might be having a stroke, and called 911. That post-discharge phone call potentially saved the patient's life!

  If we had not instituted post-discharge callbacks, in most cases we would never have learned important information and would not have been able to help. Callbacks were a win-win-win-win: they enabled us to provide great service, they built patient loyalty, they improved care, and they provided an opportunity to receive feedback that improved hospital operations for future patients.

Use Volunteers to Enhance Patients' Service Experience

People don't need to be on your organization's payroll to positively affect patients' service experience. Volunteers are a fantastic resource and can be deployed to make sure that patients feel comfortable, cared for, and respected. Here are a couple of impactful service-oriented tasks we gave to our volunteers at Hospital X:

- Each day, we ordered hundreds of newspapers for volunteers to deliver to the patients' rooms. Volunteers were also encouraged to spend as much time with each patient as the patient would like. This initiative had several big benefits. First, the newspaper itself helped patients pass the time during long days confined to a bed. Second, many appreciated the volunteer's company and the chance to chat with someone about nonmedical matters. Finally, it was an unexpected gesture that made a small but significant difference in the patient's morale. And small differences always add up to a larger cumulative effect!
- Occasionally, if patients were not able to cut their own food or feed themselves, their meals would be cold by the time a patient care assistant (PCA) was able to help them. Enter our awesome team of volunteers, whom we trained to assist with feeding patients. Now, these patients were eating a warm meal *and* enjoying company and conversation for an hour. Volunteers reported having great purpose during their time at Hospital X. PCAs could focus their time on other necessary tasks instead of on feeding patients. And because PCAs were now doing their own work, nurses didn't have to cover for them while they were feeding patients. This was a service win-win-win-win, and with zero expense!

Tailor Service to Specific Groups of People

Service isn't one-size-fits-all. In fact, it's often most meaningful when it takes into account people's unique past experiences and current needs. People want to be acknowledged. They want to know that their caregivers recognize and respect the things that matter to them. When you can show a patient that you see them as a unique, well-rounded individual and not just as a chart on the door, you will have gone a long way toward providing a meaningful and memorable service experience. Here are some ways we achieved that at Hospital X:

- Upon registration, the registrar made a note of patients who were or had been members of emergency services, law enforcement, or the military. Each day a list of these individuals and their room numbers was automatically printed inside the gift shop. The gift shop then delivered a single rose in a small vase to each of these heroes, along with a brief note thanking them for their service to our country. The notes were preprinted, but as CEO of the hospital I made sure to hand-sign every single one. The caregiver who delivered the flower would also ask the patient if they would like a visit from one of the hospital executives. Thanking these men and women for the service they had provided *us* was a small but significant way to provide thoughtful service to *them*.
- If a patient had a birthday while staying at Hospital X, we provided them with a small cake, lit a candle for them to blow out, and asked staff members to sing them "Happy Birthday." Nobody *wants* to spend their birthday in the hospital, and if the occasion isn't acknowledged, this milestone can feel even more depressing. Patients routinely told us that their birthday celebrations were both unexpected and very meaningful.

- Carrying (and certainly delivering) a baby is physically and emotionally exhausting. Often new mothers and (if applicable) their partners haven't enjoyed a night out in the recent past—and even if they have, the birth of a baby is an event to celebrate! After each new mom had rested and recovered, we treated her and her significant other to what we called "Date Night." (Those of us who are also parents sometimes joked that it should have been called "Last Date Night," because new parents can find it difficult to go out to dinner with an infant!)

  Instead of delivering the usual meal on a tray, caregivers brought a small table into the room and set it with a white tablecloth, real ceramic plates, glasses, and a battery-operated candle. The couple could choose a meal from a more upscale menu too. Steak or salmon? Crème brûlée or a chocolate hazelnut mousse? And to add a final touch of "fancy," we served a glass of wine or beer if the mother's physician approved. (Of course, we also provided this dinner service to mothers whose partners were not present and encouraged these moms to include another loved one as their "date.")

  Years later, mothers have told me and other caregivers how much Date Night stood out in their memories, and how much it meant for them and their partners to be acknowledged at a time when almost all the focus tends to be on the baby.

Remember That Service Isn't *Just* About the Patients

In healthcare we tend to think about service as being centered around our patients—and rightly so. However, I would caution against focusing so closely on patients that you ignore or remain unaware of other groups who are affected. I strongly believe that in healthcare, true service is about positively engaging four different groups:

1. Patients (referred to as *loved ones*)
2. Patients' families and other support people
3. Caregivers (in other words, *ourselves!*)
4. The community

Healthcare organizations should ideally provide 360 degrees of service. Yes, shifting people's attitudes, breaking old habits, and adopting new outlooks about service will probably take some effort up front, but the benefit is tremendous. Everyone in the healthcare ecosystem will become more engaged and experience deeper satisfaction. Let's take a closer look at how to provide service to each of the three nonpatient groups:

Service to families: Often, patients are accompanied by family members, friends, or other support people. We can provide service to them by acknowledging their help and concern, communicating what's happening, and making an effort to welcome and include them. Their service experience goes hand-in-hand with the patient's experience. If one party has a poor experience, the other's perception of service will also suffer. But if the patient *and* their family feel that they have been treated with compassion, care, and respect, their opinions about their care, their providers, and the organization will be positive.

Here are some best practices for connecting with families:

- Notice who is present with the patient. Learn their names and their relationship to the patient. Greet them when you walk in the room.
- When possible, make accommodations for family members who spend significant amounts of time with their hospitalized loved ones—especially if the family member is spending the night. One obvious way to do this is by providing an in-room couch that pulls out into a bed. If that's not in your budget, there are numerous "smaller" services you can provide to family members that still make

a big impact. I'll share a few that we incorporated into our culture at Hospital X:

- In the procedural waiting rooms, we installed several multiport chargers for portable devices. We also provided handheld portable chargers at no cost but did hold a security deposit. It was fully acceptable to not return the portable charger if the person wanted to keep it. (The chargers were branded with the hospital logo for additional "marketing.")

- We created a space called the Library that was stocked with books on healthcare, some novels, and a desk area with public-use computers as well as personal laptop charging ports.

- After receiving feedback from some patients, we converted a small room into a breastfeeding or pumping area. The room had soft music, dimmable lighting, and a comfortable lounger.

- We offered one extra meal tray per day to the families of our patients. The idea was to make it easier for family members to stay with their loved ones, and it was a much-appreciated gesture. People often commented on how thoughtful it was to offer family members a meal.

• If a patient's family or support person is in the room, ask physicians to include those individuals in the conversation and caregiving plan (rather than have them be spectators on the sideline). Family members greatly appreciate being able to meet and converse with the physician.

Furthermore, when a patient's family is educated about the patient's illness or injury as well as the steps needed to resolve it, the patient's care improves both inside the hospital and post-discharge. Physicians can explicitly ask family members to be an extra set of eyes on the patient and to reinforce certain care plans. For example, a patient on fall precautions might not want to "bother" the hospital's caregivers and thus will not inform the nurse or PCA when they need to go the bathroom. If this patient's family has been educated on the reason for the fall precaution and the risk to the patient if it is not adhered to, the family will be empowered to contact a caregiver for assistance.

The value of getting family members involved in patient care was really brought home during the COVID-19 lock-downs. With visitors unable to enter the hospital, leadership teams received feedback from caregivers that their jobs became more difficult without the assistance of patients' families. Remember, the more engaged and knowledgeable a patient's loved ones are, the more empowered they will be to help.

Service to ourselves (caregiver to caregiver): To help employees provide valuable service to one another within a healthcare system, my best piece of advice is to train caregivers to manage each other up. In other words, have them take every opportunity to compliment their colleagues and set each other up for success in the eyes of the patient.

For example, if a patient needs an X-ray, the radiology tech might ask, "Who is your physician?" If the technician is familiar with that provider, he could say, "Oh yes, Dr. Jones! She is an excellent orthopedic doctor. So many patients tell me how caring and empathetic she is. Did you know she won an award last year?" Or, when a physician enters a patient's room and sees that Sally is that person's nurse, he might say, "I see that Sally will be your nurse. She has been on this floor for over a decade. You'll be in great hands."

Managing up is an effective form of caregiver-to-caregiver service because everyone benefits. The person *doing* the managing up is reminded of why their colleague is outstanding. The person *being* managed up is recognized and valued. That caregiver will also have a head start on building rapport with the patient, perhaps even prior to their first interaction. And the patient perceives that person's care as being skilled and compassionate. All of this reinforces the organization's purpose and improves the patient's perception of the service being provided.

Beyond managing up, caregivers can provide impactful service to one another simply by looking for ways to step in and provide a helping hand outside of their normal job roles. Often, assisting another provider doesn't require much time or effort—but it can make a big difference in the other caregiver's day.

I recall one instance when a nurse was preparing to infuse a medication that necessitated a second check from another nurse. When the nurse was ready to start the infusion, he had to find a colleague to double-check that it was the correct medication, the correct dosage, the correct timing, and going into the correct patient at the correct rate.

Present in the room was a case manager talking to the patient about the patient's care and discharge in a couple of days. When the nurse started to leave the room to find another nurse, the case manager spoke up and offered to help, as she was also a licensed nurse. The case manager then validated the medication to be infused into the patient. Did it slow down her day by two minutes? Most likely. Did it allow the nurse to provide the infusion five minutes sooner? Most likely. This is a great example of one caregiver serving another caregiver, making the nurse's day just a little easier.

Systems Support Service

As leaders, one of our jobs is to help caregivers do *their* jobs as effectively as possible. One way we provide that service is by ensuring that efficient, reliable, and sustainable processes for clinical and nonclinical staff are standardized throughout the organization. When Provider A has one way of doing something but Provider B prefers

continued

---

continued from previous page

a different method, nurses and other support staff can become confused and frustrated.

That doesn't set up anyone for success. It usually results in inefficiencies (if not outright mistakes) and a poor service experience for patients, which affects the organization's reputation and profitability, which in turn reduces the budget for future training and system-building. Do you see the 360 degrees of service coming into play? (Look back at chapter 5 for more information on how leaders can provide service to employees.)

If you would like to learn more, I highly recommend *Zero Harm: How to Achieve Patient and Workforce Safety in Healthcare* by Craig Clapper, PE; James Merlino, MD; and Carole Stockmeier. This book is a must-read on creating a culture and developing processes to deliver the safest care possible. It links the delivery of customer service with the delivery of safe care.

As important as the saved time was to the nurse, the gesture probably had a greater impact on his day.

Service to the community: A healthcare system is a community asset. I've always believed that it is part of our duty (and our purpose!) to serve the area where our patients live. It's good business too. The more people see their healthcare system serving, educating, and empowering their community, the more they will view that system as a valued partner, and the more they will entrust us with their care. Here a few ways Hospital X served the community:

- Each member of the executive leadership team (including myself) served on one or two nonprofit boards in our community. This obviously benefited the community organization, but also provided another avenue by which Hospital X could engage the community and many of its leaders. It was another small way in which the hospital would become part of the fabric of the community.

One executive chose to serve on the board of a local technical college. The college wanted to develop more programs, and the hospital was always challenged with finding enough medical assistants. At the executive's suggestion, Hospital X and the technical college worked together to develop a program that benefited both institutions. The college provided the didactic education that future medical assistants would need, and the hospital provided on-site clinical education.

The result was a win-win-win: the students were employed quickly, the hospital had an opportunity to hire several new medical assistants each year who were already trained in a culture of excellence and already familiar with the hospital or clinic's processes, and the college gained a great reputation for having high postgraduation employment rates. Odds are, none of this would have happened if our executive was not on the board's strategic planning committee.

- Hospital X regularly provided healthcare seminars to the community. These included monthly community education series covering topics like joint replacement, weight loss, diabetes, sleep disorders, and smoking cessation. Community members received valuable education at no cost while building a relationship with the hospital. And if a participant needed a physician in the discipline of the seminar they had attended, we were able to provide a quick connection to the appropriate program. After about a year, we had to cap each seminar's attendance for fire code reasons, so we increased their frequency to twice per month.

- We also engaged local students in order to supplement their education in topics such as healthcare, science, and technology. For example, a local high school robotics class came to the hospital to learn about the da Vinci robotic surgical system, watch a video of a surgery using the robotic system, and eventually have an opportunity to use the equipment themselves. The educational material and footage of the students was sent home on a CD (this was before cloud storage) for parents to enjoy as well. Another win-win for the community and the hospital.

- Hospital X felt strongly about supporting other organizations that strove to better the community, and regularly participated in their fundraising events. I'll never forget the time when our chief operating officer (COO) bravely entered *me*, Kevin Joseph, into a "Dancing with the Stars" competition to raise money for a local organization.

  While I appreciated the COO's enthusiasm for engaging Hospital X in community events, I was more than a bit anxious as I'm not known for my sense of rhythm! I also found it suspicious that he volunteered me instead of himself. However, as karma would have it, only a couple of weeks prior to the competition, the organizer approached me to let me know that one of the other dancers had dropped out. Did I know someone who could take his place? I had the perfect person to fill the gap! As it turned out, the COO and I both did our part to integrate our hospital into the fabric of the community.

HARNESS THE POWER OF SERVICE RECOVERY

Despite your best efforts, your organization will not be able to deliver impeccable service all the time. Caregivers may be well trained and aligned with your organization's purpose, but they are still human. Sometimes they'll make mistakes. Let's look at some numbers. Consider the following:

- The average patient has over 100 different interactions with caregivers during their hospital stay.
- A hospital has an average of 300 patients admitted at any given time.
- Each patient's average length of stay is four days.

Based on these numbers, over the course of one year, 27,375 patients will have been admitted, giving that hospital an annual total of 2,375,500 patient–caregiver interactions. It's inevitable that somewhere along the line there will be mistakes and service mishaps.

Two Types of Patient Complaints—Two Categories of Service Recovery

In this section I'm talking about incidents where the patient is unhappy with their service experience, but there was no negative outcome of care. In other words, the patient did not experience a complication or injury.

What happens when a service complaint is focused on a complication, injury, or poor care (e.g., a lost specimen, an object retained in surgery, mixed-up test results)? In these events, leadership should *always* be brought into the service recovery as soon as possible. (In other words, don't leave this type of service recovery up to frontline caregivers.) I also highly recommend developing a process that ensures the involvement of the risk management department.

Regardless of the cause, what happens when the ball is dropped? In most cases, patients don't know or understand *why* they experienced poor service—they just know that they feel ignored, patronized, misunderstood, confused, unsafe, and so forth. Left unaddressed, those feelings will naturally translate into a perception of poor service. The good news is that you can harness the power of *service recovery* to salvage the patient's experience—and boost it to surprising heights.

Marketing research shows that customers experiencing great service generally report medium-high happiness levels. If they're disappointed with their service experience, their happiness levels are much lower. Now, here's the surprising part: Some customers who have a poor service experience that is followed by prompt and genuine service recovery report the highest happiness levels of all. That's right: These people are *more* satisfied than they would have been if everything had gone well from the beginning. This phenomenon is called the *service recovery paradox* (Riesterer 2019). Additional research by Lee Resource Inc. reveals that while 91 percent of unhappy customers will not willingly return to an organization, 95 percent of unhappy customers *will* return if their concern is resolved promptly (Miller 2022). Furthermore, 83 percent of customers feel more loyal after their concern is resolved (Harold 2021). Granted, the service recovery paradox does not always happen and will only happen if the poor experience is not extreme and the issue is addressed promptly and with genuine concern from the organization's representatives.

Obviously, I don't recommend disappointing patients on purpose so that you can benefit from the service recovery paradox. (For one thing, not all disappointed people will experience the service recovery paradox—some will remain dissatisfied.) The point is to ensure there is a process in place that facilitates a rapid response to any concerns voiced by any of the four service groups: patients, caregivers (clinical and nonclinical), patients' family members and support people, and the community. Here are some tips to keep in mind:

- **Train caregivers to look for situations where service recovery might be warranted.** According to 1st Financial

Training Services, 96 percent of dissatisfied customers don't complain to anyone—rather, they leave without sharing their negative thoughts and feelings (Mindful 2022). Therefore, for every person who complains to someone in your organization, there are approximately 25 unsatisfied people of whom you're not aware. But just because these people don't complain to you doesn't mean they aren't talking to their families, friends, and online connections about their poor experience. For this reason, all caregivers need to be proactive about searching for and identifying situations that might have caused a patient to be frustrated or disappointed.

For example, did a patient have to wait in a long line to be seen? When I was practicing emergency medicine and a patient had waited an extended period of time for me to evaluate them, I would apologize and provide the reason behind the delay: "Mrs. Fitz, I apologize that you have been waiting here for an unacceptable amount of time. I was focused on patients who had just arrived from a bad car accident." Even if you're late because your spouse is sick and you had to take over school drop-off duty for your children, say so! Most people are understanding as long as you "give them the why." In doing so, you show that you do not take their valuable time for granted.

Another way to provide proactive service recovery would be to approach someone who looks lost inside the building. If they are trying to find a particular destination, walk them to where they should be and apologize that the location was not easy for them to find. The takeaway here is that a caregiver does not have to be directly involved in a situation for it to be classified as a service failure. All that matters is that the patient, visitor, or employee had a negative experience.

- **Ensure that caregivers know when and how to escalate service recovery.** According to studies conducted by TARP Worldwide Inc. in 2006 and 2007, of those who do raise a concern, 90 to 98 percent *only* complain to a frontline provider (not a supervisor, director, or other leader) (Zeithaml, Bitner, and Gremler 2009). But frontline caregivers don't always have the knowledge, resources, or authority to directly address a service failure. Make sure that they can immediately escalate questions, concerns, and problems to the right people. (And as I discussed in chapter 6, make sure that all caregivers feel comfortable sharing "bad news" with leaders. Otherwise, many complaints will never be passed on and thus will never be addressed.)

    Does every caregiver have access to their manager? Does every manager have the mobile phone numbers of the entire executive team? You might even consider sharing the executive team's phone numbers with every caregiver in the organization, to be used in situations when that leader's immediate attention is required. (As I shared earlier in this book, I've done this with my own phone number and have never encountered a situation where the privilege was misused or abused.)

- **Make sure that service recovery is prompt.** And by *prompt*, I mean as close to the incident as possible. According to the White House Office of Consumer Affairs, "56%–70% of the customers who complain to you will do business with you again if you resolve their problem. If they feel you acted quickly and to their satisfaction, up to 96% will do business with you again, and they will probably refer other people to you" (Miller 2022). Not surprisingly, the more time that passes before a resolution is achieved, the more frustrated the patient becomes and the more people they tell about their poor experience (or, in today's culture, the more likely they are to post their experience on social media, where it can reach an unlimited number of people.)

Plus, addressing an issue promptly sends the message that you and your organization genuinely care. A resolution that occurs one day after a service failure has a much greater impact than an identical resolution that doesn't take place for two weeks. In the first instance, the patient thinks, *Wow, this hospital really hustled to make things right. They really care about my experience.* In the second, the patient's assumption is *Well, the hospital eventually addressed my concern, but it took a few weeks. I'm clearly not high on their priority list.* If an issue *will* take a longer period of time to resolve, contact the individual immediately and tell them so. Acknowledge that the wait is not ideal, give them the why, and assure them that you will be back in touch.

- **Do whatever is necessary to make things right.**
  According to National Customer Rage surveys conducted between 2003 and 2007, individuals who are not satisfied with the resolution of their complaint talk to an average of 18.5 people about the incident, but that number goes down to an average of eight people if there is good service recovery (Zeithaml, Bitner, and Gremler 2009). However, note that those statistics only refer to verbal conversations. We must also consider the extensive reach of social media.

  According the 2017 National Customer Rage study, 12 percent of people complained using e-mail, live chat, or social media (Alcantara 2020). That number increased almost four times to 43 percent in 2020 and will surely continue to increase in the future. The accessibility of social media platforms combined with the growing trend to showcase one's day-to-day activities will encourage people to immediately vent their frustrations about even the smallest negative experience.

Here's the takeaway: Put as much time, energy, and money as you can allocate toward resolving service issues—and do so as quickly as possible. If you can substantially reduce the number of people with whom a patient shares their negative experience, those resources will have been well spent. For example, I've heard that every Ritz-Carlton team member is given the capability to solve guest concerns on the spot, and to authorize up to $2,000 of incurred expenses, no questions asked. Whether that's true or not, the point is that employees need to know their left and right limits when it comes to making things right for the customer (or patient). They need to know what they're authorized to do on their own, and what warrants the involvement of leadership.

- **Always respond to patients' feedback.** Every complaint and concern (whether major or minor, warranted or not) should receive a personalized response. Otherwise, patients will feel that their voices are not heard or valued. Your organization will have lost an opportunity for service recovery.

  At Hospital X, we sent a note to each person who made a complaint. The language in the first and last paragraphs was generic ("Thank you for sharing your concerns" and "We will further investigate and get back to you"), but the main body of each note was specific to the patient and their experience. We also made sure to follow up on each case. If a patient's feedback resulted in a procedure change, for instance, we let them know. If it was too late to solve a particular problem, we sent a sincere apology.

  The same principle—always respond to feedback—can be applied internally as well. Remember, service isn't just about positively engaging patients. Sometimes it involves acknowledging our fellow caregivers too. I've noticed that often, caregivers will submit an incident report but will never hear back. (And that being the case, what motivation do they have to submit more reports in the future?) Just as you would for a patient with a complaint, always acknowledge and follow up.

EMPOWER THE FRONT LINE TO TAKE ACTION

As we have discussed, having service-oriented systems and processes in place is essential to ensuring that patients (and their families and their caregivers) have a positive experience. It is also crucial to make sure that service recovery is an integral part of your organization's culture. But there is one more piece to the service-delivery puzzle: making sure that all caregivers—especially those who work on the front line—are empowered to take action. Being empowered certainly applies to service recovery, but also to proactively providing exceptional, and often unexpected, service.

I have found that when service is central to an organization's purpose, it becomes the barometer by which employees make decisions. Caregivers begin to prioritize what's best for the patient instead of what would save them the most time or effort. They think about how they can support their coworkers. They take ownership of their work. But for heartfelt service to flow freely, all caregivers must be able to make decisions and judgment calls (within reason) to improve the lives of others.

In large part, empowering the front line is tied to breaking down the power gradient (see chapter 6). Do caregivers feel comfortable asking for help when they need it? Can they color outside the lines to achieve an end goal (as long as safety and quality aren't compromised)? Can they use the organization's resources without asking for permission up front? Are they trusted to make appropriate decisions regarding patient care? Do they have the authority to solve problems on the spot? Or must every action be scrutinized and cleared by a leader?

When I was the CEO of Hospital X, I came across many examples of empowered caregivers taking action to improve the lives of others. I'd like to share three of my favorite stories here.

Story #1

I met a prominent local business leader at a fundraiser. He told me, "I was admitted to your hospital a few months ago, and I want to talk to you about my experience."

I braced myself. While I had the utmost confidence in my organization and our caregivers, I had been a leader long enough to know that those nine words—*I want to talk to you about my experience*—occasionally prefaced complaints and criticism.

I listened with trepidation as the man went on: "When I was admitted to the hospital, I was really thirsty, and I asked my nurse for a caffeine-free Diet Pepsi. She told me that the hospital served only Coke products, and that only Diet Coke *with* caffeine was available. I told her that I would just take a glass of water."

Uh-oh, I thought. *I'm about to be lambasted because Hospital X doesn't serve a full selection of Pepsi products.* But I was wrong.

"Shift change was about an hour later," the businessman said. "Imagine my surprise when the oncoming nurse entered the room and handed me a six-pack of caffeine-free Diet Pepsi! It turns out that the nurse whose shift was ending called her coworker and asked her to stop at a convenience store for my beverage of choice. Kevin, I have never felt so well cared for!"

Let me tell you, that's the kind of story that makes you smile ear-to-ear when you hear it. I couldn't have been prouder of these nurses who went the extra mile to care for their patient as if he were truly their own loved one. I'm also proud of the fact that no supervisor was involved. These nurses knew what was the right thing to do, and they felt empowered to act—no need to ask for approval or permission.

Story #2

I had barely settled down at my desk one morning when I received a call from a nurse. "I broke a policy overnight and figured I'd better tell you about it," she said.

"What was the policy?" I asked.

"It was the 'no animals in the hospital' policy," she responded. "I promise, Dr. J., I *know* that the no-animals policy is in place to prevent animal bites and maintain cleanliness, but I was caring for a terminal patient who wanted to see her dog one last time. I made the decision to carry the dog from the parking lot to my patient's room so she could say goodbye to her beloved pet."

I smiled and immediately praised the nurse for her actions. "Sounds like this was a special case," I said. "You did the right thing for the loved one in your care. Well done!"

Story #3

A physician called me one afternoon to tell me that the day before, her case in the operating room had run late. It was 7:00 p.m., she had not eaten since breakfast, and the snack machine was not going to cut it. Unfortunately, the cafeteria closed at 7:00, and she arrived there at 7:10.

"The cafeteria workers saw me and apologized that all of the hot food had been removed from the serving stations," she recalled. "They then offered to make me a deli sandwich of my choice, and paused their cleanup to do so. I was so impressed and thankful! None of the other hospitals I operate in would have made the extra effort. I'm proud to be working here."

In all three of these examples, Hospital X's employees could have left another person's needs unfulfilled—and by a strict interpretation of the rules, they would not have been wrong to do so. "Sorry— we only serve Coke products." "Sorry—no pets in the hospital!"

"Sorry—cafeteria's closed." But our caregivers understood that to provide great service to a patient or fellow employee, they could and should take extra steps (and in one case, even break a rule).

Nordstrom: Showcasing Employee Empowerment

Many of us have heard the story about a Nordstrom customer who walked into the store to return a set of snow tires. The clerk looked at the price on the tires and handed the customer a refund—even though Nordstrom has never sold tires. This story (which is debatably apocryphal) is meant to illustrate Nordstrom's well-known commitment to customer service (Mikkelson 2011). Certainly, the clerk in question felt empowered to deliver on-the-spot service recovery.

I'm inclined to believe the tire story might just be true, because I'm familiar with another above-and-beyond Nordstrom service story. A friend's younger brother lost part of his foot as a child, and as a result wore two different shoe sizes. At one point, he and his mother were shopping for new shoes at Nordstrom. His mother took two pairs of shoes (same style, different sizes) to the cashier. When the cashier realized *why* this mom was buying two pairs of shoes, she called her manager over and explained the situation. The manager only charged the family for one pair of shoes. A month or so later, the family received a letter from Nordstrom saying, "Bring this letter with you whenever you shop at Nordstrom in the future. Show it to the cashier when you buy shoes, and we will only charge you for one pair."

What a great story of service that came about because employees felt empowered to help a customer! I'm sure that my friend's family felt extreme loyalty to Nordstrom and did a lot of other shopping there too. When you do the right thing, it's almost always good business.

As you have probably gleaned, great service is really about mind-set and empowerment. And like so many other subjects addressed in this book, it connects back to purpose. When we are mindful that we're here to make our patients' lives better, we will naturally provide great service and instinctively treat them as we would our own loved ones. The desire to serve is kind of baked into the psyche of most healthcare people anyway—it's our job as leaders to create an organization that makes it easy for them to do so.

REFERENCES

Alcantara, A.-M. 2020. "Customer Complaints, and Their Ways of Complaining, Are on the Rise." *Wall Street Journal*. Published June 14. https://www.wsj.com/articles/customer-complaints -and-their-ways-of-complaining-are-on-the-rise-11591998939#:~.

Harold, F. 2021. "Must-Know Customer Service Statistics of 2022 (So Far)." Khoros. Published May 25. https://khoros.com/blog /must-know-customer-service-statistics.

Mikkelson, D. 2011. "Nordstrom Tire Return." Snopes. Published April 30. https://www.snopes.com/fact-check/return -to-spender/.

Miller, I. (ed.). 2022. "Customer Service Facts." Customer Service Manager (CSM). Accessed August 15. https://www .customerservicemanager.com/customer-service-facts/.

Mindful. 2022. "Customer Service Stats That Matter: Part II. Mindful." Accessed August 15. https://getmindful.com/blog /customer-service-stats-that-matter-part-ii/.

Riesterer, T. 2019. "The Best Way to Apologize to Customers, Backed By Science." Corporate Visions. Published April 30. https://corporatevisions.com/best-customer-service-apology/.

Theodore Roosevelt Center at Dickinson State University. 2022. "Theodore Roosevelt Quotes." Accessed August 15. https://www.theodorerooseveltcenter.org/Learn-About-TR/TR-Quotes?page=112.

Zeithaml, V. A., M. J. Bitner, and D. D. Gremler. 2009. *Services Marketing: Integrating Customer Focus Across the Firm*, 5th ed. New York: McGraw-Hill Education.

CHAPTER 8

Hiring and Re-Recruiting
Your Greatest Asset

IF SOMEONE ASKED you, "What is your organization's greatest asset?" how would you respond? It's conceivable that a leader might say, "Well, our building is our greatest asset. Without it, we would not have a place to serve our patients" or, "Our greatest asset would be our medical equipment and associated technologies. Those things allow us to provide the best care and save lives."

Yes, hospital buildings, equipment, and technologies *are* valuable assets. Without them, hospitals, medical clinics and practices, and other medical systems would not be able to function. But none of those things are our *greatest* asset. If, as we established in chapter 7, healthcare is almost exclusively part of the service industry, and service is provided by people, then our employees—our caregivers—are a healthcare organization's greatest asset.

I realize this is hardly a unique statement. Most leaders will *say* that their people are their greatest asset, and I feel the vast majority of leaders truly believe it. However, for a variety of reasons, they may unintentionally have their operations set up in a way that does not allow them to *live* this value. That's why we need to take a hard look at ourselves and make changes wherever they are called for—especially when it comes to attracting, hiring, and retaining purpose-driven caregivers. It's too important *not* to do so, particularly at a time when employees want and expect their needs to be placed at the center of the organization.

Think about the last time you were involved in planning a major change initiative for your organization. Maybe your hospital was building a new wing or phasing in a new computer system. Perhaps your department was updating outdated processes and procedures or making plans to replace its equipment. No doubt you put a lot of time and consideration into this change: which option would be the best fit, how much it would cost, what its impact would be on the rest of the department or organization, and so on.

Now let me ask you: How does that compare to the time and consideration you give your employees? If caregivers are truly our greatest asset, we should prioritize a thoughtful hiring process over one that's automated and streamlined. Established employees should get the first fruits of their leaders' time and attention because if they aren't supported, developed, and appreciated, they *will* become disengaged, provide lackluster care, and eventually leave your organization.

People Are More Important than Things

You wouldn't rush the process of buying a new magnetic resonance imaging (MRI) machine. You would want to make sure that you were getting a good value for your money. You would try to choose a model that would match well with your organization's capabilities and your staff's training. And for the machine to help your organization provide care to patients for a long time to come, you would ensure that it was maintained properly and upgraded when necessary. Why would we treat acquiring and retaining employees any differently?

I know that many leaders in healthcare don't have all the resources they might want. We are trying to do more with less while adapting to changing models of care and patient preferences. There never seem to be enough hours in the day to accomplish even a fraction of our goals. Trust me, I get it. If you're reluctant to allocate more resources toward hiring and re-recruiting, remind yourself that patients notice and remember the *people* who cared for them much more than the building they were in or the medical equipment that was used in their care.

How often do you hear someone rave about how easy it was to navigate a hospital's layout, or nerd out about the intricacies of the ultrasound machine that was used to scan their liver? Hardly ever. However, you *do* hear people say things like "My nurse took such good care of me. Her kindness made all the difference"—and you hear those things often. You'll also hear some people comment on things like how clean or dirty the building was, for example, but observations of that sort are directly related to the caregivers who clean and maintain the building.

My point is, more than anything else, caregivers are instrumental in helping patients have a positive healthcare experience. If we skimp here, we will pay down the road.

If we want to provide great care, we have to put caregivers first. I first began to understand this essential truth when I read the book *Patients Come Second* by Paul Spiegelman and Britt Berrett. Admittedly, my first reaction upon seeing the title was *Who are these jerks? What do they mean, patients come second? Patients should always be our* first *priority!* But as the saying goes, you can't judge a book by its cover. Spiegelman and Berrett were correct.

If you really want to give a patient (or loved one) the best care and service, you must first commit to engaging, supporting, and developing your employees. When employees feel "recognized, valued, appreciated, and understood" (as explained by Stephen Covey—more on this later), they show up to work each day ready to go the extra mile. They will provide the best care to patients and achieve your organization's desired success metrics when they are fueled by purpose; empowered to proactively do the right thing for the patients in their care; and have the tools, training, and support they need to truly treat patients as loved ones.

On the other hand, a caregiver who feels unappreciated, unsupported, and unempowered will not have the confidence and motivation to go above and beyond for patients. In fact, that caregiver might not have the mental, emotional, or physical bandwidth to do much more than the bare minimum that his job requires. This sets the stage for mediocre, lackluster, or downright poor patient experiences.

It's clear that to prioritize our patients, we must focus, first and always, on our caregivers. Throughout the rest of this chapter, I'll share best practices for investing time, effort, and resources into hiring and retaining your organization's greatest asset.

RECRUIT THE RIGHT PEOPLE

If you have ever dabbled in do-it-yourself home improvement, you know that it's important to have the correct tools and proper materials. For instance, you can't use a flathead screwdriver to drive Phillips screws. You should probably have a multimeter tester on hand before replacing an electrical outlet. And a worn or broken tool is more of a danger than an asset. You get my point. Without the proper resources at hand, your project isn't likely to turn out the way you'd hoped. You might even encounter delays, damage your home, or injure yourself.

The same principle holds true for our greatest asset in healthcare. To provide the best care to patients (and to avoid negative outcomes and service failures), you need to ensure that your organization is staffed with the right people. The following sections discuss a few strategies I've found to be extremely helpful.

Hire for Culture Fit First and Skills Second

Hiring clinical and nonclinical staff with experience, proven skill, and credentials is only half the equation—and not even the most important half!

At Hospital X, I decided to focus on culture first and foremost, because I believed that a strong culture would naturally lead to improved outcomes and metrics. One of the first changes I made was hiring new employees who were great culture fits, even if doing so meant passing over other applicants who had all the right skills. Why? I knew that we could teach new hires how to give a breathing treatment, how to place a Foley catheter to reduce infection, or how to take a radiograph for an imaging study. But we *couldn't* force new hires to adopt qualities like work ethic, values, compassion, professionalism, and empathy. (I've always said that it's Mom and Dad's job from birth to age 18 to instill those qualities in their child, not a supervisor's responsibility once someone enters the workforce.)

To provide patients with the best care, it is essential to bring people on board who want to serve a greater purpose and who care about doing the right thing for their patients. If collecting a paycheck or being a "superstar" is a candidate's number-one goal, that person will *not* be an asset to your organization because they will not be intrinsically motivated to treat patients as loved ones, or to treat their colleagues with respect and empathy.

Granted, this can be a difficult decision for leaders who have not experienced both sides of the equation. Let's compare the process of onboarding two candidates for a clinical position. Candidate A is a strong cultural fit with adequate skills and relatively little experience. Candidate B is highly skilled with great experience but is challenged to work with others and doesn't seem to adhere to several key values that support your culture.

Candidate A receives some necessary training, as well as consistent support and constructive feedback from leaders. This person becomes a tremendous asset to the organization. She provides heartfelt, empathetic, and high-quality service to patients, and quickly becomes a role model for many of her colleagues. (Plus, I can tell you from experience that from a leader's perspective, it is quite rewarding to have played a part in the development of an all-star.)

Candidate B doesn't require additional clinical training, but leaders are often obliged to spend significant time and effort in managing her. This individual's mentoring conversations tend to be driven by negative feedback (unlike Candidate A, whose development usually revolves around positive recognition and advice on how to get to the next level). Eventually, Candidate B's leaders may be forced to terminate her relationship with the organization, which is always an unpleasant experience for the leader, the employee, and the employee's family.

It truly isn't worth hiring someone who does not fit your culture. Yes, there's often great pressure to fill a staffing or leadership "gap," but compromising for a quick fix will lead to long-term struggles. As a former colleague of mine, Steve Mombach, was fond of saying, "Hire hard. Manage easy."

Utilize 360-Degree Interviews for Hiring and Promotions

In chapter 4, I shared that I use 360-degree interviews when recruiting senior leaders. I recommend using this strategy for hiring and promoting at all levels, because healthcare is a complex team sport. It's rare that a caregiver's role does not necessitate partnership with others in delivering the best possible patient outcomes and driving the organization's success. Implementing 360-degree interviewing helps ensure that new hires will be culture fits. It also allows frontline caregivers to ask questions about what they value in a colleague, which might not be the same things Human Resources or other senior leaders value.

No matter what role you are recruiting for (clinical or nonclinical), I recommend that candidates be interviewed by their future colleagues: their leader, their peers, and others with whom they'd work closely (perhaps from other departments).

If the role is supervisory, you should also involve future direct reports in the hiring process. It might sound odd to have current employees interview their potential boss, but this is essential. Caregivers need to respect and work well with their leaders, or culture and results will suffer. Plus, when frontline caregivers are involved in selecting their supervisor, the new hire will hit the ground running with the team's support.

Peer interviewing is also a way for organizations to maximize the employee experience for caregivers who are already on the team. Younger generations in particular want a lot of input into the decisions that affect their work life. They also want to work for leaders who are empathetic and care deeply about their well-being. By involving them in hiring decisions, you can achieve both goals. And as we'll discuss in chapter 12, involving employees in decisions regarding the organization's future is one strategy to combat burnout.

Here are a few things to keep in mind regarding peer interviewing:

- When peer interviewing is performed at the front line, it's common for the interviewers to not have any experience interviewing others—which has the potential to create problems. For instance, there are questions that legally cannot be asked. Make sure to train all peer interviewers *before* placing them in this role. Ensure that they know the basic dos and don'ts as well as what is expected of them in terms of conduct. You may also want to discuss ahead of time what information you *and* they hope to gather during the interview, and even go over specific questions they intend to ask.

  Perhaps sit in on the first couple of interviews to provide the interview team feedback. However, the downside of auditing interviews is that your presence may prevent the candidate from asking questions about sensitive topics such as culture and the leadership style of their potential superior. It may also inhibit candid and transparent answers from the interview team. You will need to weigh the interview team's experience against these potential drawbacks.

- While evaluating the candidate, interviewers should "sell" the position and organization in a genuine and accurate manner. This too necessitates some education and training for the interviewers. It may sound cumbersome and time-consuming, but this additional education builds further engagement and ownership in the organization. It also helps develop caregivers' leadership skills. All of this will benefit the organization in the long run.

- It is absolutely critical that the interviewers' feedback be taken into genuine consideration. If it is disregarded, the interviewers will begin to distrust the organization and will view the process as a sham and an inconsiderate waste of their time. Personally, I always made a point to talk to interviewers whose impressions differed sharply from those of the rest of the group so I could gain a better understanding of why they did or did not favor the candidate in question. When a decision was made, I assured them that I *had* taken their thoughts into account and, if applicable, explained the reason their preferred candidate was or was not hired. This is critical to maintain trust.

Use Behavioral Interviewing Techniques

A large part of determining culture fit comes from having a general, organic conversation with the job candidate. But you'll get the most accurate picture of each individual if you utilize behavioral interviewing techniques. Essentially, certain interview questions are designed to highlight which personality traits the interviewee may or may not have.

It is wise to train inexperienced interviewers in this technique, as well as provide them with a list of potential behavioral questions to ask. We covered some behavioral interviewing questions in chapter 6, but here are a few more that work well:

- "What recent disagreement did you have with a colleague, and how was it settled?"
  - *What to look for:* Did they seek compromise or push their own desire? Did they seek assistance or settle the issue themselves?
- "What gets you up out of bed and excited to go to work? What aspects of work make you want to keep sleeping?"
  - *What to look for:* This question helps you decipher candidates' motivations and frustrations. Are they energized and willing to take on challenges? Or do they seem reluctant to face difficult situations?
- "Give an example of a time when someone asked you to do something that you thought was 'below your level.' What was your response?"
  - *What to look for:* Did they refuse the task? Did they happily agree to do it? Was their impression that the task was a waste of their valuable time? Or were they willing to do what was necessary for the organization to succeed?
- "Tell me about a decision with which you very much disagreed for reasons that you thought were valid."
  - *What to look for:* Did this person express their concerns, or did they hide them and continue on? If they did not express their concerns, what was the reason? If they did express them, how did the situation end?

Keep in mind that good behavioral questions usually require the interviewee to tell a story, instead of giving a concise answer. They also lend themselves to follow-up questions that enable you to dig deeper and understand more.

For example, someone may answer the first question about disagreeing with a colleague by describing what the disagreement was about, then explaining that they approached the person the next day to try to understand their point of view. In the end, they found a great compromise. Or, the person may say that they went to the manager, who solved the disagreement for them. Certainly, the latter answer opens the door for several additional questions, including: "Why did you not approach your colleague directly?" "What would you have done if your manager had not decided the issue in your favor?" "Was there any friction with your colleague after your manager resolved the issue? How did you handle that?"

When interviewing key executives and other senior leadership roles, organizations often administer personality tests, motivation tests, leadership style tests, and even interviews with corporate psychologists to provide additional insight into the candidate.

Develop (or Partner with) Educational Programs

Interviews can only provide so much information as they generally range from a single hour to over 25 hours, depending on the position. Even at the extreme end of that scale, it can be difficult to get an accurate, unvarnished picture of the person you're interviewing. Many job candidates are exceptional at "saying what you want to hear," especially at higher leadership levels. Thus, the best interview is one that occurs while working with the person over many months or years. This can happen through employment or a training program.

Organizations that develop their own training programs (or partner with other institutions that have training programs) are at a great advantage in recruiting:

- First, you get the first opportunity to hire the individuals who complete the program, prior to those trainees applying for jobs with other organizations.
- Second, since each trainee is a potential hire, you get to shape their education and help them develop their priorities, behaviors, values, and purpose to align with your organization.
- Lastly, there is a great opportunity to assess not only each trainee's skill, but also their cultural fit.

For example (this one is admittedly on the extreme side), I was an emergency medicine resident prior to the limitation of resident work hours to 80 or fewer hours per week. Thus, there were many weeks when I spent between 80 and 110 hours at the hospital! It isn't possible for someone to regularly work that many hours over the course of four years and *not* have their "true colors" come out. Fatigue and frustration eventually got the better of even the most capable and disciplined residents. Looking back from the perspective of a hospital system leader, I know that the hospital's physicians, directors, and other leaders were observing how we residents reacted to setbacks, disappointments, and exhaustion. They were noting how we treated patients, one another, and our fellow caregivers. Those observations no doubt influenced which of us the hospital tried to recruit, and which of us it didn't.

The same principle holds true for internships, apprenticeships, and training programs of all types in any discipline or industry. The very best "interview" is to work alongside someone. Consider developing training programs or partnering with educational organizations so that its students can receive hands-on training at your organization. This model works with clinical disciplines (e.g., nursing, respiratory therapy, pharmacy) and nonclinical disciplines (e.g., healthcare administration, healthcare law, marketing).

Assign an Ambassador to New Hires

I recommend pairing each new hire with an ambassador from their new team, shift, or department. (It's even better if this ambassador was part of the 360-degree interview process!) The ambassador is an employee who is assigned to help their new coworker learn the ropes and adjust to the culture, as well as answer any questions that might come up.

A good ambassador understands the organization, its purpose, and its values—and is a good role model for all those things. Make sure that all of your ambassadors are volunteers who have expressed a desire to help new hires acclimate. If you try to force this relationship, it won't work well and might even backfire. (The last thing you want to do is assign new employees an ambassador who gives off *I resent doing this* vibes!)

Some organizations provide compensation for ambassadors as a way to recognize and appreciate their additional efforts to better the organization. This can be a delicate balance: You want to reward the ambassador's efforts, but you don't want someone to become an ambassador solely for the compensation. Again, the success of this program depends on ambassadors having a genuine passion to onboard and ensure the success of their fellow caregivers.

If compensation is provided, consider disbursing it when various milestones are reached instead of in one lump sum. For example, 25 percent of the compensation might be provided at the start of the relationship, another 25 percent after the new caregiver is part of the organization for 6 months, and the remaining 50 percent after 12 months with the organization. Compensation does not have to be money. It can be anything that demonstrates appreciation, such as time off work.

CONTINUOUSLY RE-RECRUIT YOUR CAREGIVERS

Richard Branson (2014) has provided wise advice to "train people well enough so they can leave, treat them well enough so that they don't want to."

The point is simple: Because you have to invest a significant amount of time, money, and other resources into properly training new hires, it's essential that you keep them! As a friend told me, "If you don't have the time and money to train and retain, you certainly won't have the time and money to recruit." Retention is just as important as recruitment.

Think about it this way: I'm sure your organization regularly spends time and money maintaining and improving your facilities, equipment, information systems, and so forth. You know that to provide the best care, you can't allow things to become dirty, neglected, outdated, or in a state of disrepair. Similarly, the various aspects of re-recruiting employees are a way to "maintain" and "update" your greatest asset: your caregivers.

The following sections address a few basics about re-recruiting employees for long-term retention.

Employees Need to Be Engaged Long After Onboarding Is Complete

Too often, employees fall by the wayside after they are onboarded. Think about it: During the hiring process, many caregivers are actively recruited. They are given incentives to accept a particular position. They may even be sought after by multiple organizations. Then, during the first few days or weeks on the job, new employees are warmly welcomed. They receive special tours, training, and maybe even gifts. They are excited to engage in their new role.

But pretty soon, they are left alone to do their jobs. They may begin to wonder if the organization that was so thrilled to hire them still notices, much less appreciates, the great work they do. They may feel stuck in one place without an opportunity for growth. They certainly don't feel like they are your greatest asset. These employees then become less engaged. Subsequently, the grass at another organization begins to look greener and greener.

Our job as leaders is to make sure that doesn't happen. We need to build a culture where people are appreciated, have opportunities to grow, and are motivated to provide the best care. We need to help our employees maintain the sense of welcome, excitement, and purpose they had when they were first hired. Engagement depends on a variety of factors: the quality of caregivers' relationships with leaders and coworkers, your willingness to provide training, how well your systems and processes work, and more. None of that should be left to chance. Our organizations must develop plans to engage and continuously reengage our teams.

When Turnover Is a Good Thing

Yes, there is such a thing as positive turnover. If a caregiver is learning, thriving, and developing leadership skills but there is no growth opportunity for them at their current organization, it's our responsibility as leaders to help them find that next role. It's the right thing to do—both from a "taking care of your greatest asset" standpoint and from a "helping them align with their purpose" standpoint. People remember how they are treated on the way out, and they *will* talk about an organization after their exit. Plus, we never know if their career paths will bring them back to our organizations in the future.

The External Environment Can Significantly Impact Retention—So Adapt Accordingly

Re-recruiting caregivers is especially important during this time of rapid change in healthcare. Not only are organizations adapting to new technologies, models of care, and the changing preferences of patients in the wake of the pandemic, but the balance of power is also shifting from employers to employees. (This is actually true in every industry.)

As I write this book, the Great Resignation is creating staffing shortages and fueling an increasingly intense war for talent. Now and in the future, employers must be able to attract and especially *retain* good people. This may mean dramatically restructuring various parts of your organization to put employee engagement and well-being squarely in the middle of everything. It's also crucial to hire leaders who understand the need to proactively (rather than reactively) drive change in your organization's priorities and culture.

As we'll discuss later in this book, helping employees manage stress, burnout, and mental health issues is a huge factor in keeping them engaged, productive, and doing their best work. These problems were rampant before COVID-19, and now they are exponentially worse. As leaders we have to acknowledge the pressures and hardships people are facing, not just at work but also at home, and take action to make their lives better. In other words, we need to approach and re-recruit each employee as a "whole person"—not just as a nurse or a technician or a food service worker. The next section highlights a current example of what I mean.

Flexibility Is No Longer a "Perk"—It's a Must-Have for Retention

Multiple studies demonstrate that younger generations prioritize personal time and flexibility over loyalty to an organization. If you don't meet their preferences and expectations, they may move to an organization that will. And please don't fall into the trap of assuming that millennials and Gen Z are simply being selfish. Remember, caregivers of all generations have full lives and myriad responsibilities outside the workplace. If leaders truly want to treat our employees as our greatest asset, shouldn't we do everything in our power and within reason to ensure that they are satisfied and supported even after they clock out?

For instance, flexibility in work hours might allow parents to drop off their children at school or attend their afternoon sporting events. Imagine the difference between an employee who thinks, *I am so grateful to have a job that allows me to eat breakfast with my daughter and take her to school* and an employee who thinks, *I am so resentful of the fact that I can't be there for my kids*. Now consider the potential differences between these two employees' attitudes and performances. Which person would you want to provide your care if you were a patient? Which one will be motivated to stay with your organization long-term? When you look at it this way, meeting employees' preferences doesn't seem so outlandish after all. Instead, it's a powerful recruitment and retention tool.

That said, offering flexible work schedules can be a bit of a challenge—especially for frontline caregivers. Fixed schedules are an important component of maintaining continuity of care, but do all shifts need to be 12 hours long, from 7:00 a.m. to 7:00 p.m. or from 7:00 p.m. to 7:00 a.m.? Or could some units have both 12-hour shifts and 8-hour shifts? Greater flexibility will necessitate putting more effort into managing the schedule, but it may also attract better talent and reduce departures from your organization.

Another change that leaders need to consider is the rise of remote work. Due to disruptions forced on all industries by the COVID-19 pandemic, working from home has become an expectation for many. What positions in your organization could be transitioned from in-person to either partially or fully remote? What training would be needed for remote workers and their leaders? How often would remote workers need to meet in person to maintain organizational culture and build intradepartmental or interdepartmental relationships?

Scheduling flexibility and the option to work remotely are just two of the many changes leaders need to consider as the nature of the modern workplace evolves. We must keep our eyes open and our ears to the ground so we remain aware of the innovative adaptations that are occurring in healthcare around the country. We should also look at other industries to see what practices we can adopt into healthcare.

If Turnover Is a Problem, We Need to Look in the Mirror

If an organization is having difficulty retaining talent, leaders must resist the impulse to blame departing employees (e.g., "All they care about is money," "People don't have any loyalty anymore," or "There just aren't enough qualified employees out there").

Instead, we should hold a mirror up to ourselves and to the rest of our organization's leadership and culture. We need to take responsibility for the turnover and try to determine why caregivers might be leaving the organization. Are there pain points or inefficiencies we can address? We may even find that the issue isn't something negative we *are* doing, but rather involves positive things we *are not* doing. For instance, good caregivers want opportunities to learn and grow—which brings me to my next piece of advice.

Provide Internal and External Sources of Learning

During a meeting, a chief financial officer asked the CEO, "What happens if we invest in developing our people and then they leave us?" The CEO responded, "What happens if we don't, and then they stay?"

Continuous training and investment in caregivers (both clinical and nonclinical) is essential to deliver the best care possible. However, development opportunities don't just help employees become more confident and skilled, they also offer a fantastic way to re-recruit. When caregivers see investment in their growth and future, they are more motivated to spend that future at their current organization.

I would guess that most, if not all, healthcare organizations send their employees to conferences. Conferences can certainly be beneficial, but if you aren't thoughtful about which employees you are sending to each conference and why, they don't always provide a good value for your money. External conferences are best suited to provide very specific training to a few individuals.

For example, in the past I have sent billing and coding specialists to a conference so they could learn about specific topics such as updated processes for documentation and critical care coding. I also sent some of the critical care physicians with the coding specialists so the physicians could learn how to document more accurately, which would in turn allow our organization to receive appropriate reimbursement. Both the caregivers and the coders were on the same page—and, of equal value, they had the opportunity to develop stronger relationships through their time spent together at the conference.

To educate a larger swathe of your employees about broad but critical topics (e.g., change management, crucial conversations, cultural transformation), I am personally biased toward internal learning opportunities like internal conferences, classes, article reviews, and book clubs. The content of internal events can be tailored to your organization's needs and goals, and a greater number of people can attend because travel and lodging are not an issue. Plus, internal conferences provide a wonderful opportunity to build relationships within your organization as everyone learns together. If your organization doesn't employ an expert in a particular discipline, bring external speakers to your internal conference.

Each Caregiver Needs to Feel Individually Recognized, Valued, Appreciated, and Understood

In his book *Primary Greatness: The 12 Levers of Success*, Stephen Covey (2016) writes, "The deepest hunger of the human soul is to be recognized, valued, appreciated, and understood." I believe Covey's observation is applicable to our personal and professional lives. As my mother taught me when I was a child, everyone wants to be acknowledged, respected, and regarded as a unique individual whose life and contributions matter. (You can refer back to chapter 1 for the full story.)

When caregivers receive this type of consideration from their leaders, directors, and supervisors, they recapture the sense of being valued and sought-after that they may have felt during the recruiting and hiring process. That being the case, do your organization's caregivers *feel* that they are seen, celebrated, and developed based on their individual merits and desires? Before you answer, know that the most critical word in that question is *feel*.

I recall a conversation in which an executive told me that he recognized, valued, appreciated, and understood every member of his team. "That's wonderful, but it may not matter," I responded. "What matters is that your team *feels* recognized, valued, appreciated, and understood. If they don't *feel* that you are doing all of those things, your efforts don't exist in their minds."

For now, know that this is not a one-size-fits-all process. You will need to figure out how to genuinely connect with each individual. For instance, what makes one person feel appreciated (e.g., being recognized publicly at a departmental meeting) might make another feel self-conscious and uncomfortable. In chapter 10, we'll take a closer look at how to make sure each individual feels recognized, valued, appreciated, and understood.

Purpose Is a Powerful Tool for Retention

Ideally, all caregivers in your organization are driven by a personal purpose and aligned with your organization's overarching purpose. If someone *isn't* connected to purpose, they probably lack sustained motivation and engagement. Rather than being excited about the job they do each day, they endure it until it's time to go home. These aren't the kinds of feelings that inspire people to remain at their organization long-term.

As leaders, it is our job to help clinical and nonclinical caregivers understand and stay connected to their purpose in the organization. This task is of great importance in re-recruiting them. When caregivers are excited to wake up each day, go to work, and positively change the lives of patients, they probably aren't thinking seriously about jumping ship. I encourage you to reread chapter 1, this time with the goal of retention in mind.

Empower Caregivers to Make Their Own Decisions

People rarely want to be treated like robots: always being told what to do, when to do it, how to do it. As anyone who has spent time with children can attest, the desire for agency, control, and independence manifests at a very young age. If children are not provided the opportunity to make their own decisions within established guidelines, they will lash out with frustration—and perhaps a tantrum.

The same thing is true for caregivers! If we don't empower them and allow them to make their own decisions within established guidelines, they will lash out by leaving the organization. (Some might even throw the adult version of a tantrum by posting derogatory things about your organization on social media.)

If caregivers are the most valuable part of our organization, shouldn't we always be striving to help them realize their potential? Don't we want to use our greatest asset at its highest capacity? I certainly believe so. When people are empowered to make their own decisions (and the occasional honest mistake), they become owners of the process and the result. They are energized, put forth greater discretionary effort, and become more closely connected to their purpose. On the other hand, employees who are micromanaged or burdened with a plethora of restrictive rules and regulations quickly become timid, fearful, and disengaged.

So how do we strike the balance between being *too* controlling and not giving caregivers enough guidance?

Start empowering employees during onboarding. I recommend starting the process of empowerment during onboarding so that new employees understand that it is a part of the culture. At this point, new hires are receiving *a lot* of rules, regulations, and expectations. They are hearing multiple variations of "Do this, not that." It's especially important to balance the scales by asking for their opinions, including them in appropriate meetings, and allowing them time to voice questions and observations.

Ensure that one person isn't making decisions for a group. For example, do the nursing caregivers on a unit meet on a regular basis for shared decision-making? Or is the unit manager solely in charge of the unit's development? Caregivers will feel less like "renters" and more like empowered "owners" if they are included in making decisions that affect their jobs and their futures.

Guide caregivers with a helping hand instead of an iron fist. I believe that a good leader always provides three things: the direction, the *why* behind the direction, and the support a caregiver needs to travel in that direction. But ultimately, it's the caregiver's responsibility to take the first step in the right direction . . . and the next step, and the next, until the task is complete.

What I mean is that good leaders rarely prescribe *how* something should be done. They encourage caregivers to find their own solutions and follow their own preferred methods, as long as those things are within reason (or when practicing medicine, within the standard of care). Showing employees this level of trust is a powerful retention tool *and* a great way to ensure that patients receive thoughtful, high-level care.

At one point in my career as an emergency medicine physician, a resident approached me to discuss a patient whose X-ray indicated the presence of pneumonia. The resident asked me what antibiotic he should give. I answered, "What antibiotic do *you* want to give?"

Although the question made the resident uncomfortable, it also made him think and forced him to rely on his own education and experience. After the resident told me which antibiotic he felt would be best, I asked him to explain his thought process to make sure it was sound, and not just a guess. I told him that I would have given a different antibiotic and explained my own reasons why. Finally, I explained the pros and cons of a few other antibiotics that might realistically be prescribed for this patient (cost, duration of therapy, frequency of dose, side effects, etc.). I encouraged the resident to discuss these antibiotic options with the patient before making a final decision. Just as I was engaging the resident to be a decision-maker in the care delivery process, engaging the patient in decision-making also builds ownership.

"In the end, as long as the medication you prescribe is appropriate and within the standard of care, it's up to you and your patient," I finished. "There are often multiple 'correct' ways to treat someone. Think about all the antibiotics we've discussed, and then make your own choice with the patient." He did—and I noticed that his care of that patient was filled with purpose, empathy, and consideration. In short, this resident took charge and treated the patient as if she was one of his loved ones.

Imagine if all caregivers (clinical and nonclinical) in your organization were empowered to act similarly! Whether you are practicing medicine or providing leadership, give everyone space to make their own decisions within appropriate parameters. They will develop confidence and critical thinking skills, achieve consistently positive results, and experience greater professional satisfaction.

Empowered Caregivers Can Change Patients' Lives

You may recall two stories I shared in chapter 7. In the first, a caregiver went against policy to bring a dying patient's dog into the hospital so the patient could say goodbye. In the other story, nurses took the initiative to purchase caffeine-free Diet Pepsi (which the hospital did not offer) for a patient who had requested it. While both of these stories were originally told to highlight exceptional service to patients, they also illustrate the tremendous impact empowered caregivers can have on those they serve.

At another point when I was CEO of Hospital X, nurses learned that the spouse of a very ill patient had suddenly died at their house. Understandably, the patient was exceptionally distraught and only wanted one thing at that moment: to see her deceased husband. Without feeling the need to request permission, the nurses did what they knew was the right thing. They contacted the morgue and arranged for their patient's husband to be brought to the hospital so the patient could spend time with her husband in a large conference room.

At the end of the day, the "right" way to invest time, effort, and resources into your organization's greatest asset boils down to one simple principle: Treat all caregivers as you would want to be treated. Look for ways to engage, support, and develop them. Listen to them, recognize them, and empower them. Communicate with honesty, transparency, and humility. When you do these things, your greatest asset will be fueled by purpose to provide the best possible care and service to patients—and they'll be in it for the long haul.

I'll end this chapter by saying that the topic of re-recruitment is a broad one. I could probably write an entire book on this subject alone. And in a way, I have. While they aren't labeled explicitly as "retention tools," this book is full of ways to continuously re-recruit employees. For instance, connecting caregivers to their purpose, breaking down the power gradient to bring all caregivers into the conversation, and providing honest, constructive feedback are *all* things that keep healthcare employees engaged and fulfilled in their organizations. In the next two chapters, I'll share several suggestions to help you improve communication and stay connected with clinical and nonclinical caregivers. Good communication and staying connected with your greatest asset is essential for retaining top talent and elevating their engagement.

REFERENCES

Branson, R. 2014. "Train people well enough so they can leave, treat them well enough so they don't want to," Twitter, March 27, 11:23. https://twitter.com/richardbranson/status/449220 072176107520?lang=en

Covey, S. R. 2016. *Primary Greatness: The 12 Levers of Success*. New York: Simon & Schuster.

CHAPTER 9

Enhancing Communication to Strengthen Culture and Improve Outcomes

IF YOU'RE IN a leadership position, chances are you're a fairly good communicator. Any leader worthy of the name wants to support their employees and does not withhold important information on purpose.

But on so many employee engagement surveys, respondents say they are not happy with the communication they receive. According to a recent Gallup report, only 7 percent of American workers strongly agree that "communication is accurate, timely and open where they work," and only 26 percent strongly agree that "their manager's feedback helps them do better work" (Robison 2021).

Why is there such a big chasm between leaders' best efforts to communicate and how employees perceive that communication? I think that for most leaders, basic communication skills aren't the issue. You wouldn't have been promoted to a leadership position if you struggled to express yourself and couldn't convey information to others.

In my experience, closing the communication gap is a matter of "little" things making a big difference. Small variations in how, when, why, and with whom you communicate can drastically alter how your employees perceive your message and whether or not they get on board with your suggestions and direction.

In this chapter we will look at some strategies to help you level up your communication. (Also, be aware that more tips for better communication are scattered throughout the book since communication is crucial to flattening the power gradient, delivering feedback, holding employees accountable, and much more.)

WHY IS GREAT LEADER COMMUNICATION SO IMPORTANT?

There is more at stake than survey results. You know this, but as a busy leader, you may be questioning whether it's *really* worth using your precious time to grow your communication skills from "good" to "great." It is—and here's why:

- **Communication is a foundational building block of any service business.** As we have established, healthcare organizations rely on caregivers to provide prompt, purposeful, empathetic, and high-quality service to patients. Great communication keeps caregivers aligned, agile, motivated, and empowered (which boosts productivity for your organization and clinical outcomes for your patients). Without great communication, your team may become confused and overwhelmed. Misunderstandings and mistakes will happen more frequently, and your team will be unable to move quickly in the same direction.
- **It reduces the power gradient.** Great communication travels 360 degrees. Leaders need not only to relay information to others, but also to hear honest, freely given feedback from their bosses, peers, and subordinates. As we discussed in chapter 6, an established power gradient can cause issues such as a decrease in safety, poor morale, and a pervasive lack of trust. You may also recall that poor

and unclear communication was a significant contributing factor in the Tenerife plane crash.

- **Great communication supports a culture of well-being.** The better leaders are able to communicate, the more clearly they can convey the organization's values, purpose, standards, and expectations. When this happens, stress and uncertainty are reduced. People know what is expected of them and where the boundaries are, and engagement and morale will improve.

- **It builds strong relationships.** Great communication between leaders, caregivers, and patients creates strong bonds and increases trust in all directions. People stay engaged and connected. They see themselves as part of a valued (and valuable!) team. They act like owners and are more likely to stay with your organization long-term.

- **Great communication is essential in today's complex work environment.** Healthcare is evolving at a rapid pace. Today's best practices will soon become obsolete. Technology needs to be constantly updated. Remote work in non-frontline positions is on the rise. Patients' goals and expectations are changing. Leaders must be able to sort through, manage, and disseminate this constant flow of information in a way that leaves caregivers informed but not overwhelmed.

- **It is essential when navigating tough times.** Communication is always important, but it is especially crucial in times of great change, trauma, or disruption. The past few years certainly fit those criteria: COVID-19, social and political unrest, natural disasters, international crises, and more. Almost all of these things disproportionately affect those of us in healthcare. When you handle tough situations the right way, not only do you help caregivers get through the immediate crisis, but you also give them the tools to become a stronger, more unified, and more resilient team than they were before.

Overall, I'd say that being a great communicator is one of the things that separates people who *manage* or *administrate* from people who *lead*. Managers or administrators maintain the status quo and check things off their to-do lists, but leaders are able to motivate, inspire, and develop others to drive performance through communication.

STRATEGIES TO HELP LEADERS COMMUNICATE MORE EFFECTIVELY

Let's look at some best practices to help you become a better communicator. You're likely already doing some of them! I urge you to adopt what's useful for you and skim over the rest.

Always Give People the "Why"

In other words, share your rationale on all decisions. Communicate your thought process to all stakeholders. Explain why other options were not chosen, especially if your decision was not their preferred one. The more honest and transparent you are, the more your team will trust and respect you. What's more:

- Hearing a breakdown of your thought process can be educational because it showcases your critical thinking skills. Explaining the "why" can help develop people by teaching them *how to think*, not just what to do.
- The people with whom you work (whether they're your own leaders, your peers, or your reports) want to know the reason behind your decisions. Even if they disagree, knowing that you have taken the decision seriously can help gain their buy-in. If those who disagree have provided input or suggestions that were not followed, explain the

"why" behind your decision (and make sure to genuinely thank them for their input). And for people who *do* agree or who are ambivalent, sharing the "why" builds even more engagement and ownership.

- Providing the "why" behind a decision shows respect and is a great way to flatten the power gradient. At some point we have all been on the receiving end of "because I said so" leadership—and it doesn't feel good. Without the "why," people feel taken for granted and perhaps not worthy of an explanation. When you share the "why," you are respecting the other person's ability to be an independent thinker and person of action.

  Here is a story to illustrate. Hospital X was a typical community hospital but was also part of an academic healthcare system. Our organization's leadership had great appreciation and respect for medical education but didn't initially want Hospital X to have residents and fellows. Leaders were concerned that it would become known as a "training hospital." Frankly, some had very strong opinions on the subject. They wouldn't blindly accept— nor should they have accepted—a dictum without understanding why it would be beneficial.

  As CEO, it was my responsibility to convey why residency and fellowship training programs would be an asset to Hospital X so that our leadership team could make an informed decision. Here is the point-by-point explanation I gave. Note that I gave details and specific examples wherever possible:

  - Point 1: Quite often, large academic institutions employ physicians whose medical specialties are rarely seen in community hospitals. Partnering with academic institutions will provide access to these specialists. Not only will community members have access to better care, Hospital X will be able to expand its service for programmatic growth. Certainly, this would be a differentiator for our community hospital when compared to our competitors.

- Point 2: One of the missions of our parent organization is to educate future healthcare providers. The great majority of their training takes place at a large and complex hospital that cares for the most critical patients in the region. Future providers will get a much different—but equally valuable—experience here at Hospital X.

  For example, anesthesia residents currently receive exceptional training experience taking care of surgical patients who are having a heart transplant or undergoing an eight-hour radical neck dissection for cancer. But they have less experience in a community hospital where procedures like elective knee arthroscopies and joint replacements are more commonly performed. In addition to the differences between procedures, anesthesia residents will also learn how to turn over an operating room at a quicker pace. In the community operating room, there may be eight to 15 procedures performed in one room over the course a day. Thus, rapid turnover is necessary. Contrast that to a transplant room or a complex cancer operating room, where there may be only one or two cases performed each day.

- Point 3: Finally, our hospital will be able to speak to the community about the exceptional specialized academic physicians who are now practicing at their community hospital.

In fact, at one future point Hospital X created advertisements touting, "Our physicians train the other physicians" and "Hospital X employs the same physicians as Academic Institution A," which was well-known regionally and nationally for stroke, trauma, critical care, cancer, and other services.

Connect Back to Purpose

As often as possible, link your "why" to your organization's purpose (or mission, or values). This will give changes, goals, and initiatives a deeper meaning and will prompt greater engagement and buy-in from your team. Instead of doing something "because the boss said so," caregivers will want to do it because they'll see how it will make the organization a better place to work, make their jobs easier, improve the patient's experience . . . or all three!

You may recall that in chapter 1, I shared several examples of how Hospital X engaged with the community. Those initiatives could have easily been seen by our employees as "just one more thing to do." But our leadership made a conscious effort to connect the "why" behind community outreach to our organization's purpose, "to change the lives of others." I truly believe this made a big difference in how enthusiastically caregivers got on board.

For instance, one leader stated: "I know that training young adults with special needs to work at the hospital is outside our wheelhouse of providing direct healthcare. But it's certainly within the scope of our purpose. We can change the lives of these young people in so many ways. Their time here at Hospital X will help them gain confidence, give them the experience of working on a team, and teach them valuable job skills."

After the "why" was provided and discussed, Hospital X's leadership team understood and largely agreed with the decision to support medical education at our institution. A few individuals disagreed with the "why," which was their right. But all appreciated that they had been a part of the conversation and were treated as respected members of the team.

Answer Promptly

Giving people a prompt answer is easy—and even enjoyable—when the answer is yes. Every leader enjoys feeling like a hero when they can say, "Yes, you can take those days off." "Yes, that's in our budget." "Yes, we're hiring the candidate you liked." A yes answer can be a complete assent to the request, or it can include small adjustments. For instance, "Yes, we will implement the changes you suggested. Everything except for one item is in our budget right now; we'll plan on launching that final item next quarter."

But when you are not able to give someone their preferred answer, the temptation to drag your feet comes into play—and there are all sorts of "legitimate" excuses you can use to justify delaying. "I'll just wait till tomorrow to deliver the news—I don't want to ruin their evening." "I have a lot of important things I need to do first—I don't have time to talk to them now." And worst of all, "If I don't force the issue, maybe they'll just forget about it." (This almost *never* happens.)

Trust me: Don't put off the conversation. Get back to the other person as soon as possible, give them the answer, and tell them the "why." A *prompt* no is unpleasant, but a *slow* no is worse. The conversation isn't going away. Waiting only makes it harder for you to initiate and for the other person to hear.

The worst thing leaders can do is to never respond to a question or request. No answer is still an answer. It's disrespectful, implies a power gradient, and breaks down relationships and trust. I see "slow nos" and "no answers"—especially if they are habitual—as a form of leadership malpractice, which we'll discuss in detail in chapter 11.

When you know the answer but withhold it from an employee, one or more negative outcomes might occur:

- The employee is left in a protracted state of uncertainty, stress, or anxiety.
- You send the message that the employee is not a priority for you.
- Without an official answer, the employee makes assumptions that may not be correct.
- Your slow response breaks down trust. *Why didn't my leader tell me this sooner? What else might they be keeping from me? My time was wasted because I could have been working on a different plan instead of waiting so long for the answer.*

Having Difficult Conversations Is a Skill Leaders Need

Often, leaders are guilty of the "slow no" because they dread having difficult conversations. Maybe they don't want to disappoint someone, are uneasy holding them accountable, don't want to be seen as the bad guy, or fear that the other person might become angry. But being able to navigate tough conversations is a skill all leaders need. If you haven't had any training on how to approach difficult conversations, *Taking Conversations from Difficult to Doable: 3 Models to Master Tough Conversations* by Lynne Cunningham, MPA, is a great practical resource.

Anticipate People's Need to Know

As we've established, leaders are subjected to a constant flow of information. You must be intentional about sifting through everything so that you can proactively share the right information with the right people. Get in the habit of asking yourself, *Who else needs to know this? What information do I have that might help someone else do their job better?*

Above all, try to anticipate situations that might make caregivers wonder, *Why didn't anyone tell me this? Why am I just finding out now?* Unfortunately, there will always be people who operate in "gotcha" mode with their leaders, so don't wait for employees to notice on their own that changes are occurring. Being up front and proactive helps you control the narrative and keep their trust. Plus, most people will respect you for reaching out directly with updates, even if the updates are undesirable.

Admit When You Don't Know Something

As a leader you are expected to have a high degree of knowledge and competency, but you are *not* expected to have all the answers, all the time. When you don't know something, acknowledge it. Then promise to find an answer and get back to the other person. You may worry that admitting ignorance will cause caregivers to lose respect for you, but this is almost never the case. Instead, they'll respect you for your honesty and—assuming you follow through on your promise to find an answer—for your integrity.

Depending on the situation, this can also be a good opportunity to develop your employee: "Here's how I went about finding the answer: I talked to these people, searched in these publications, ran these tests, etc."

Make Sure Your Communication Is as Transparent and Complete as Possible

We can all agree that leaders should communicate in a clear, accurate, and timely manner. Like giving employees the answer they want to hear, this is easy to do when you have something positive to share. Everyone enjoys announcing good news, emphasizing wins, and celebrating accomplishments. (Side note: Make sure you are doing these things as frequently as possible! Never miss an opportunity to recognize a caregiver or boost your team's morale.)

But it's just as crucial to be honest about bad news. People *can* handle the truth. This is especially true for healthcare workers, who are tough, adaptable, and resilient. They need to know they can trust you, their leader, to be fully transparent—even when you're sharing something they don't want to hear. When leaders delay or skim over the truth, people fill in the gaps on their own. They make assumptions that may not be true, and they come up with theories that may not be correct. Then they may spread this misinformation as though it were fact.

What about times when you can't be fully transparent? If there is an information gap, admit it and explain why. Then give people a timeline for when the gap will be filled, if possible. Here are some things you might say:

- "I don't know, but I'm looking into it. I'll give you an update before the end of the day."
- "Some of this information is confidential. I'm telling you everything I am authorized to share."
- "I am waiting to get the results of the survey. Once I receive those results, I will be able to make a decision."
- "I'm still working on this. I expect to have an answer by Monday."

Err on the Side of "More"

In other words, communicate frequently and with moderate redundancy. During my years as a leader, I found that it's usually most effective to touch base with your team at shorter intervals, and to make your communications brief. You'll get more communication accomplished over the long run, *and* you'll have more touch points for connecting with caregivers. Let's take a look at why both frequency and redundancy are important factors in great communication:

- **Frequent communication keeps people informed.** It enables you to roll out information in smaller chunks that may be more digestible. You can keep employees abreast of changes and updates as they happen. On the other hand, if you rely on big information dumps, you will find that most of it is not absorbed. Why? People tend to focus on the first thing you tell them or on what they find most interesting. Their attention wanders. They have numerous responsibilities of their own and don't have the mental bandwidth to download a laundry list of "important points."

  So how often is "frequent?" It depends on the nature of your leadership role. If you are a shift supervisor whose direct reports are frontline caregivers, you might hold several huddles each day to make sure everyone is up to speed and to discuss issues that may have arisen during the day. As the chief medical officer (CMO) of a healthcare system, I sent a short two- to three-minute video to the entire organization of 13,000 caregivers each morning during the height of the COVID-19 pandemic. Daily communication was necessary because information and processes were literally changing by the day. However, between surges when there was calm before the next storm, the videos went out weekly.

  Experience has taught me that it is better to overcommunicate than undercommunicate, but also to be careful not to "force" communications. If there isn't a necessary update, spend your time doing something else. (Remember that your time *and* your employees' time is very valuable!) When communications start to lose value, your audience will start skimming the newsletter, skipping the video, or not opening the e-mail. As a result, the audience will miss important information when it is distributed.

- **Redundant communication ensures that people receive and remember the message.** Often, people hear an announcement, but their minds are elsewhere. They'll skim an e-mail and miss something important. Or they *think* they remember what you told them, but they've misunderstood or misremembered an important detail. That's where redundancy comes in. If people hear a message multiple times, the chances that they accurately receive and remember the information rise considerably.

    The more important the message, the more crucial redundancy is. When big things like strategic initiatives are at stake, I make sure to communicate the same thing many times in many different venues. It's better for some people to be annoyed ("I already know that!") than for a ball to be dropped ("I forgot!"). That said, redundancy doesn't have to be obnoxious. It's often as simple as sharing a few quick reminders at the beginning of a meeting or huddle or sending a brief "Don't forget!" e-mail or text.

Make It Multimodal

You have several different modes of communication at your disposal, and I've found that each is best suited for specific types of communication. For the purposes of this chapter, I'll focus on how you can use each mode to communicate with a group, team, department, or organization (as opposed to communicating directly with another person or a few individuals).

- **E-mail:** In today's professional world, e-mail is ubiquitous. It can be a quick, easy way to convey important information to your team or organization. But it's also easy to misuse or abuse e-mail (even if you don't intend for this to happen). Here are some tips for using e-mail in a way that keeps people informed without overloading or irritating them:

- My top tip for sending e-mails to a large group: Keep your message short. TL;DR (too long; didn't read) is a real hazard. Remember that busy caregivers don't have time to wade through dense paragraphs, so clearly state up front what you want them to know or. Put it in the subject line if possible. Is an action item needed? Is the message informational only?
- If you think that even brief e-mails are not being read, consider using a program that monitors e-mail open rates. The resulting data will enable you to see what's working and what's not (e.g., are certain topics ignored more than others?) and, when appropriate, to hold chronic e-mail ignorers accountable.
- E-mail is not efficient for back-and-forth conversation or discussion. If you anticipate there will be many questions or comments, or if replies keep going back and forth, then it is time to either pick up the phone or set up a meeting.
- Situation, Background, Assessment, and Recommendation (SBAR) is a well-known communication tool to succinctly organize information. When used as a guide, it helps guarantee that all necessary information is included in the e-mail and that it is organized. SBAR also assists with brevity. I have found that people are more likely to read an e-mail in SBAR format than one of the same length that isn't well organized. Make SBAR a part of your culture.
- If there are multiple people on the e-mail, specify who has which action and who is only included as an FYI. If possible, create a standard e-mail culture in your organization or department. For example, there is an

action necessary for all those in the *To:* line. Those who are cc'd are included for informational purposes only.

– Only include those on the e-mail who truly need to be included. Often the sender thinks they are being considerate by including other individuals, but this is actually inconsiderate because reading (and possibly responding to) the e-mail consumes the recipient's valuable time.

– Once you have the right people on the e-mail, you should still be considerate of their time. Remove people from the e-mail when it is no longer necessary to include them. Often the sender doesn't want to drop someone else off the e-mail because he doesn't want to hurt that person's feelings. To prevent this, explain your rationale in one last communication. For example, "Mary and Bob, I am dropping you off this e-mail because your action items are complete. If there is any information that you need to be updated on, I will be sure to reach out to you. Don't hesitate to reach out to me." Yes, it is much easier to click "reply all," but bear in mind the inefficiencies that a bloated inbox can cause.

– Use the bcc feature with extreme caution. In my opinion, blind copying someone is disingenuous. You are including a third party in the conversation without the primary recipient's awareness. I find it difficult to think of a reason why a transparent, candid, and authentic leader would need to use this e-mail function (the obvious exception being an informational e-mail that is sent to the entire department or organization, with no expectation of a reply). Leaders need to treat others the way we would like to be treated ourselves—or better yet, treat others how they would like to be treated!

- Evening and weekend e-mails can make the recipient feel they must respond before the next workday (even if the sender doesn't expect such a prompt response). If something absolutely must be addressed on the weekend or on a holiday, then it is most likely urgent enough to warrant a phone call or text instead. Many people, myself included, do work on weekends and holidays. However, when I send out e-mails on those dates, I use the "send later" function to ensure that the message is delivered during working hours.

- **Text messaging:** Although texting is the preferred mode of communication for many people, be careful not to overuse it. Group texts and organization-wide texts can quickly become a burden or feel intrusive. Plus, there's no way to guarantee that everyone will see the text (or that they will opt in to your organization's text messaging list, *or* that they even have a phone!). Therefore, texting is *not* a good way to convey critical information. Instead, think of texting as a technique for redundancy. It allows you to instantly send small bits of information that will be reiterated elsewhere.

  Texting is also an effective way to follow up on a situation or request. For instance, you might send a text message to inform your team that an important document or e-mail is awaiting their attention in their e-mail inbox, since it's not uncommon for e-mails to remain unread for longer periods of time: "Good afternoon, Team! There is an important e-mail that needs your attention sometime today. It is titled 'Emergency power outage tomorrow.'"

- **Newsletters:** Despite all the technological advances that have transformed the workplace, newsletters (whether physical or digital) are still one of the best ways to announce things like Employee of the Week and monthly birthdays, and to remind people about upcoming events and deadlines.

You can certainly use newsletters to highlight critical or urgent matters, but (again) use this mode of communication as a redundancy since there is no way to guarantee that everyone will read each article.

- **Town Meeting (TM) forums:** At one healthcare system where I was a leader, several senior leaders visited each site (hospitals, ambulatory clinics, support staff, corporate, etc.) on a quarterly basis to hold TM forums. The purpose of the forums was to facilitate bidirectional dialogue. Information was provided to all caregivers, and questions were asked of the audience. Since TM forums were costly and time-consuming, the system eventually moved to holding biweekly videoconferences with bilateral communication.

  Because caregivers could see and hear the leaders, communication via body language and intonation was preserved. Plus, leaders were able to communicate more frequently with caregivers across the system. Caregivers themselves could type in real-time comments and questions; sometimes, we even pulled specific caregivers into the video chat.

  Because virtual TM forums were so successful, the system soon made physician forums virtual too. Instead of asking the physicians to travel from different sites, some of which were an hour away, the physicians could stay in their offices to join the virtual meeting. Attendance rose dramatically.

- **Video communication:** Toward the beginning of the COVID-19 pandemic, I began recording a one- to two-minute video message each morning. It was e-mailed to each of the 13,000 caregivers (clinical and nonclinical) in the healthcare system, and a link to the video was also posted on our website. I usually included information on the spread of COVID-19, changes in our organization's processes, updates on miscellaneous critical items such as personal protective equipment supplies, and other relevant announcements and reminders. As often as possible, these messages were connected to the organizational purpose.

I also made sure to share words of encouragement and admiration. Especially during the pandemic, it was important to acknowledge just how hard our caregivers were working, and how much the leadership, myself included, appreciated their courage and commitment. Sometimes I recognized individuals who had gone above and beyond. Since the video messages were more engaging than e-mails, they had a very high "watch" rate.

Video communications are best used by leaders who oversee several departments, several sites, or the organization. This is because senior leaders cannot have consistent personal conversations with all caregivers given the quantity or the geographic spread of their employees. For departmental leaders, updates in huddles or other forums are best, as in-person communication is more personal and provides better opportunities for questions and discussion.

- **Podcasts:** When most of us think of podcasts, we envision professionally produced, longer-form audio episodes. If you have the time, expertise, and inclination, you can certainly create this type of podcast and share it with your organization. But bear in mind that podcasts can also be shorter and simpler—and similar to video messages, they're an engaging way to communicate with larger groups.

  I know a chief medical information officer (CMIO) of a healthcare system who e-mailed regular updates about the electronic medical record, voice dictations, and other clinical care technologies to all 1,400 physicians. At first, the information was communicated solely via e-mail in a paragraph format. However, the CMIO eventually included a link to a one-minute podcast that featured him verbally conveying the same information. Using e-mail data analytics, we noticed that the number of practitioners who opened the e-mail increased with the addition of the podcast. Feedback from practitioners themselves indicated that they had greater interest and capacity in their day to listen to the podcast than to read another e-mail.

- **In person:** Despite all the options technology affords us, I think in-person communication is still the gold standard for connecting with others. There's no substitute for being in the same space with others, looking them in the eye, and reading their body language and energy while you communicate. If you are an upper-level leader, you probably don't have many opportunities to speak directly to everyone in your organization—and that's where a good cascade system, which we'll talk about next, comes into play.

Have an Effective Cascade System in Place

Design and implement a system that allows you to "cascade" information throughout the entire organization, from top to bottom—and from bottom to top. These systems ensure that every employee receives the same message at the same time, directly from their leaders.

Have you ever been in a situation where, for instance, one department head announces a new initiative two days before another department head does? This lack of coordination in rolling out the announcement can have numerous negative consequences. Some employees will hear about the initiative from colleagues in other departments instead of from their own supervisors. As the message is passed along, it may become garbled. And the longer it takes for employees to receive the "official" announcement, the more their trust will break down: "Why didn't my leader tell me this sooner?" "Why is this department the last to know anything?" "Is this true? My supervisor hasn't mentioned it." "It sure would have been nice to have this information a few days ago."

When I was CEO of Hospital X, we developed a daily huddle system that allowed us to cascade information throughout the entire hospital system. Tier One had daily huddles. (Tier One consisted of frontline departments and the lowest levels in the organizational hierarchy—e.g., a primary care office in the ambulatory world, the cardiac unit in a hospital, or the risk management team within corporate support services.) These huddles took place at the beginning of the shift and lasted 15 to 20 minutes. Three processes were covered:

- Looking backward (e.g., What has been going well? What do we need to change? Has anything occurred that others need to know about?)
- Looking forward (e.g., What's happening in the near future? What goals are we working toward? What actions do we need to take? Are there any obstacles with staffing levels, equipment, or delays?)
- Following up (e.g., Are there any discussions from previous huddles that need to be continued? Any previous questions that can now be answered? Any additional information to share? Any updates on upcoming challenges?)

Later, Tier One reported up to Tier Two (e.g., the medical office building comprising all the clinics, the hospital building with all the departments, or the entire legal team). Tier Two reported up to Tier Three (the regional hub), and finally Tier Three reported up to Tier Four (the executive team). During each report, the three processes outlined earlier were covered. To keep the flow of information controlled and efficient, only one person from each tier reported up to the next, and the tiered huddles were separated by about one hour.

Tier Four (the execs) could also use the huddle system to cascade information downstream. We would send what we called "Meeting in a Box" to all huddle leaders and ask them to present the contents at their next huddle, thereby ensuring that the information was being presented to all caregivers at the same time. Meeting in a Box was essentially an outline for these leaders to use as they spoke. It ensured that standard messaging was used and that there was clarity around important points. This process of cascading information downstream was also used by Tier Three and Tier Two huddles.

One note: The structure of each organization will dictate how many tiers are needed to effectively cascade information. Your organization might require more or fewer tiers.

Assign Projects a Stoplight Status

You may already be familiar with stoplight reports. They promote transparency and are a great form of continuous communication regarding projects and their progress toward completion.

- **Green means "Completed."** Putting a green light next to completed projects is important so that people *know* they have been done. Otherwise, employees often don't realize how much has actually been accomplished. You'll hear things like "Nothing ever gets fixed around here" and "Whatever happened to that project we were working on?"
- **Yellow means "Aware and working."** This status is assigned to everything that's in progress. It's useful for reminding caregivers what you'd like them to focus on, and it also reassures them that leadership hasn't forgotten about their concerns and goals.
- **Red is "Not at this time" or "Can't be done."** If you assign a project Red status, you should always include the reason it was postponed or permanently shelved. Maybe it was prohibitively expensive, was not in line with the organization's strategic vision, would be detrimental to the culture, or is illegal. Or perhaps leadership thinks the idea is a good one and would like to take more time to think about how it might be implemented!

Using the stoplight system forces you to get away from the "slow no" and the "no answer," which we talked about earlier. If you commit to assigning everything a status, nothing stays in limbo and it's harder to put off tough conversations. A best practice is to place dates adjacent to each project name. This clearly communicates when a project was completed, how long it has been in process, or how long it has been sitting in the Red category.

Stoplight reports work at all levels: team, unit, department, division, organization, and committee. You can even use them to organize your individual projects and priorities. At the hospital system where I was the CMO, each Tier One huddle had a "huddle board." We posted current stoplight reports on the huddle boards, along with important departmental or organizational communications and other departmental items.

Myers-Briggs Can Help You Be Heard

My final practical to become a Certified Physician Executive (CPE) required me to present a business plan that "spoke to" different Myers-Briggs personalities. In case you aren't familiar with it, the Myers-Briggs describes a person's personality across four dimensions, accounting for a total of 16 distinct personality types.

Let's take a brief look at the two dimensions that determine how people take in information and how they use that information to make decisions. Individuals are either S (Sensing) or N (Intuition), and T (Thinking) or F (Feeling):

S vs. N (Sensing vs. Intuition)

- **S:** These individuals are detail oriented and prefer factual information. They seek out practical solutions and appreciate specific and literal communication.

continued

continued from previous page

- **N:** These are "big picture" people—they prefer more conceptual and theoretical information. Because they have an intuitive rationale, they're more apt to go with their "gut feelings" than make data-backed decisions.

T vs. F (Thinking vs. Feeling)

- **T:** These people are logical thinkers with strong reasoning skills. They consider different options and pay attention to the pros and cons of each. They are likely to choose what they consider to be the best answer without being swayed by its effects on others.
- **F:** When making decisions, these individuals consider how their choices will affect others. They balance data-backed options with creating or maintaining harmony among groups of people.

So, for example, you may be sending out information that is factual and detailed. Sensing individuals will appreciate it and connect with your message, but Intuitive individuals might not be as interested or motivated to engage.

The point is that we are usually focused on the *message* that we're sending, but we also need to be thinking about how people *receive* information. Effective communication requires two parties. If the other person doesn't truly "hear" what you're saying, true communication didn't happen. Great communicators will convey their message to an audience with an effort to relate to both of the dimensions of information processing: Sensing and Intuition, and Thinking and Feeling. If this is done well,

continued

continued from previous page

the information's recipients will be more likely to grasp what is being communicated, will better understand the "why" behind decisions, and will have greater engagement moving forward. The next time you need to make an important presentation regarding issues such as strategy, culture, a business plan, or a critical change in direction, try to speak to those two dimensions of the Myers-Briggs test overviewed here.

Remember That Words Are a Small Part of How We Communicate

In chapter 6, I shared research by Dr. Albert Mehrabian that suggests 55 percent of communication is based on body language and facial expressions, 38 percent happens through intonation, and just 7 percent via spoken words (World of Work Project 2022). It bears repeating that we should always strive to be aware of what we're conveying through our body langue and tone. We all know what it's like to speak with someone whose face or posture sends a message that contradicts their words.

We can also extrapolate from Dr. Mehrabian's research that when you send an e-mail or a text, only 7 percent of your communication potential is at your disposal. When you make a phone call, you have 45 percent. But when you speak in person or via video, you have 100 percent. Sometimes you don't have a choice regarding which mode of communication you use. But whenever it makes sense, communicate in person or via video. This is especially important when conveying information that is important, sensitive, or has the potential to be confusing.

Get Out Among Your Team and Stay Visible

Being present and available is an important component of being a great communicator. If your people can't easily see and access you, you'll lose numerous opportunities to connect with them, invite 360-degree communication, and gain their trust. And no, having an open-door policy isn't enough—*unless* you broaden the term's definition. Don't think of *open-door* as an invitation for others to come to you. (Most won't.) Instead, think of your door being open so that you can walk through it and go to the front lines where caregivers are working!

Being highly visible is *especially* important in times of crisis, stress, or change. When things are uncomfortable and uncertain, employees need to see and talk to their leaders frequently. It's your responsibility to keep them informed and reassure them as much as possible. (If they don't hear anything from you, most people will assume the worst.) Don't send out a spokesperson or rely on indirect modes of communication like e-mail, either. When information comes straight from you, you'll alleviate anxiety and be able to prevent misinformation from spreading.

I'll end this chapter on an encouraging note: When it comes to communication, practice helps you get closer to perfection. The best way to become a great communicator is to keep doing it. The more you speak in front of others, the more your confidence will grow. The more you write e-mails to your team, the clearer and more concise your writing will become. And over time, you'll be able to identify what works and what doesn't. (Remember that you are unique and so are your employees—so what a peer or mentor swears by might not be as effective for you.)

If you're ever unsure, just ask your team: "What information would you like to have? What information do you feel that you lack? How would you like to receive that information? What am I doing well, and what would you like me to do differently?" Then, respectfully listen while *they* communicate with *you*.

REFERENCES

Robison, J. 2021. "Communicate Better with Employees, Regardless of Where They Work." Gallup Workplace. Published June 28. https://www.gallup.com/workplace/351644/communicate-better-employees-regardless-work.aspx#.

World of Work Project. 2022. "Mehrabian's 7-38-55 Communication Model: It's More Than Words." Accessed August 11. https://worldofwork.io/2019/07/mehrabians-7-38-55-communication-model/.

CHAPTER 10

Building and Strengthening Relationships with Caregivers

As we established in chapter 7, healthcare is almost exclusively a service industry. Good service is based on developing good relationships—with patients, certainly, but also with our fellow caregivers. For those of us in leadership roles, these caregiver relationships are especially important. The more connected your people feel to their organization and its leadership, the longer they'll stay, the better they'll perform, and the more strongly aligned they will be with your organization's purpose.

My decades of leadership have shown me that caregivers want to work with leaders who are present and who engage them. They want to develop relationships with us that are based on mutual respect. They want to be treated as individuals, and with empathy. They want their thoughts and opinions to be heard and taken seriously. In other words, caregivers desire a sense of meaningful connection with us—their leaders—because that sense of connection makes them feel like they are, indisputably, our greatest asset.

We leaders also have a lot to gain from building connections with caregivers. As I've pointed out multiple times in this book, talking to clinical and nonclinical caregivers at all levels helps you learn things about your organization that you would otherwise not be aware of. The insights of your employees can help you pinpoint (and solve) problems, as well as identify opportunities for growth and improvement.

And when caregivers feel you are accessible and approachable, they will tell you what they need to do their jobs better (which, in turn, makes *your* job of serving and supporting *them* much easier). All of these things build trust and break down the power gradient.

For all these reasons, I see connection as a way to live out my personal and professional purpose "to change the lives of others." When I led Hospital X, I wanted my employees to see me as Kevin— a guy they could talk to and be honest with—not as Dr. Joseph or as the CEO. When people spoke, I listened respectfully with genuine interest. I wanted to understand their input and concerns, because I knew that each new perspective expanded my understanding of what was happening throughout the organization.

I am grateful to say it must have worked. By the time I left the role, people from Environmental Services would come by my office, give me a high five, and say, "Hey, what's up, Dr. J.?" Plant Operations and Security team members would pat me on the back. Employees from every department would pop into my office to say hello, or start a conversation in the hallway. In other words, everyone in every level of the organization felt seen, heard, and accepted. This laid the groundwork for a culture of trust where people were highly engaged and mission driven *because they felt connected and valued.*

I was not alone in becoming more connected with caregivers. The rest of the leadership team also committed to demonstrating through their words and actions that they would like to hear from employees across the organization. Our entire leadership team wanted caregivers to feel comfortable bringing news, concerns, and requests to our attention. We wanted others to understand that we were not going to view them as "bothering" us, and we were not going to shoot the messenger if they told us something we didn't necessarily want to hear. In fact, quite the opposite was true: We always thanked caregivers and other leaders for approaching us with their concerns, no matter what they were. (Note: Creating the culture of trust and connection I've just described was possible only because of the effort and discipline that went into creating the leadership team. Refer to chapter 4 to review the importance of an exceptional leadership team and for tactics to assist in creating that team.)

I've found that some leaders proclaim "my door is always open" and think that makes them connection-friendly. It doesn't. True connection happens only when you are the kind of leader employees aren't afraid to approach—and the kind of leader who proactively approaches them.

Let's Broaden Our Definition of *Open Door*

Many leaders use the term *open door* to convey that others are welcome to enter their office at any time, but if you ask me, this definition is too passive. It implies that everyone else needs you, when the truth is that you as a leader need them more. Ideally, *open door* means that your door is always open so that you can proactively leave your office and go to the front lines, where the rest of your team is located. If you rely on others coming to you, you won't experience much meaningful connection.

The good news is that there is no "right" way to connect beyond having frequent, authentic, 360-degree interactions throughout your organization. Meaningful connection can take on many forms. The following sections discuss some connection tactics that have always worked well for me.

MAKE ROUNDING A REGULAR PART OF YOUR ROUTINE

I think most leaders in healthcare know what rounding is. If you don't, here are two helpful resources:

- "Rounding for Outcomes: How to Increase Employee Retention and Drive Higher Patient Satisfaction" by Barbara Hotko, RN, MPA; https://www.huronlearninglab.com/hardwired-results/hardwired-results-01/rounding-for-outcomes
- "Employee Engagement and Leadership Rounding" by Amy Vanderscheuren, MHA; https://www.theberylinstitute.org/blogpost/947424/315036/Employee-Engagement-and-Leadership-Rounding

Rounding is an invaluable tool to build relationships, disseminate information, ask and answer questions, find out what is and isn't going well, develop employees, and so much more.

When I am rounding in my capacity as an organizational leader (as opposed to making clinical rounds with physicians, nurses, and other providers), I refer to what I'm doing as *connecting* instead of *rounding* because that term gets to the heart of what I'm trying to accomplish. (Plus, in my own experience, I've found that the term *rounding* has become so commonplace that many people no longer stop to think about what it means.)

As a leader, you should regularly connect with (or round on) all of your direct vertical and horizontal coworkers. Aim for 360 degrees of connecting. If you are vice president of Clinical Programs, for instance, this might mean connecting with your own supervisor (the CEO), other vice presidents with whom you closely work, and all the departmental directors who directly report to you each week.

I also recommend connecting with those who are two levels "below" you in the organizational structure; in other words, connect with the caregivers who report to your direct reports. Just be sure to inform your direct reports that you'll be rounding two levels down, out of respect for their own leadership.

It's important to build positive relationships with all of these people. Stay familiar with what they are doing, ask questions about what they need from you, and recognize all the great things they are accomplishing. When you conclude your connecting (aka rounding) conversation with each person, they should *feel* "recognized, valued, appreciated, and understood," as Stephen Covey (2016) puts it.

You should also make it a priority to regularly connect with caregivers who *aren't* directly connected to you on the organizational chart. Obviously, leaders can't connect with every caregiver each week or month. But you *can* make a habit of leaving your office and being present on the front lines on a regular basis. Set aside an hour every day, a half day every week, or a full day each month so that you can connect with clinical and nonclinical caregivers: physicians, nurses, imaging technicians, billing specialists, data analysts, food service workers, and more.

During my regularly scheduled "connection times" at Hospital X, I would walk around various departments and speak to the caregivers I encountered. As I've mentioned before, I also made a habit of spending time in areas where people gathered, such as break rooms, cafeterias, and nurses' stations. Especially as our efforts to break down the power gradient took effect, I often didn't have to approach caregivers and strike up a conversation myself. When people saw me, they came forward to tell me what was on their minds, or just to say hello. I often heard some variant of "Kevin, I'm so glad I saw you today. I've been wanting to speak with you about something, but I haven't found the time to send an e-mail or call you."

Of course, there will be times when you are not approached for a conversation, and you will have to be proactive about engaging the caregivers (both clinical and nonclinical). This interaction doesn't need to be formal or complicated—just start a conversation. For instance, you might ask how a caregiver's day is going or compliment them on something good you observed them doing. If someone with whom you would like to chat is busy, tell them that you will be in the break room for the next hour, and ask them to stop by when they have five minutes.

Remember, the primary purpose of connecting is to build a relationship so you can learn through that relationship. If you engage in genuine dialogue without a prescribed checklist of items to discuss or questions to ask, you'll usually find that you learn what you *really* need to know.

Connecting Supports a Culture of Well-Being and Combats Burnout

The levels of burnout, stress, and frustration are higher than ever for those of us in healthcare. It's important that we stay vigilant for signs that a caregiver is struggling, under unusual stress, depressed, or burned out. Connecting (rounding) on a regular basis helps leaders do this. The better you know someone and the more frequently you check in with them, the better equipped you'll be to notice when their wellness might be suffering. In the end, it is our responsibility to look out for each other. A colleague of mine, Dr. Ed "Mel" Otten (who is the most brilliant individual I have ever met) once posed the question "How can we work together to take care of patients if we can't take care of each other?" (In chapter 12, we'll delve into the reasons burnout is so prevalent, as well as strategies leaders can use to address and prevent it.)

MAKE QUICK CONNECTIONS WITH PHONE CALLS, TEXTS, AND E-MAILS

This connection tactic is pretty self-explanatory, but that doesn't make it any less effective. It only takes a minute or two to send a message that says, "Hey, I was just thinking about you and the issue you brought to my attention last week. I wanted you to know that I'll be discussing it with the CEO the next time we meet."

You could also send a text or e-mail to follow up on a conversation about something personal: "How was your daughter's wedding?" or "Welcome back from spring break. Hopefully the ski conditions were great." This demonstrates that you were paying attention to what the other person said in a previous conversation *and* that you care enough about them to circle back on something important that happened in their personal life. We are all very busy juggling many tasks of varying sizes and complexities, so make a note in your calendar after the initial conversation to reconnect via text, phone call, or e-mail.

As I've shared before, it's also a good idea to make sure caregivers have your mobile phone number. I believe you'll find that this privilege won't be abused but rather will give people a way to directly reach you in situations that warrant your immediate attention.

Welcome to My Office . . . I Mean, My Laptop

I joke that my office is really my laptop, because I travel to different parts of the hospital system on a daily basis. In chapter 6, I shared that whenever I can, I set up my "laptop office" in communal areas like cafeterias and staff lounges because I want caregivers to see me as an accessible colleague instead of as an unapproachable leader in an ivory tower. Another benefit of not holing up in an empty office or conference room is that I can connect with caregivers who are usually on a break and therefore have a few minutes to speak with me. Whether the conversation is about a professional topic or just casual small talk, the relationship will develop and the power gradient will decrease.

SCHEDULE EVENTS THAT FACILITATE CONNECTION

At Hospital X, we held several regular events that gave caregivers a chance to interact with leaders. These events were especially valuable because connecting with leaders was the only "job" caregivers in attendance had to do (unlike a rounding conversation, during which a caregiver might be distracted by other tasks or deadlines). Two events that were always big hits were breakfast with the CEO and welcome breakfasts for new caregivers.

Breakfast with the CEO

Each month at Hospital X, I hosted Breakfast in the Boardroom with around 20 caregivers (clinical and nonclinical) from various departments. I asked Human Resources to randomly pull the names of four to six people, all from different departments, who had been with the organization for more than six months. I also asked HR to eliminate the names of any individuals who had experienced any recent disciplinary action. An RSVP invitation was then sent to the caregivers on the list. Finally, we connected with each potential attendee's department leader to ask if that person's absence would result in any significant staffing issues that could not be overcome.

I found it beneficial to have multiple clinical and nonclinical departments present at the same Breakfast in the Boardroom event because these different types of caregivers learned a lot from each other. Plus, meeting and connecting with colleagues from other departments underscored to everyone that we were all working together for a common purpose.

While we ate, we had an open conversation that usually lasted between one and two hours. I wanted the caregivers to get to know me and develop a better understanding of the hospital's leadership team. And as I'm sure you've guessed, I also used the opportunity to learn more about the organization. I asked questions like *What's going on in your departments? What are you hearing "on the street?" What can I do or change that would help you do your job better?* and *How can we better the organization, and what concerns you about the organization?*

I was usually able to squash some rumors, provide clarification, and empower the caregivers with knowledge. And thanks to their feedback, I often learned of small, easy-to-fix issues that made their jobs easier. It certainly didn't hurt that the caregiver who brought up each concern became a hero to their colleagues, or that the leadership team also looked like heroes after we addressed those concerns! Overall, Breakfast in the Boardroom was a great way to connect with caregivers, build trust, and break down the power gradient—all while enjoying coffee, bacon, and eggs.

One final suggestion: The host of this type of event doesn't *have* to be the CEO. That privilege could be rotated among all the senior executives. This would enable clinical caregivers to get to know leaders with whom they might not otherwise come into contact, such as the chief financial officer or general counsel. And nonclinical caregivers could connect with clinical leadership such as the chief nursing officer or the chief medical officer.

Welcome Breakfasts for New Caregivers

When you make a meaningful connection with new caregivers during the onboarding process, you set a positive tone for their future communication with leaders. You also make a strong statement about the power gradient (namely, that you don't want it to be a part of the work culture).

An effective way to do this is to hold a welcome breakfast once a month. Invite the new hires, their ambassadors, their departments' leaders, and senior executives. Every new hire who attends will receive the message that they are a valued and supported member of the team.

At Hospital X's welcome breakfasts, we asked new recruits questions like *What are your challenges so far? What would you like leadership to know? Do you have any questions about your role, the department, or the organization that haven't been answered?* and *What have you seen done better at other organizations than at this organization?* This last question is especially valuable because each new colleague has a fresh set of eyes. They can provide input on opportunities for improvement and share tactics and processes from other organizations.

Expect new hires to be hesitant to answer some of these questions, at least initially. They are new to the organization and may not yet be confident in the culture of transparency and honesty. They may also be concerned about retribution or the power gradient. Engaging in a frank conversation will start to confirm your organization's culture to them. I also recommend emphasizing the type of culture your organization is striving to build at the beginning and at the end of the discussion. Thank new hires for their participation in the welcome breakfast and encourage them to propagate the culture of candid communication going forward.

BE ESPECIALLY VIGILANT ABOUT CONNECTING DURING AN EMPLOYEE'S FIRST YEAR

In addition to the monthly breakfast for all new employees, I also recommend that the new caregiver, their leader, and their ambassador meet every month or so for the first year. This is a critical time for employee retention because new caregivers are settling in, learning the culture, figuring out what is expected of them, and integrating into their new teams. They may also be training to acquire new skills. Their satisfaction during the first year determines whether or not they become fully invested in your organization and its purpose—and whether or not they will stay long-term.

Try to keep these monthly meetings relaxed. The goal is to support recent hires and develop a relationship with them. You can have conversations about what's going well, what isn't, and how the leader and ambassador can provide better support to advance their success. Regular first-year meetings are also a great opportunity to recognize and appreciate the new hire, and to deliver feedback in a comfortable, nonthreatening setting.

TAKE EVERY OPPORTUNITY TO RECOGNIZE AND APPRECIATE CAREGIVERS

Recognition and connection go hand in hand. When you look at how to connect with caregivers, recognition is a necessary and significant part of the equation. If caregivers are our greatest asset, the least we can do is tell them how much we appreciate them!

Have you ever heard of the book *The 5 Love Languages* by Gary Chapman (2015)? It explains that different people have different "love languages"—in other words, different ways of *feeling* and *experiencing* love from other people. Chapman explains that your partner may feel most loved when you give them your undivided attention, for instance, while you may feel most loved when they perform acts of service such as cleaning the house or watching the kids so that you can have a break. In this scenario, you might instinctively do practical things to help your partner because that's how you prefer to receive love. Meanwhile, your partner's need for love is partially unmet because what they *really* want from you is to spend dedicated, distraction-free time together. The point is that for relationships to really thrive and flourish, you need to "speak" the other person's love language.

Similarly, I believe there are "recognition and appreciation languages" that those of us in the professional world should be aware of. Some people thrive on public recognition, while others really dislike being singled out in front of a group. Some employees might prefer that you say "thank you" in a brief conversation with them, while others would get greater gratification from being mentioned in an organizational newsletter or weekly departmental e-mail.

The same thing goes for rewards when they have been earned: one caregiver might love tickets to a baseball game, whereas their coworkers would prefer a gift card to a grocery store or an extra paid vacation day.

Leaders need to determine what each caregiver's "recognition language" is so that they can "speak" it whenever possible. This doesn't need to be a complex equation; it's often as simple as knowing whether someone prefers to be recognized publicly or privately; formally or informally. Don't be afraid to ask questions like "How would you prefer to be recognized when you do something great? Would you mind if I talked about your accomplishments in a staff meeting, or would you prefer not to be the center of attention?" You can also identify people's recognition language by observing them. Do they seem to light up when you pull them aside and thank them privately? Do they look happy when you highlight their achievements in a group setting, or do they seem uncomfortable?

Group Recognition Can Be a Valuable Tool—but Use It with Care!

Sometimes it's appropriate to recognize multiple people at once: perhaps a shift has met a safety goal, or a department has earned exceptional patient satisfaction survey scores. When this happens, feel free to go all out. Hang banners, have pizzas delivered, and personally thank each individual. Just be careful not to over-rely on group recognition, because it can deflate the impact of your appreciation. For instance, don't effusively thank an entire patient care team for going above and beyond if one nurse's empathetic service was largely responsible for the patient's satisfaction. In this scenario not everyone contributed equally, and the team knows it.

Just remember: What feels most meaningful to you might not feel as meaningful to them. Instead of following the Golden Rule (Do unto others as you would have them do unto you), follow the Platinum Rule (Do unto others as they want done unto themselves)! This will help you forge the strongest connections with caregivers, and it also goes a long way toward re-recruiting them.

Recognition is another topic that could fill a whole book. Here, I'd like to focus on one type of recognition: thank-you notes. If there is such a thing as a universally effective type of recognition, thank-you notes are it. No matter what someone's "recognition style" might be, I don't think I've ever encountered a person who didn't feel valued and motivated after receiving one. And since thank-you notes can be kept and read many times over, they often make a longer-lasting impact than verbal thanks.

A thank-you note doesn't need to be long or complicated; in just a few sentences you can specify exactly what a caregiver did that you noticed and appreciated. Specificity is much more impactful than a generic "Thank you for your hard work! I appreciate you" message. Provide details about the specific event or behavior that caught your attention. For instance, you might write the following:

> Yifei,
> Your supervisor told me about how much time you spent explaining your pediatric patient's care plan to her parents. Your patience, kindness, and empathy greatly helped to alleviate their anxiety and answer their questions. You are a wonderful example of our organization's purpose "to change the lives of others," and I am deeply thankful that you are a part of our team.
>
> With gratitude,
> Kevin

It's usually quickest and easiest to send your thanks in e-mail format. I encourage you to send thank-you e-mails as often as you can "in the moment." (Don't wait and run the risk of forgetting!) The preceding example took less than two minutes to type but has the potential to uplift the recipient for an entire day—or longer.

Handwritten notes take more time and effort to compose—and for that reason, they are often even more impactful than e-mails. I place handwritten thank-you notes into three different "escalation of appreciation" categories, depending on what you are recognizing the caregiver for:

1. A handwritten note that is given to the caregiver in the workplace
2. A handwritten note that is sent to the caregiver's home
3. A handwritten note that is sent to the caregiver's family at home

Let's look at numbers two and three in more detail.

Sending a Note to a Caregiver Through the Mail

A card that is sent to a caregiver through the mail isn't just seen by the caregiver; chances are that it will also be shared with the caregiver's spouse, children, parents, and roommates (if applicable). The caregiver will thus receive twice the recognition: first from the note itself, and second from their loved ones' compliments and congratulations. The extra effort that went into sending the note to the caregiver's house is also recognized and appreciated, which makes the note more meaningful.

Sending a Note to a Caregiver's Family at Their Home

This is a form of recognition that I use only occasionally, in very specific circumstances—usually when a caregiver has gone far above and beyond in their efforts and accomplishments. Here are two examples of notes I've written to families in the past:

Dear MacNeill Family,
I know that your husband and father Ian has been working a significant number of overtime hours the past few weeks, and I understand that he has had to miss many family meals, bedtimes, and an important soccer game. The ICU has been exceptionally busy, and Dr. MacNeill's skills as a physician have been instrumental in saving the lives of many patients at the bedside. I wanted you to know that your sacrifices as a family during this time have not gone unnoticed or unappreciated. Your support of your husband and dad are instrumental in helping him fulfill our organization's purpose of "changing the lives of others."

With gratitude,
Kevin

Dear Persaud Family,
I wanted to write a note to make sure you know what a hero your wife and mother Riya is. As you know, she works here at Hospital X as a front desk registration clerk. Yesterday, a distraught woman ran up to the desk holding an infant who was blue and limp. Mrs. Persaud had just taken a CPR course, and she immediately started CPR on the infant—with success. The baby recovered, and all the physicians and nurses who were involved in his care were very impressed by Mrs. Persaud's actions. They are in agreement that her quick actions changed the infant's outcome. We are grateful and honored that she is a member of our hospital's team. I hope you'll tell her how proud you are of her. It's not every day a family member saves a baby's life!

With gratitude,
Kevin

I have found it helpful to set aside blocks of time on my calendar to compose thank-you notes, instead of trying to fit this task into the gaps in my schedule. (Inevitably, that strategy leads to me having written no thank-you notes at the end of the day.) Find a time that works for you, and stick to it. For instance, spend the first five minutes of the day writing thank-you notes, or the last 30 minutes of each Friday.

A final point about appreciation and recognition: Don't worry about going overboard. It's almost impossible to recognize caregivers too often, as long as you are genuine in your thoughts, specific in the details, and timely in your delivery. You may be familiar with the 3-to-1 Positivity Ratio, which states that it takes three positive experiences to counterbalance just one negative experience (Robinson 2020). In other words, caregivers need three "Good jobs," "Thank yous," or other acknowledgments to offset one "Could we talk about how to improve next time?"

Never forget that your organization has 360 degrees of connections. Healthcare is a service industry based on relationships, not just with our patients and their families, but also with each other. The strength of those connections, in all directions and at all levels, directly influences your organization's ability to live out its purpose. When leaders are connected to one other, to clinical and nonclinical caregivers, and especially to those who work on the frontlines, your organization will have the foundation it needs to deliver quality care and exceptional service. Make connecting a part of your culture.

With strong connections, information and ideas will flow freely. Leaders and caregivers will know how to support one another. Problems, challenges, and opportunities for improvement will come to light. Healthy working relationships will be the rule, not the exception. Caregivers will feel valued, heard, and appreciated. Morale, engagement, retention, and quality metrics will all improve.

But for any of this to happen, connection needs to be top-of-mind for leaders at all times. Remember, we build relationships so that we can learn through those relationships. And just like learning, creating and maintaining connection is a continuous, never-ending, and infinitely rewarding process.

REFERENCES

Chapman, G. 2015. *The 5 Love Languages: The Secret to Love That Lasts*. Chicago: Northfield Publishing.

Covey, S. R. 2016. *Primary Greatness: The 12 Levers of Success*. New York: Simon & Schuster.

Robinson, B. 2020. "The 3-to-1 Positivity Ratio and 10 Ways It Advances Your Career." *Forbes*. Published October 16. https://www .forbes.com/sites/bryanrobinson/2020/10/16/10-ways-the-3-to -1-positivity-ratio-can-advance-your-career/?sh=35eabba670c4.

CHAPTER 11

Providing Constructive Feedback
with Fair Accountability

"You are doing a fantastic job." "You are on track to meet the goals we set together." "I am pleased with your performance." "You are exceeding my expectations." "Your work is improving." "I hear wonderful things about you from your patients and coworkers." "Our organization is a better place because you are here."

It's always a pleasure to deliver this kind of feedback to caregivers. As leaders, we look forward to the opportunity. Recognizing and praising someone's positive performance is uplifting for both parties, and it's an important tool in developing and retaining high-achieving employees. In fact, recognition is so important that it takes up a large portion of chapter 10.

But what about other types of feedback, like check-ins, annual reviews, and constructive criticism? They probably aren't your idea of fun, but we can all agree that they're necessary and even beneficial. By mastering the art of giving thoughtful feedback we not only help people improve their performance and develop professionally, but we also go a long way toward building strong, trusting relationships.

Don't forget about the difficult discussions leaders must have with caregivers when someone does not meet expectations, crosses a line, or exhibits consistently low performance. Holding employees accountable is often unpleasant, can feel thankless, and may challenge our resolve and conscience. However, if leaders don't do it fairly and consistently, the purpose- and values-driven culture we are trying to build will quickly crumble.

In this chapter, we'll take a closer look at two main topics: the types of feedback that every employee receives (informal, formal, evaluative, coaching, etc.) and the serious feedback leaders must give when holding employees accountable to organizational standards. We'll discuss why these types of feedback are important and offer some guiding principles to help you approach each one in a way that's helpful and fair to you *and* your employees.

DELIVERING EVERYDAY FEEDBACK

First, let's take a look at the type of performance feedback leaders deliver on a daily, monthly, or annual basis. For purposes of structuring this chapter, I'm calling this *everyday* feedback—to distinguish it from the *accountability* feedback we'll cover later. (Hopefully, the latter type isn't an everyday occurrence; if it is, the employee in question is likely on borrowed time!)

Delivering everyday feedback can be more of an art than a science. the following sections share some things I've learned during my years of leadership.

All Feedback Should Be Rooted in "Leadership Integrity"

Leaders owe it to everyone in the organization to be honest, transparent, and forthright. It is our responsibility to provide clear expectations, accurate and timely feedback, appropriate training, opportunities to develop and improve, and empathetic guidance to anyone who is struggling.

Failure to do any of these things is unfair to caregivers, the organization, and ultimately the loved ones (patients). In fact, it's a form of what I think of as "professional neglect" or even "leadership malpractice." People cannot drive for better outcomes without candid feedback or clarity around what right looks like. We can't hold caregivers accountable for standards we failed to adequately communicate up front. (Again, this is what we ourselves would want from our own leaders!) So before we turn our focus to coaching, developing, and guiding others, we must first take a look in the mirror.

Let me be very clear: I certainly don't believe that leaders set out to neglect their employees, and I am not here to judge you if you believe that you may have been neglectful at some point in your leadership tenure; I've been there, too. Here are three reasons professional neglect might creep into your leadership, even if you have the best of intentions:

- **Other pressing issues demand your attention.** At any given time, you're working toward meeting goals, improving metrics, and adapting to the rapid changes in healthcare. Every day, there are a multitude of reports to sign, tasks to complete, meetings to attend, and fires to put out. Without you consciously recognizing it, it's easy for your focus to gradually slide away from caregivers. It's not that you *intend* to neglect them; they simply get shuffled to the back burner as these other things demand your attention.
- **You've never had much (or any) formal leadership training.** Many leaders have never been trained in how to empower, develop, engage, and hold employees accountable. This is especially true for leaders like me who moved into healthcare administration after beginning their careers on the clinical side of the house. I was the medical director of Hospital X's Emergency Department when I was asked to become the organization's CEO, and as I described in chapter 2, there was initially a lot (and I mean *a lot*) I didn't know about my new role.

I can attest to the fact that while physicians spend a significant amount of time learning the practice of medicine, there isn't space in the curriculum to learn about leadership.

Instead, it is often assumed that physicians are leaders simply because of their position—some are even told this explicitly. For example, an emergency medicine physician leads the codes in the Emergency Department. In the Operating Room, surgeons and anesthesiologists are firmly in charge. Although this type of situational leadership is expected, it cannot be translated into nonclinical leadership.

Having earned my MBA, I can also tell you that formal leadership training isn't a major part of the curriculum in most business schools. You'll learn a lot about how to market, manage, and otherwise run a business, but much less about how to connect with and influence the people who work for you. (You can refer back to chapter 2 for a list of leadership resources that have been helpful to me.)

- **You focus on things that are easily measurable.**
  Consciously or not, we assign everything in life a place in our personal priority system. There's often a tendency for leaders to focus on things that are easily measurable, such as finances and clinical outcomes. These things are attractive because they are objective and tangible. Even if the process of achieving a metric is challenging, it's easy to see what needs to happen. For instance, *We need to lower our readmissions by 10 percent.* Or, *We can't spend more than $50k when implementing the new training program.*

  That's usually not the case for culture and employee engagement. These areas are more difficult to measure. You can't glance at a spreadsheet or report and immediately ascertain where you stand and what you need to do next. But as I stated earlier in this book, your organization's culture is the foundation for moving all other metrics—including finances and clinical outcomes. As Elliot Eisner wrote, "Not everything that is measurable matters and not everything that matters is measurable" (Eisner and Cuban 2020).

Despite the temptation to focus your energy on more concrete issues, employees must remain a top priority. I've found that the difficult part of prioritizing is not deciding what to do, but rather deciding what *not* to do. Focusing on caregivers (clinical and nonclinical) should never be in the latter category.

Measuring the "Unmeasurable"

I have some good news for the "numbers people": While it's true that things like culture and employee engagement are very difficult to measure accurately and frequently, you *can* gauge where they stand by using surrogate markers. For example, I worked at one organization where we wanted to measure how comfortable caregivers were in speaking up without hesitation or fear. We had an annual survey that included this information, but its frequency was inadequate. So instead, we measured the percentage of incident reports that were filed anonymously. We knew that we were making cultural progress as that percentage decreased.

We wanted to measure employee engagement too. This information was also gathered in a periodic survey, but again, the survey wasn't distributed with adequate frequency. Therefore, we used the percentage of unplanned paid time off (PTO) days as a surrogate marker. Unplanned PTO is usually taken for one of two broad reasons: (1) an

continued

continued from previous page

unforeseen illness, emergency, or other special circum-
stance, or (2) the employee simply didn't want to come
to work (perhaps because the weather was beautiful and
hanging out by the pool seemed like a better option). We
figured that the amount of illness- or emergency-related
PTO was unlikely to change much over longer periods, so
a decrease in the overall percentage of unplanned PTO
days meant that people were more engaged in the success of the organization. They didn't want to abandon
their colleagues or their patients, and hopefully, they felt
more driven to come to work each day because they were
connected to their purpose.

In both of these examples, surrogate data points were
measured monthly instead of relying on the annual survey.

Think Continuous Feedback Instead of Annual Review

I think of the annual review as a formality. It's just one day out of the
year. When developing, guiding, and holding caregivers accountable,
the other 364 days are just as important. My best analogy is Valentine's Day. If February 14 is the only time you tell your significant
other that you love them, express your appreciation, and turn on the
romance, then you missed the boat. (But please, don't extrapolate
from my comments and tell my wife that I think Valentine's Day
is just a formality!)

My point is that all caregivers should always know how they're
doing in their roles at work. What are they doing well? What do
they need to work on? What goals should they be working toward?
What is the next level in their career, and what steps should they be

taking now to get there? If they aren't meeting expectations, what is the plan to help them make up the deficit? The answers to these questions shouldn't be a surprise that comes once per year. (Isn't that what we would prefer for ourselves?)

I'll take this concept one step further. Let's say a caregiver isn't performing to the expected standards. That person's leader thinks, *I'll just wait and bring up this issue at the annual review.* Maybe the leader wants to delay a difficult conversation, doesn't think the caregiver's performance issue is a "big deal," or is simply focused on other things. Whatever the reason, the result is that the leader is not providing feedback to the individual for weeks or even months. In this scenario, who is actually responsible for the subpar care that a patient receives, the lack of clarity in financial reports, or the business development department's struggle: the caregiver or the leader?

If you don't need to convey criticism to a particular employee (remember, compliment in public but criticize in private), continuously providing feedback in the moment is vastly preferable to giving delayed feedback because the situation or event on which the feedback is based is fresh in everyone's mind. Thus, the dialogue about what happened, why it happened, what better options exist, why they are better options, and so on, will be much more robust.

The importance of continuous feedback in the moment underscores the vital role of rounding and connecting with others. If a leader spends more time in an office than "out in the field," they are missing opportunities to learn from the organization, and for the organization to learn from the leader through continuous in-the-moment feedback. Chapter 10 provides more detailed information on this critical aspect of leadership.

That said, there *is* a place for the annual or semiannual review. These meetings are a good time to, for example, set serious goals, listen to any concerns the caregiver might have, and discuss changes that might need to be made to the caregiver's role.

The Four Feedback "Buckets"

When I am assessing a caregiver, I organize my feedback into four "buckets":

1. **The Do More bucket:** These are things the individual does that are excellent and need to be continued and/or expanded. Perhaps share these things publicly so that other caregivers will know to emulate the behavior. And in most cases, the caregiver receiving the feedback will appreciate being recognized in front of their coworkers.

2. **The Adjust bucket:** These are recommendations of small performance-improving adjustments the individual can make to things they're already doing.

3. **The Start Doing bucket:** These are things the individual does not do now but should start doing. If someone else is doing these things, consider having them demonstrate or educate the person receiving the feedback (this also builds leadership in the person providing the training).

4. **The Stop Doing bucket:** These are things the individual is doing that should stop.

When I'm providing feedback to someone, I try to think of something that falls into each of the four buckets. Occasionally I cannot think of an item for a particular bucket (and that's okay), but I have found that overall, this method of organizing my thoughts about the feedback conversation enables me to provide more comprehensive, constructive feedback than if I had "winged it."

A quick tip: If utilizing feedback buckets appeals to you, consider sharing this methodology with your team (or the

continued

continued from previous page

entire organization) to set expectations. When caregivers know that you will be discussing what they can tweak, what they can start doing, and what they should stop doing, they won't be blindsided by what might be perceived as out-of-the-blue criticism. The conversation will be more comfortable and productive for both parties.

When It *Is* Time for Annual Reviews or Formal Evaluations, Solicit 360-Degree Feedback

In Chapter 8, we talked about utilizing 360-degree interviews for hiring. The principle is similar for providing feedback. When it's time to deliver more formal performance reviews or evaluations, don't just rely on your own observations. Reach out to the caregiver's peers, direct reports, and anyone else with whom they work closely. This 360-degree feedback is valuable for all positions, from leadership evaluations to frontline caregivers' performance reviews.

For example, if you are a vice president preparing for a departmental director's evaluation, you should speak with the directors of other departments as well as the managers, supervisors, and coordinators who report to that person. Ask questions like "How does Mr. Guerrera work with leadership? With his colleagues in other departments? With his subordinates?" or "What are Mr. Guerrera's most outstanding strengths, so that we can provide him recognition?" (This question may also provide you with thoughts on how to spread the employee's unique leadership attributes across the organization.)

You should also ask what Mr. Guerrera could improve upon to make him a better leader. The answer to this question often provides great insight as it will come from a very different viewpoint than you have as Mr. Guerrera's direct leader. Often, you'll find that the 360-degree feedback you receive aligns with your own impressions—but not always.

When I was at Hospital X, one of my VPs told me that a particular director was outstanding: "Mr. Smith always does what I ask, meets his goals, and is a great team player." But when the VP talked to a different director who worked closely with the person being evaluated, she got a completely different story: "I really dread working with Mr. Smith. He is disrespectful, doesn't answer my e-mails, and thinks his job is more important than mine." The VP was stunned. She had no idea that Mr. Smith's colleagues thought so poorly of him. Why? Mr. Smith was good at managing up. He presented himself well to his bosses, did everything *they* asked of him, and served the people in his unit (but no one else). Until she sought 360-degree feedback, the VP hadn't known that there were horizonal issues.

It is essential that these 360-degree conversations remain confidential. Feedback provided to leaders by a person's peers or subordinates must not be traced back to the source. Not only might a breach of confidentiality affect caregivers' working relationships, but it also might result in others not being honest when evaluating their peers and leaders in the future.

Tailor Your Feedback to the Situation

Feedback can range from a casual observation to a very serious discussion, and there's an ideal time and place for each type of feedback to occur. For instance, you wouldn't want to pull a nurse manager aside during the middle of her shift and say, "We need to talk about something serious that will affect your future at this organization." Not only is the nurse manager likely to be busy mid-shift, but your conversation might distract her for the rest of the day and cause her to provide subpar care.

When I provide feedback, I divide it into a few different types:

- **On-the-go feedback** occurs at the time of the event. You notice something, you say something. This type of casual feedback works well for compliments and appreciation. You might also use it to deliver relatively minor constructive criticism: "I noticed that you were having trouble performing that task. Next time, try this instead." Just make sure you aren't correcting the caregiver within earshot of their colleagues if the correction is something the caregiver should have known. If the correction is akin to a "trick of the trade" or unique knowledge, then certainly educate all those present.

- **Casual but private feedback** is given when you want to discuss something in more depth with another person, and it is usually preplanned. This type of feedback is often used to address an aspect of the person's behavior or performance. It might also be initiated out of concern for the individual. (Essentially, use this type of feedback for a conversation that isn't appropriate to have in the presence of others.)

  For example, "John, I have noticed that you are frequently interrupting others in meetings, which is disengaging them from closely listening to what you are trying to say." Or, "Suman, I have noticed recently that you are getting frustrated a bit more easily. You have also missed several of your children's soccer games and have not had much time off over the past couple of months. What can I do to help you?"

  Depending on the situation, casual but private feedback can be scheduled days in advance or via a simple "Let's meet to discuss this at 2:00." You may want to consider having this type of conversation in a conference room or other small meeting space because, as we discussed in chapter 6, people tend to feel more confident and comfortable when they're not on their leader's "turf." With this type of feedback, you don't want the caregiver to feel ambushed or attacked.

- **Serious feedback** isn't given very often, but when the situation warrants it, you may want to set the tone by asking the other individual to meet in your office, across from your seat at your desk. This is one of the few occasions in which you may want to emphasize that a power gradient exists. When serious feedback is necessary, your goal is to make it clear to the other person that your authority within the organization supersedes theirs and/or that you may have to implement consequences if they fail to take action as a result of the feedback.

One situation that requires leaders to deliver serious feedback is when you have already provided constructive feedback to help a caregiver change or improve (perhaps in a previously described casual but private feedback session), and the issue is still present. The goal of this conversation might be to inquire why the behavior has not changed and what the caregiver plans to do differently. At this point, leaders will usually reiterate their expectations and explain the consequences if the change has not occurred within a specified amount of time. Expectations, timing, and consequences are all necessary points of discussion in order to provide accountability later.

It is often useful to have documentation of times when you have delivered serious feedback, especially if it seems likely that you will have to impose consequences in the future. Be specific during the meeting and take good notes immediately after it concludes. I often send myself an e-mail of my notes so that they are time stamped and can be put in a folder.

A brief note: Serious feedback often overlaps with holding employees accountable. We'll talk about accountability in much more detail in the next section. However, I wanted to cover serious feedback here because sometimes it *is* enough to prompt the desired change. Certainly, avoiding the imposition of consequences is the preferred outcome.

- **Mentoring feedback** is given to individuals you want to guide and develop. (You may or may not be in a formal mentoring relationship with them.) To help reinforce the fact that I am giving feedback as a friendly ally instead of as a "boss," I often have these conversations outside the other person's normal work environment over coffee, breakfast, or lunch. You can suggest mentoring to a rising high performer, but let the majority of the initiative to continue the relationship come from them. Mentoring is much more fruitful when the mentee seeks out the opportunity and initiates discussions.

I do recommend that mentoring relationships not overlap with accountability relationships. In other words, don't mentor your direct reports or their direct reports. In these cases, mentoring may cause future conflicts of interest or prompt accusations of favoritism and will not be as "natural." The mentee will always be aware that their mentor is the same person who rates them, evaluates them, or promotes them, and this awareness *will* affect their candor—especially if they're experiencing something they think you may perceive as "negative," like job dissatisfaction or an issue with a coworker.

Before Giving Negative Feedback, You May Want to Dig Beneath the Surface

I was once in a meeting with a several physicians and executives. One of the physicians was normally a very calm person; in fact, I admired how he always presented himself as thoughtful and professional. On this day, though, he was quite aggressive, raising his voice and angrily attacking several relatively small issues.

continued

continued from previous page

I didn't address this out-of-character behavior during the meeting. (Remember, whenever possible, it's best to praise in public but criticize in private.) I did call the physician the next day. I was tempted to begin the conversation by asking why in the world he had behaved so poorly. But since the physician's conduct was unexpected and unusual, I simply asked, "How are you doing?" Over the next few minutes of the conversation, I learned that the physician had just been diagnosed with cancer. He later mentioned that he had not been acting like himself. As you can imagine, I reframed my intended discussion to focus on my concern for him as a person.

Always consider each person, what you know about them, and their history before delivering criticism. If a behavior seems to be an anomaly or out of character, it's worth your time to find out what else might be going on in their lives—and how you might be able to support them. This is another reason why connecting with (rounding on) others is important: It gives you a baseline knowledge of people as individuals.

HOLDING CAREGIVERS ACCOUNTABLE

What happens if you have provided timely, specific, and repeated feedback, but a caregiver's performance or behavior does not improve? You must hold that person accountable.

Did you cringe when you read the word *accountable*? I'll be the first to admit that holding caregivers accountable isn't a particularly fun part of leadership. But accountability must be a fundamental part of your organization's culture if you want to attract and retain the best people. When a leader ignores a caregiver whose values, purpose, behavior, or performance do not align with your organization's expectations, that person won't be much of an asset (much less your *greatest* asset). Such caregivers might even become a liability if they provide poor care or service. Plus, their behavior will negatively affect the rest of the organization.

Understand Why Holding Caregivers Accountable Is So Important

One of my mentors, Quint Studer, often says, "What you permit, you promote." In other words, when you fail to hold a low performer accountable, you tacitly give the rest of the team permission to replicate the undesirable behavior or to deliver lower quality outcomes. Meanwhile, other caregivers will quickly become disengaged and demotivated when they see "slackers" skating by without repercussions. As Perry Belcher has stated, "Nothing will kill a great employee faster than watching you tolerate a bad one" (Leonard 2020).

Leaders need to consistently provide low performers with feedback and opportunities to improve. And on the relatively rare occasions when a person can't or won't meet the organization's standards, that individual must move out. (More on this later.) When we don't hold someone accountable for failing to do their job, then we are failing to do *our* job, and the rest of the organization will realize it.

Sooner or later we'll still lose employees, but they'll be our now-cynical high performers. Talented, purpose-driven caregivers don't want to work at an organization where quality care and high performance are not recognized and valued. Ultimately, *not* holding caregivers accountable is one of the quickest ways I know of to dilute an organization's culture.

What Do Culture and Health Have in Common?

I liken an organization's culture to an individual's health: They are both essential to well-being and performance. They both take significant time and effort to build and maintain. However, it takes very little to prompt a backslide.

You've probably experienced a time when you were dedicated to getting in better shape. If so, you'll recall how much time and effort it can take to see progress. You've also probably experienced how a few weeks of poor food choices, lack of exercise, or disrupted sleep can negatively affect your health. In a fraction of the time it takes to make progress, you can slide backwards and lose the benefits of your previous efforts. Once you're back on the wagon, it can take weeks longer to make up lost ground, much less experience new gains.

Similarly, the ripple effect of just a few low performers can break down a culture that has taken months or years to build. As with personal health, it can take a long time for an organization's culture to "get into shape," and a short time for it to slide backwards if continuous efforts and discipline aren't sustained. Just as good health enables us to enjoy great personal success and happiness, a strong culture is essential for an organization to meet its goals and live out its purpose.

But here's where my analogy diverges. When you're getting back into physical shape, there's usually some element of muscle memory to help you. You know which healthier foods you should eat more of; you know what it looks like to incorporate yoga or a trip to the gym into your daily routine. That's not the case with an organization's culture. If your people lose faith in their leaders, gaining their trust a second time is even more difficult than if you were starting from scratch.

Now let's get into the nitty-gritty of *how* to hold caregivers accountable. Many leaders struggle with this because (like so many aspects of leadership) we're never explicitly taught the best practices. Plus, it isn't something that comes naturally to most people. Having accountability conversations—not to mention following through with consequences—is awkward, uncomfortable, and can be contentious. Our natural inclination is often to minimize the discomfort, but in doing so, either we aren't fully honest with the caregiver or we allow their undesirable behavior to persist. Following are some pointers to help you navigate the difficult task of holding caregivers accountable.

Don't Wing It

When giving feedback to low performers, leaders must know beforehand what they want to convey and what their goals for the conversation are. Give yourself time to think it through. Review notes from prior conversations with the caregiver, if available. What is unacceptable about this person's performance? (If an organizational standard or standard of care is being violated, have the employee handbook or appropriate regulation ready to share.) How often is it happening? How severe is it? What needs to improve, and what does the timeline look like? What are the consequences if the improvement doesn't occur within the discussed timeline?

Once you have answered these questions, organize your thoughts regarding what you want to say, how you want to say it, and the order in which you want to discuss your main points. Be as specific as possible and have documentation of the caregiver's performance ready to share with them. It's okay to refer to your notes during the accountability conversation. In fact, this can help you resist the temptation to end the conversation early if you receive pushback or become flustered.

Do Document It

Earlier in this chapter I shared that when I am delivering serious feedback, I often summarize the conversation in an e-mail to myself immediately after the feedback has been given. This provides a time-stamped record of the conversation in case documentation is needed down the road. I suggest doing this with every accountability conversation so that there is no question later (from you or the caregiver) about what was discussed.

In some instances, documentation may take the form of a performance improvement plan (PIP). This sends a stronger message and provides better documentation since you and the caregiver put your signatures on a detailed description of what was said, what the action items are, and what the consequences will be if the issue isn't corrected within a certain period.

Enlist the Caregiver in Developing Solutions

Remember, we're talking about *personal* accountability here. Generally, people are much more willing to change when they played a role in creating an action plan (or PIP). You "own" what you help create, not what someone dictates to you.

During accountability conversations, ask questions like the following:

- Can you help me understand what has been happening?
- What barriers are keeping you from meeting this standard?
- What equipment, accommodation, training, or support would help you achieve this goal?
- What do you think is a reasonable amount of time for you to improve your scores?
- What is the first step you think you need to take? How often would you like to check in going forward?

- Is there anything you don't understand or don't agree with?

That said, there will be times when you must overrule the caregiver's suggestions and set expectations the caregiver doesn't agree with. As a leader, it's your responsibility to hold the line.

If Things Don't Improve, Determine Whether It's a "Will" or "Skill" Issue

In other words, is the caregiver ignoring your feedback on purpose? Are they consciously choosing not to meet your expectations, even though they have the ability to do so? Or is their performance subpar because they lack knowledge, experience, support, or something else? Do they clearly understand what is expected of them?

Hopefully you're dealing with a skill issue, because skill can be improved. You can—and should—give caregivers the training and development they need to perform at their highest competency. (In chapter 8, we discussed why it's so important to spend time, effort, and resources on providing comprehensive training and support.) The good news is that a caregiver with a strong will but subpar skills is usually more than willing to make a good-faith effort to improve.

On the other hand, you can't develop someone's will. As is the case with values, professionalism, empathy, and other qualities that determine an employee's culture fit, someone either has the will to improve or they don't. If will isn't present, you will need to decide whether that person should continue to be a part of the organization.

Discuss and Enact Consequences

If an employee will face consequences should their performance or behavior not improve, you owe it to them to explain what those consequences will be. Be specific and thorough—don't just state the potential minor consequences. For instance, if your organization has a progressive discipline plan that moves through conversation, written warning, suspension, and termination, inform the employee of all four stages and explain what each entails. Be clear about what improvements are expected, and what the timetable for enacting the consequences will be. Again, be sure to document this conversation and give the employee the opportunity to help you develop a solution.

Sometimes You Have to Skip a Step

Whenever possible, you should move through your organization's progressive discipline plan and offer lower performers support so that they have the best odds of improving. But as all leaders know, sometimes employees commit a serious offense such as using slurs, sexually harassing a coworker, drug use, unethical conduct, or theft of company property. In these instances, it may be appropriate to skip several steps in the progressive discipline plan (e.g., suspend the employee without a prior written warning). You may even need to dismiss the employee "on the spot."

Stick to the Subject at Hand

Normally, I advise leaders to balance criticism with several positive statements. Holding employees accountable is the exception to this rule. Avoid sandwiching accountability between compliments, and keep the conversation strictly focused on the employee's misaligned or poor performance. Providing accolades during this type of conversation tends to muddy the waters and confuse the employee. They might think, *Kevin said my performance needs to improve, but then he complimented me on how friendly I am to patients and thanked me for my great attitude. I can't be doing that badly.*

This doesn't mean you have to be unrelentingly stern, severe, and unforgiving during accountability conversations. You can and should infuse them with empathy, and as far as possible, treat the employee as a partner in their own development. Just make sure that the employee's subpar performance and the improvements you're asking them to make are the sole focus of the discussion.

Give the Individual Time to Ask Questions and Address Your Concerns

You'll probably be doing most of the talking at the beginning of an accountability conversation as you explain why the employee's performance needs to improve and what will happen if it doesn't. After you've said what you need to, give the employee a few moments to reflect on your statements. Then, invite them to address your concerns and ask any questions they may have.

Be prepared for some employees to try to deflect blame, especially if other people are involved in the accountability issue: *This isn't my fault; I wouldn't have said what I did if my coworker hadn't rolled his eyes.* Or, *I would be more productive if the rest of my team did their work on time. Why aren't they in here too?* When this happens, you need to separate the employee's actions from those of their colleagues. You can assure the employee that if anyone else has failed to meet a standard or expectation, they too will be held accountable. Then keep the conversation focused on the employee's individual performance and be clear about what they could have done differently.

Before ending the discussion, ask the employee to recap the main points: what they did wrong, what they should have done differently, consequences if improvement doesn't happen, a time frame to fix the issue, first steps to take, how they would like to be supported going forward, and so on. If the employee has misunderstood anything you've talked about, now is the time to correct it and answer any remaining questions.

Schedule These Conversations Thoughtfully

Accountability conversations can be very difficult for employees to hear. A best practice is to have employees take the rest of the day off, if possible. Most people will have trouble focusing on their work for the rest of the day, which can be dangerous in healthcare. Plus, allowing a caregiver to go home reinforces the idea that you care about their personal well-being, not just the organization's metrics. That being the case, try to schedule accountability conversations in the latter half of the caregiver's shift. If you can have the discussion right before the weekend or the caregiver's day off, even better.

Don't Allow Low Performers to Stay

You've given an employee continuous, accurate feedback about their performance. You've explained what they need to improve and have given them the resources and opportunities to do so. They are aware of the consequences of failing to meet organizational standards. But despite everything, it has become apparent that the employee is not a fit for your organization. This is one of the tasks we leaders dread the most: terminating a caregiver's employment.

Someone once asked me if terminating someone ever gets easier. My answer was, "Yes . . . and no." The *process* of terminating a caregiver's employment gets easier with training and experience. You learn what to say, how to say it, and how to navigate the paperwork. You become more confident that your decision was the right one. You understand more clearly why you can't allow low performers and poor culture fits to stay.

But the actual *discussion* wherein someone is terminated should never get easier. The day this meeting is not a challenge to your conscience is the day you need to step down from leadership. I always remind myself that the average American household has 2.5 members, and that everyone has a network of loved ones. When I tell a caregiver they are not a fit for the organization, I am most likely changing others' lives as well. Perhaps the caregiver will have to move out of state for a new job and leave their ailing parents behind. Or maybe their child has special needs that place a heavy financial burden on the family. Everyone has challenges that we are not aware of, and that's part of why the termination process should never get easier.

All of this underscores why leadership integrity (and caring for your greatest asset in general) is so important. When you inevitably have to terminate someone's employment, you want to be certain that you have done everything you possibly could to avert this scenario. If you didn't provide authentic, candid, and timely feedback, as well as resources for improvement, then the responsibility for the termination lies at least partially on your shoulders—and that's a burden none of us wants to bear.

REFERENCES

Eisner, E., and Cuban, L. 2013. "On Teaching (Elliot Eisner)." National Education Policy Center. Published June 19. https://nepc.colorado.edu/blog/teaching-elliot-eisner.

Leonard, S. M. 2020. "Killing Morale: 5 Ways Leaders Put Their Teams at Risk." ClearanceJobs. Published November 3. https://news.clearancejobs.com/2020/11/03/killing-morale-5-ways-leaders-put-their-teams-at-risk/.

CHAPTER 12

Recognizing and Addressing Burnout

ONE OF THE challenges of writing this book is the temptation to say too much. Healthcare leadership is a complex job, requiring knowledge in many diverse areas. One such area is burnout (and wellness in general). When I set out to write this chapter, I struggled with how much territory to cover. Obviously, healthcare leaders cannot be expected to be burnout experts. Still, the past few years have exacerbated the condition so much that I'd be remiss not to include a chapter that hits the high spots.

Frankly, I've come to believe burnout is the greatest threat our industry is facing now. And I'm certainly not the only one. US Surgeon General Vivek Murthy stated, "Confronting the long-standing drivers of burnout among our health workers must be a top national priority . . . And if we fail to act, we will place our nation's health at risk" (American Hospital Association 2022).

Burnout is dramatically affecting the lives of caregivers and, ultimately, the patients who count on them. This is why leaders must be able to do several things to combat its presence in the workforce: recognizing red flags, interceding when needed, and creating a culture that makes burnout less likely to take hold in the first place. We'll discuss all of these throughout the chapter.

This is an urgent situation. Leaders can no longer afford *not* to make burnout and other mental health issues a priority. Especially in light of the COVID-19 pandemic and the Great Resignation, we must get out in front of these issues. If we wait too long, people will leave. Today's employees insist on working for organizations that prioritize their needs and create a rewarding workplace environment—and helping to ensure wellness definitely falls into these categories.

Burnout is not a new issue, of course. Healthcare always has been and always will be a stressful career, and over the years it has taken a toll on some individuals. Yet, as we'll discuss shortly, the problem has gotten worse over the past decade or so and has rapidly worsened over the last few (incredibly difficult) years. And the COVID-19 pandemic is surely not the last crisis our industry will face. We live in a chaotic world. The scope, pace, and intensity of disruptions we must weather will only increase—meaning that burnout will always be a danger.

A QUICK BURNOUT CRASH COURSE

First things first: Let's talk a little about what burnout *is* and *is not*. The term was made famous by New York psychologist Herbert Freudenberger in the early 1970s. Around the same time, another psychiatrist, Christina Maslach—who would go on to codify burnout in the famous MBI (Maslach Burnout Inventory)—was also "discovering" the condition on the other side of the country. In an interesting *Washington Post* article, Jonathan Malesic (2022) puts Freudenberger and Maslach's work in historical perspective and explores it through a cultural lens.

In 2019, the World Health Organization (WHO) redefined burnout as "a syndrome conceptualized as resulting from chronic workplace stress that has not been successfully managed." The press release went on to say that burnout is "characterized by three dimensions (WHO 2019):

- feelings of energy depletion or exhaustion;

- increased mental distance from one's job, or feelings of negativity or cynicism related to one's job; and
- reduced professional efficacy.

Soon thereafter, a Healthline article by psychologist Juli Fraga (2019) explained that "changing the definition of burnout can help dismantle the misbelief that it's 'nothing serious.' It can help remove the incorrect assumption that those who have it don't need occupational support."

There is no doubt that burnout is incredibly destructive. It affects the following:

- **The well-being of the individual caregiver.** Burnout not only makes the sufferer tired and irritable, but it can also cause physical symptoms such as headaches and gastrointestinal issues. It can lead to depression, substance abuse, and in extreme cases, even suicide. In many cases there are likely downstream effects on the family as well.
- **The success of the organization.** It stands to reason that when people are burned out, they will become disengaged. Lack of employee engagement in any industry will hurt productivity, drive up operating costs, increase turnover, lead to dissatisfied customers, and more. But we aren't just talking about any industry. We're talking about healthcare, where the stakes are life and death—which leads me to the next point.
- **Patient quality of care.** That's right: When healthcare providers are burned out, patients pay a price. There is plenty of evidence that burned out clinicians display a decreased sense of empathy, which generates lower patient experience ratings. Worse, they can make mistakes that lead to poor clinical outcomes like more hospital acquired infections and even higher mortality rates.

STRESS AND BURNOUT ARE DIFFERENT

Sometimes significant stress is confused with burnout, but there is a difference, in both diagnosing the issue and treating it. It's important for leaders to know and recognize that difference. Smith, Segal, and Robinson (2021) have identified the following distinctions between stress and burnout:

- Stress is characterized by overengagement, while burnout is characterized by disengagement.
- People experiencing stress are often emotionally overreactive, while those experiencing burnout have muted emotional reactions.
- Stress produces a sense of urgency and hyperactivity. Burnout engenders feelings of helplessness and hopelessness.
- Stress damages physical health and energy levels. Burnout damages emotional health and the ability to stay motivated.
- Stress often leads to anxiety disorders, whereas burnout causes detachment and depression.
- Stress may result in premature mortality. Burnout can cause a person to feel as if life is not worth living at all.

When doing research for this chapter, I saw a quote I thought was apt: "Stress is having too much on your plate—too much work to handle, too many responsibilities, too many hours spent working. Burnout is the opposite. You typically feel like you don't have enough—not enough motivation, not enough energy, not enough care" (Integris Health 2021).

For this reason, stress is easier to manage than burnout. When you're stressed, you're overwhelmed, but you still have the motivation and energy to address the situation. You can go for a walk, take a meditation class, call a friend to vent, or rethink your time management strategy. Not so with burnout, which causes you to lose your motivation, energy, and passion. Even though there may be things you *could* do to help your situation, it's just too hard to muster up the wherewithal to do them.

Although I won't dwell on it here, a third issue is increasingly being discussed: *trauma*. In the wake of COVID and its many disruptions, more and more healthcare workers have progressed from stress and burnout to a state of trauma. To greatly simplify, while stress disrupts us temporarily, trauma puts us in survival mode. It makes us feel threated and unsure of the future. If you'd like to learn more about trauma, I recommend two books by Drs. Mark Goulston and Diana Hendel: *Trauma to Triumph: A Roadmap for Leading Through Disruption (and Thriving on the Other Side)* and *Why Cope When You Can Heal? How Healthcare Heroes of COVID-19 Can Recover from PTSD.*

WHAT IS THE STATE OF BURNOUT IN HEALTHCARE NOW, AND HOW DID WE GET HERE?

As I mentioned earlier, burnout has probably always been with us (even if we didn't know what to call it) and it became "official" in the 1970s. But around 15 years ago it started to manifest itself in healthcare with many changes in the healthcare system.

It's probably no coincidence that the rise in burnout during this time frame coincided with four big changes:

- Increased regulatory oversight
- Increased need for documentation
- Increased use of electronic medical records
- Increased number of physicians moving from an independent practice to health system employment

While it's difficult to prove that these four factors contributed to the recent spike in burnout, the timing does coincide. Anecdotally, many healthcare leaders and caregivers attribute some of their burnout to these four changes over the last 15 years. It makes sense to me. For one thing, these changes greatly intensified the pressure on already-overburdened physicians. For another, they destroyed the sense of autonomy they had previously enjoyed and cut into their time with patients—one of the aspects of their job that makes it meaningful and rewarding.

So, burnout was already at a high level, and then COVID showed up and things got a lot worse. In March 2022, Medscape released the results of a survey it conducted the previous year involving more than 13,000 physicians (Yasgur 2022). It revealed that the number of physicians who reported suicidal thoughts rose from 14 percent in 2019 to 22 percent in 2020. The survey also reported that almost 1 in 10 physicians said they had "thought about or attempted suicide."

Also, the survey found that 21 percent of physicians overall said they were depressed. The report stated:

> Before the pandemic, a team at Penn State College of Medicine conducted simple screenings for depression in multiple hospital systems. Those screenings pointed to a 10% rate of major depression among physicians. "Now, we're seeing a 30%–33% depression rate," says Daniel Shapiro, PhD, vice dean for faculty and administrative affairs, and professor of medical humanism, at the Penn State College of Medicine (Hershey). (Yasgur 2022).

It's no surprise that COVID has put burnout, and mental health in general, on the front stage. The stresses of the pandemic pushed healthcare systems and their processes, and thus the caregivers, over the edge of capacity. Many factors came together to create a perfect storm for burnout. For instance:

- The strain of working long, exhausting hours in harrowing conditions (including in some cases lack of personal protective equipment)

- The feelings of despair and inadequacy that come with not being able to help everyone, and with witnessing the sheer number of deaths
- The fear of catching COVID-19 oneself, and the fear of giving it to family
- The strain of trying to balance work obligations with personal life complications like finding childcare during a pandemic when schools and day care centers are closed
- Concern over children's education when all teaching was online
- More difficulty in decompressing due to gyms being closed, sporting events and arts performances cancelled, and restaurants and bars closed (and then only open for takeout)
- The uncertainty factor: not knowing how bad the pandemic would get, whether needed resources would be available, how high death rates would go
- The possibility of another variant leading to yet another spike in cases, just as the virus appeared to be slowing

This confluence of factors led to increased burnout, which resulted in shockingly high healthcare attrition rates, which resulted in staff shortages that left the remaining caregivers stretched even thinner. This created a spiraling cycle. The more people that leave the industry, the worse conditions are for the remaining ones. Eventually, when enough people leave, the quality of care begins to decrease.

Burnout in a single individual has been demonstrated to lead to increased risk of patient safety errors (or other errors in nonclinical areas of healthcare). Clearly, this isn't good for the patients or the person making the error. Burnout of many individuals results in turnover of staff, leading to even fewer staff, which results in greater risk of errors (clinical and nonclinical) across the organization. This is why, as I mentioned earlier, I think burnout is the greatest threat to healthcare.

That said, it's not always easy to recognize burnout in a team member. An analogy I like to use is water flowing through limestone and wearing away at it, creating holes and fissures. It all happens underground. You're not even aware of it until a sinkhole occurs and the weight of the earth above it causes a collapse. The weight has always been the same, but the foundation beneath it has been weakening, sight unseen, for years. It's up to leaders to detect the running water and intervene before a collapse occurs.

The good news is that because of the pandemic, media and society have started talking a lot more about burnout in healthcare. It has also gotten more attention from researchers over the past few years, with many theories being tested. There's a lot more to learn—but the momentum being created means progress is almost certain to happen.

Tackling the Burnout Stigma: The Time Is Now

A big part of helping people cope with burnout is helping to break the stigma surrounding it. The good news is that this is already happening in many industries. Lately, some athletes who are respected, admired, and at the top of their game have been speaking up about their own issues. In 2021 alone, tennis champion Naomi Osaka withdrew from the French Open citing burnout, and gymnast Simone Biles withdrew from team competition at the Tokyo Olympics to prioritize her mental health.

With the ice already broken, it would be great if healthcare industry role models could also speak out. Unfortunately, physicians and nurses may be even more susceptible to stigma than athletes. Healthcare is a "buck up and deal with it" industry. Caregivers think, *I am a healthcare provider and thus don't need another healthcare*

continued

continued from previous page

provider and wonder, *Will patients not want me to take care of them if I have a mental well-being issue?* Further, there's the worry that getting help means seeing one of their colleagues. Many caregivers hold a deeply ingrained belief that being strong and resilient is just part of the job, and if they can't cope they will be seen as a failure.

As an industry we need to get more intentional about breaking the stigma. We need to normalize discussions around burnout, anxiety, depression and other mental health issues. Part of the solution is educating. Another part is transparency. We need more people in healthcare to step up and say, "I think I have this issue." Leaders may need to role model this behavior. (See more on this subject later in the chapter.)

Let's explore what we as leaders can do to address burnout in our organizations.

AN ANTI-BURNOUT PLAN

As leaders, our goal is to recognize and address current cases of burnout and make changes to prevent future burnout. I've organized what needs to happen into four main "prongs."

1. The three *A*s: assessment, awareness, action
2. Efficiency of operations
3. Culture and engagement
4. Personal strength and balance

Before we address each prong, let's take a quick look at what *not* to do when addressing burnout.

How *Not* to Address Burnout

There's a lot of misunderstanding about the causes of and effective treatment for burnout. Therefore, it's hardly surprising that leaders sometimes make mistakes. As you begin to create an anti-burnout plan at your organization, be sure to avoid these missteps:

- Don't just ignore the problem and hope it will go away. It won't. However, many of your best caregivers might.
- Don't tell physicians they need to build up resilience. They've been through four years of undergrad, four years of medical school, and between three and nine years of residency and/or fellowship training. They wouldn't have made it that far if they weren't resilient! (The same principle holds true for nurses and other clinical and nonclinical employees.) Resilience doesn't mean withstanding stress and pushing yourself to the breaking point.
- Don't perpetuate a "suck it up and move on" attitude. This only adds to the stigma.
- Don't tell people to relax or meditate. While there is nothing wrong with these practices, they're not cures for burnout.
- Don't shame, alienate, or otherwise penalize people for needing to take a break, ask for additional support, or make other changes.
- Don't assume taking a couple of days off is the solution. Burnout didn't just occur overnight and won't go away overnight.

continued

continued from previous page

All these "solutions" put the blame squarely on the person who is burned out. The underlying message is "If you're burned out, you're the problem." In reality, it is probably the organization that is exhausting the caregiver on every level.

Prong 1: The Three *As*—Assessment, Awareness, Action

The first prong in our plan requires a laser focus on the burnout that already exists in our organizations. We need to root out the problem, draw attention to it, and of course take action to help those who are burned out or perhaps on the brink of burnout.

First, *assess* burnout. Leaders must be able to recognize where their people are right now in terms of mental health. I recommend using the MBI (https://www.mindgarden.com/314-mbi-human-services -survey), which is a questionnaire we and our team members can take confidentially to assess degree of burnout. The version called MBI-HSS (Human Services Survey) is the most widely used. There is also a version derived from it called the MBI-HSS (MP) that's designed specifically for medical personnel.

Another survey to consider is the Utrecht Work Engagement Scale (UWES), which assesses an individual's risk for burnout. It measures personal attributes and personality and combines that information with the degree of employee engagement. If someone is not highly engaged, then their risk of burnout increases significantly; this is another critical reason for leaders to focus significant effort and resources to build the engagement of their caregivers, both clinical and nonclinical.

Another helpful resource (and good starting point) is Quint Studer's *The Well-Being Handbook: Tools & Tactics to Help You and Your Organization Heal from Burnout, Stress, and Trauma.* This downloadable e-book is available for free at www.thegratitudegroup .com/tool/ebook-the-well-being-handbook. It offers a few informal assessments for detecting mental health issues on both an organizational and an individual level.

Once we know where our people are in terms of burnout and other wellness issues, we'll have a better handle on what treatment is needed and where we might need to make changes inside our organizations. However, assessments alone cannot do all the work. Having strong relationships with our caregivers goes a long way toward recognizing burnout, which brings us to the next *A*.

Make *awareness* a priority. In this context, *awareness* means making regular connections with people and paying attention. We need to be very intentional about this. The better we know our people, the more likely we'll notice that something is wrong. For example, keep an eye out for the following:

- They're missing a lot of workdays.
- They seem tired, sluggish, and unable to focus. They might complain that they're having trouble sleeping or that they're tired all the time.
- They're obviously disconnected. Their performance may be suffering, and even if not, there's a sense that they're "going through the motions" with their work.
- They're socializing with coworkers less than they used to.
- They're making a lot of mistakes.
- They're super irritable.
- They're defensive when you offer feedback.
- They make a lot of bitter or cynical remarks.
- They're showing physical symptoms, such as headache, nausea, or weight gain or loss.

These are fairly obvious red flags. Be aware, though, that early signs of burnout may be more subtle. Lately there has been a lot of talk about *languishing*, which is not burnout but can feel similar. Languishing is the opposite of flourishing. Sociologist Corey Keys, who coined the term, described it as "emptiness and stagnation, constituting a life of quiet despair" (Abrams 2021). In a widely read article published in the *New York Times*, Adam Grant (2021) called it "an absence of well-being" and "the neglected middle child of mental health."

Most leaders want the people we lead to flourish. We don't want a team of burned-out caregivers. This is why, as I discuss in chapter 10, it's so important to be diligent about connecting with caregivers via frequent rounding engagements. When we make an effort to connect with people regularly, we are more likely to detect changes in their behavior that might signal burnout. Also, when we build strong relationships with people, they'll be more likely to open up and tell us if something is wrong.

Professional speaker and brand and leadership consultant Tim McClure is widely quoted as saying that "the biggest concern for any organization should be when their most passionate people become quiet" (Mills 2016). Silence is concerning because it is a demonstration of apathy and disengagement, which are key symptoms of burnout. So, when you are connecting with your team and they respond to questions like *How are you doing today?* or *How are the resources on your unit?* with silence or "Fine," keep digging.

Take *action* against burnout. If you discover that someone is burned out, act without delay. You will probably start by helping them figure out a solution. Maybe the person needs a different schedule that fits better with obligations like childcare or elder care. Maybe they're struggling with a new skill and need some training. Maybe they'd be happier working in a different department. (A change of scenery can sometimes be a huge energy booster.) Maybe they need to work fewer hours or have a lighter load, or just need permission to draw some boundaries around their personal time.

Perhaps they feel that they don't have a voice, either in creating new processes or finding solutions, because they are not included in the conversation or feel they cannot speak up because of a power gradient. Maybe their purpose isn't fulfilled by their current position.

The most important rule? Always ask. Don't assume. There is no "one size fits all" solution for burnout. I read something I really liked about following the Platinum Rule. Unlike the Golden Rule—"Do unto others as you'd have them do unto you"—the Platinum Rule is about doing unto others as *they* want done to them. This takes into account the reality that everyone has different needs, circumstances, and preferences: what works for Caregiver A may not work for Caregiver B.

If your organization has an employee assistance program (EAP), refer struggling caregivers to it. If your organization does not have an EAP, then give it consideration. Make sure the program is easily accessible, its existence is known throughout the organization, and it has the expertise to assist those struggling with burnout. Make sure to familiarize yourself with your organization's offerings. Many leaders don't know much about their organization's EAP. Educate yourself so you can tell others.

Another important aspect of taking action is getting intentional about reducing stigma. It's critical to bring burnout into the open. This means communicating frequently and in various ways (at meetings, in e-mails, on your website, etc.) about the signs and symptoms of burnout. Urge people to look out for these red flags in their coworkers—quite often we can see in others what we can't see in ourselves.

At one of my past organizations, we held a physician dinner to discuss burnout. Several doctors volunteered to speak about their symptoms. This helped alleviate the stigma that others in the audience might have felt, and it made them feel more comfortable speaking up. It also helped people see what burnout looked like in their colleague—for example, one doctor described a sense of "decision fatigue" that manifested at home—which in turn made others realize, "Hey, I have that too!" It was beneficial for both the physicians speaking about their burnout challenges and for those in the audience.

Another way to reduce stigma is to be vulnerable. Share your own struggles. Talk about your own burnout. Say, "I'm not doing well. I'm struggling with _____." When people see that you're not concealing your burnout, it opens the door for them to be frank as well. It also opens the door for others to assist you.

All this helps you create that crucial sense of psychological safety. People need to feel they won't be judged or otherwise penalized for admitting to burnout. Otherwise, they'll never open up, they'll continue to struggle, and the entire organization (and the patients) will suffer the consequences.

Prong 2: Efficiency of Operations (Fewer Bad Days)

The next prong in our burnout action plan is ensuring that your operations are as efficient as possible. A well-run hospital helps stave off burnout simply because it isn't adding to the difficulties caregivers already face. Healthcare work is inherently tough and heart-wrenching. But caregivers should not have to deal with preventable frustrations on top of everything else. In other words, caregivers are going to have *sad* days, but they don't have to have *bad* days.

Many people think burnout is caused by the daily tragedy that we witness: diagnosing someone with cancer, telling someone their spouse has died from a heart attack, telling a mother her baby is stillborn, telling someone they may never walk again because of their stroke. These circumstances create sad days, but sad days are typically not what cause burnout. Caregivers went into this field knowing they would have to do and see all of these things. (In extreme circumstances, sad days *can* slowly add up to burnout, particularly when they are severe and serial. The relentless nature of COVID-19 hospitalizations and deaths is a case in point. But hopefully, COVID-level disruptions are the exception, not the norm.)

Burnout is caused by bad days, not sad days. A bad day is when someone cannot find the EKG machine, the blood sample was clotted during testing and thus another sample is needed, the X-ray took a long time to get, a piece of equipment is broken, the operating room is delayed, and so forth. On bad days, you spin your wheels and aren't able to efficiently do what you need to do. You go home frustrated and mentally and emotionally worn out. Over time, an endless string of bad days is a sure recipe for burnout.

Our responsibility as leaders is to eliminate (or at least greatly minimize) the bad days by creating efficient and reliable processes. Efficient and reliable processes also result in better clinical outcomes with less chance for error, improved patient satisfaction, improved caregiver satisfaction and engagement, and reduced cost. Here are a few tips for creating more efficient processes:

Listen to the issues raised by the front line. So many of the "big picture" issues in this book boil down to one simple goal: understanding what frontline people need and giving it to them. Strategies and tactics that lead to us listening (and genuinely hearing) include regular connecting (rounding), holding breakfast in the boardroom, a good cascading system with daily huddles, being present and available, breaking down the power gradient so that people speak up, aligning purpose, and more.

Eliminate as much waste as possible. I have in the past developed a Lean Process Design Department for a healthcare system. As you may already know, Lean thinking is about eliminating wasteful practices to prioritize the delivery of value to customers. This department looked at the whole organization, not just frontline care. Here are just a few examples of waste the department targeted:

- Excessive steps to and from the medication dispenser (yes, these folks got down to minute details like counting the physical steps a nurse takes).
- Redundant credentialing applications for all the hospitals in a healthcare system. If a physician wanted privileges at three hospitals, he would have to fill out the packet three

times. This was wasteful. While delineation of privileges may be different at different hospitals, the physician's date of birth and address is the same.

- Long patient waits. For example, when a patient is scheduled for evaluation of a breast mass, can she get the mammogram and perhaps visit the oncologist or breast surgeon on the same day? Why make the patient wait weeks for the next appointment when this will negatively affect her quality of life through worry?
- Non–value-added steps in patient processes. Lean also benefits patients by, for example, eliminating multiple registrations of a patient during the same day of visit, from outpatient lab to outpatient imaging to inpatient admission, and so forth.

Designing processes to be Lean not only is better for the caregiver, but it usually also results in better outcomes and use of time for the patient. In addition, it often results in reduced expense for the organization. This, of course, subsequently leads to greater revenue when the patients who are more satisfied and have better outcomes share their experiences with their neighbors!

Make sure people are doing their job and not someone else's (especially in times of short staffing). For example, hospitals commonly need sitters to provide certain patients with supervision and companionship. These caregivers are primarily tasked with monitoring the patient to make sure they don't get out of bed and fall.

Unfortunately, because virtually every hospital across the country is short on sitters, the patient care assistants (PCAs) who are supposed to help the nurses must function as sitters instead. This is not what the PCAs want to do. Not surprisingly, the result is a lack of PCAs. That, in turn, means that registered nurses (RNs) are doing their own job—the duties that only a nurse can do—*and* the PCA's job. They are frustrated and very busy, and the patients are not likely getting the best possible care.

At Hospital X, we solved this problem by creating a "tele-sitter" program. We purchased several portable video monitors that enabled one sitter to monitor multiple patients. (This is similar to how one nurse monitors multiple cardiac patients via telemetry.) This allowed the PCAs to focus on their work and the RNs to focus on theirs. Both PCAs and RNs were able to spend more time with patients. Not only did the tele sitter program solve the immediate problem, but it also made for happier caregivers on all levels. People naturally want to work at the top of their licensure and do the job they are hired to do.

As we discussed in chapter 7, volunteers can also fill staffing gaps. Remember the story of Hospital X having volunteers feed patients who couldn't feed themselves, instead of relying on a nurse or PCA to do this task? This made our processes more efficient and allowed the PCAs and nurses to focus on their core responsibilities—all of which contributed to the delivery of excellent care. Meanwhile, the volunteers were also fulfilled because they wanted to interact with patients. And finally, patients were happy because they got a timely meal and company. A win-win-win, for no additional cost.

Prong 3: Culture and Engagement

Culture is a huge and multifaceted topic. In fact, every chapter in this book connects back to it. As I said in the very first chapter of this book, I believe it is crucial for organizations to design and perpetuate a culture that engages people and helps them tap into their sense of purpose. When leaders do it well, they create an environment that constantly replenishes caregivers, which in turn helps to ward off burnout. Much has been written on the subject of purpose as an antidote to burnout; for example, bestselling author Daniel Goleman (2022) describes purpose in terms of the oxygen that "stokes the fires of employee engagement" even more than good pay, time off, and other factors: "It is a source of intrinsic motivation. Because it comes from within, it tends to be more powerful and its results are more gratifying in the long run."

Before I cover some of the other burnout-busting cultural building blocks we cover in *this* book, I'd like to start with a word about trust. Everything we've talked about until now is directly related to building more trusting relationships between leaders and caregivers. Working in healthcare is a bit like leading soldiers into a war zone every day. If we haven't built that trust from the beginning, people won't willingly follow us. This is why rounding and other methods of making regular connections are so vital, especially in tough times. From what I've observed, leaders who were highly visible and worked alongside people during the COVID-19 pandemic found that they developed stronger, more trusting relationships—and the trust went both ways.

There is plenty of evidence that where there is trust, there is less burnout. A GreatPlaceToWork.com article shares research suggesting that "burnout at a company with a low-trust culture is nearly twice as widespread as burnout at a company with a high-trust culture" (Kazi and Hastwell 2020).

The following sections touch on some other cultural building blocks that I believe engage and replenish caregivers and reduce burnout.

Empathetic leadership. When leaders can put themselves in employees' shoes, they are much more likely to come up with customized solutions for their burnout. This means being accessible, being a good listener, and at times shifting how we think about "problematic" employees. When we realize that underneath their bad behavior is someone who is struggling, it can change how we look at them and makes us want to help.

Collegiality. Feeling like "part of the team" is extremely important. In 2021, Dr. Stephen Beeson did a presentation for The Gratitude Symposium in which he talks about how powerful collegiality, community, and belonging actually are. In fact, he says they are "the most powerful countermeasure to burnout." I urge you to listen to his inspiring speech at https://gratitude-symposium.heysummit .com/speakers/stephen-beeson.

Caregiver involvement in large decisions. Making sure people have a say in large decisions is beneficial in several ways. First, it's natural to prefer to be a part of determining our own future rather than being told what our future holds. It also further engages people in the organization and provides them with the reason behind decisions (and when people understand the "why," they are more likely to engage). Finally, involving people in large decisions gives them a greater sense of control, which minimizes frustration and fear of the unknown.

Empowerment. Along the same lines, people need to be empowered to make their own decisions. Most often, the individual closest to the situation knows the pros and cons of a decision better than anyone else. Plus, the less bureaucracy there is, the less delay there will be. Throughout this book I have told stories about frontline caregivers taking action because they were empowered to make their own decision: breaking a no-animals policy to bring a dog into the hospital for a patient nearing death, a nurse buying a different type of soda for a patient, and so forth. We need to trust our people to have the common sense to do the right thing.

A low power gradient. This is so essential to a well-functioning organization that an entire chapter of this book is dedicated to it. Lowering the power gradient also contributes to lowering burnout. The comfort of being able to voice an opinion or concern to anyone and the feeling that everyone is just as important as anyone else is a powerful and fundamental part of caregiver well-being.

Good communication (especially in times of crisis). Without communication, engagement is difficult. The unknown is stressful and anxiety producing. People need to know where the organization is going, why a decision is being made, what changes are taking place in the internal or external environment, and so forth. They need status updates on progress or failures. Where there is an unknown, people speculate and fill in the blanks, typically assuming the negative rather than the positive. Communication is another critical topic warrants its own chapter in this book.

Accountability. Good people want to know that everyone is appropriately held accountable, including themselves. Behaviors and outcomes that are permitted are naturally seen as being acceptable. If poor behavior and outcomes are accepted, then those with higher expectations will become disengaged and leave the organization. Generally, your all-stars are committed, engaged, and hardworking. When they see inadequate behavior or performance that is not held accountable, it adds to their daily frustrations and can lead to burnout. These problems are compounded when the all-stars need to pick up the slack of a low performer. That said, standardization of appropriate accountability methods also needs to be in place. Development of a "just culture" must be a priority of all organizations.

Recognition. Just as we need to hold people accountable, we also need to recognize and reward positive actions and results. This demonstrates appreciation toward an individual or group for their efforts and success, but it also reinforces the behaviors and outcomes that we want to reproduce. It can also blunt burnout to a certain degree. People who are recognized, valued, appreciated, and understood gain personal gratitude for their efforts and have their sense of purpose reinforced.

Integrity and respect. These cultural building blocks are the foundation for trust and positive relationships—and as discussed elsewhere in this book, healthcare is a relationship business. Relationships between caregivers, and between patients and caregivers, are at the center of everything. If the parties do not have integrity and respect for each other, these relationships will not be strong enough to deliver the best care. Feeling respected and treated with integrity, which includes fairness and equity, is necessary to adequately treat burnout. On the flip side, a lack of respect and integrity can promote burnout.

Fairness and equity. Treating people *fairly* means treating them appropriately. For example, is compensation for a particular position appropriate for the individual's experience and responsibility? *Equity* is being treated the same as others like you: for example, everyone in that role with the same experience and responsibility is compensated similarly. We can have fairness without equity (or vice versa), but we need both. They're crucial for the integrity of the organization and culture. Plus, humans are wired to value fairness and equity. Where it is absent, people cannot thrive.

Workplace pride. Everyone wants to be proud of what they do and who they work for. This is another reason communication, celebration, and recognition are important. If leaders don't take the time to acknowledge and celebrate caregivers' achievements, recognition for a job well done has to happen internally. For example, a person will need to look in the mirror and say, *Wow, I saved a life today*—or *Wow, if I didn't catch that error, the financial plan could have been a disaster for the entire year*. However, if a leader celebrates and recognizes both individual and team accomplishments, the recognition and pride in success also come from an external source.

Don't stop with recognizing the individuals or groups that achieved the accomplishment; share their success with the entire organization. Not only will those who contributed to the success get greater recognition, but also other caregivers will develop a greater sense of pride in their colleagues and their organization. This may help counteract burnout, because when a person or a team is proud of their accomplishments, it makes their work feel more meaningful and their efforts worthwhile.

As mentioned in chapter 8, Stephen Covey (2016) says that the "deepest hunger of the human soul is to be recognized, valued, appreciated, and understood." Notice that all four aspects of feeding the soul are in the aforementioned points on culture.

One more suggestion before we move on to Prong 4: I have cited Quint Studer elsewhere in this book (including earlier in this chapter) and I am going to mention him again. In 2021, he wrote *The Calling: Why Healthcare Is So Special.* In it, Studer talks about how to create a culture of replenishment—in other words, one that keeps people going when times are tough. I think it is a wonderfully readable book on a complex topic. I also firmly believe that a culture of replenishment is a powerful remedy for preventing and mitigating burnout. Thus, I recommend that you give it a read.

Prong 4: Personal Strength and Balance

This last prong is a little different from the other three. So far, we've focused on things leaders and organizations can do to help caregivers prevent and heal from burnout. Now I'll switch gears and discuss how leaders can (1) shore up their own physical and emotional well-being to make burnout less likely to take hold and (2) encourage caregivers to do the same.

Some of these suggestions are meant for you, the leader, to put into practice in your own life. Only when you are healthy can you help others help themselves. Once you've mastered these tactics you can also share them with those you lead. The others are steps you can take to foster wellness in your team.

Get clear on your personal True North. To create a strong foundation for your well-being, it is important to define your own values and your own purpose. Many people never think to do this. They go through life with only a fuzzy, unformed notion of what they stand for and want to achieve in the short time they're here on Earth. I feel this is a tragedy. It is only when you take the time to clarify your values and purpose that you can stay true to yourself.

Yes, your True North can shift over time—life events such as marriage or having children or losing a loved one can provide a different perspective—but solidifying it now can help you make decisions that will hopefully assist you in keeping burnout at bay. I urge you to revisit chapter 1 and review the section on articulating your personal purpose, paying close attention to the Ikigai model. Write it down: both your purpose and your values. Let them guide your steps.

Work to shore up the five aspects of good health: physical, relational, mental/emotional, spiritual, and financial. To be strong and in balance, it's important to pay attention to these five areas. If you are to be "healthy" overall—which provides the personal strength and resilience to withstand the stressors that can lead to burnout—you must be healthy in each of these five areas. If you aren't, you will feel stressed, sick, or unfulfilled to some degree.

I have seen these building blocks of good health referred to as *capitals*, based on the idea that they are types of wealth. I've also seen them called *pillars* and *dimensions*. It really doesn't matter what we call them. The point is to pay attention to each area, work on improving them as needed, and strive to keep them in balance.

- **Physical:** Sometimes our physical health is out of our control as a result of genetics, personal injuries, effects of aging, and so forth. However, there is much we can do that's also *in* our control: exercise, good nutrition, adequate sleep, and avoiding tobacco, overconsumption of alcohol, and other kinds of substance abuse. It is important to seek regular healthcare as well. If there is anything you're doing (or not doing) to harm your physical health, it's time to be honest. You only have one body to last a lifetime. Are you taking care of it? What steps can you take right now to get stronger and healthier?
- **Relational (family and friends):** We all need fulfilling relationships with others (yes, even introverts who value

their alone time!). It's through these relationships that we learn, grow, play, and enjoy the full spectrum of human experiences. It is also through these relationships that we survive difficult times. There is evidence that a sense of community and the support of others drive our personal wellness, our success, and even our longevity. How are your family relationships? Are you making time for friendships? Do you have people you can call on and rely on for any situation?

- **Mental/emotional:** Good mental and emotional health is what it takes to be strong in the face of adversity. Ideally, we feel a sense of stability in our mental and emotional state where the highs are not excessive and the lows are not crippling. We feel in control, so to speak. I also believe that much of mental and emotional well-being stems from our own True North discussed earlier: having a clearly understood (and written) purpose statement and values, and living by them.

However, there are also plenty of science and medicine-based solutions that can help with mental, emotional, and behavioral health. Many professionals can provide assistance: counselors, psychologists, psychiatrists, and other specialists. They offer medicinal and nonmedical treatments that work very well. We shouldn't hesitate to take advantage of these options when needed and encourage others to do so as well. Getting professional help saves lives.

I am part of a group of men who meet once per week. During a meeting, one of the guys stated that he needed assistance. One hundred percent of us supported him without judgment. Unfortunately, many people feel they *will* be judged if they seek help. We need to realize that seeing a professional for mental health issues is no different from seeing a cardiologist for heart issues. Another viewpoint is that a person who admits they need assistance and seeks it is actually a stronger person than someone who denies assistance or minimizes its role; we need to be strong and encourage others to be strong. How is your mental and emotional health? Are you letting groundless concerns about what others might think stop you from seeking needed help?

- **Spiritual:** Some people do not have a background of faith. We are all on our own journey, and nobody can presume to understand (or judge) another person's life view. What I know is my *own* faith is central to who I am. I also know most people have some form of faith or spirituality that may provide a directional component to their life, a sense of purpose, and a measure of comfort in the face of mortality. If you do have a particular faith, is it strong? If you don't have one, have you considered exploring various paths? How are you nurturing your spirituality?

- **Financial:** The goal here isn't to be rich (often, a single-minded pursuit of wealth creates as many problems as it solves!) but rather to be financially secure enough to not have to worry about putting food on the table, having a roof over our house, and affording our medications. Secondarily, it's great if we can provide for other priorities such as education for our children, entertainment, saving for retirement, and so forth. Are you managing your money as mindfully as you could? Do you need to take steps to increase your earning potential? Conversely, are you *too* obsessed with making money, perhaps at the expense of strong relationships with your loved ones or having enough downtime to truly enjoy life?

Create a second victim program. When an adverse medical event such a patient death occurs, especially one due to a medical error, the healthcare provider involved becomes a "second victim." Caregivers suffering from second victim syndrome (SVS) may experience ongoing mental, emotional, or even spiritual turmoil. They may show symptoms like shame, sadness, guilt, fear, anger, anxiety, and depression. They can have PTSD-like flashbacks, become unable to concentrate, and lose their confidence. SVS is "associated with increased rates of burnout, substance abuse, and even suicide" (Wilson 2020).

Often, people suffering from SVS will either suffer in silence or end up leaving their job. I have seen physicians within months of completing their training, who are finally starting to practice medicine, quit the profession. I've also seen pharmacists and nurses quit. These are huge losses for healthcare.

As leaders, our job is to support these second victims. One healthcare system in my past created a rapid response team for caregivers who might fall into this category. Our thinking was, *We have rapid response for urgent situations for patients, why not for caregivers?* The team was composed of trained colleagues, chaplains, social workers, and other support people who were on call at all times. They were always available for a personal discussion and were also deployed to units during more notable events to provide real-time support for the caregivers.

Set a healthy example for others. We can preach all day long that a good work–life balance matters in the fight against burnout. But if we don't *practice* it, no one will believe what we say. Employees typically take their cue from what their leaders do, not what they say. When they receive e-mails from us when they're off work, they may think we don't respect their downtime. They may even feel compelled to respond right away. That's because if we are sending e-mails on weekends, holidays, and evenings (or whenever we are supposed to be "off"), we are conveying a message that working during personal time is normal and even expected. Seemingly small things like limiting e-mail delivery to working hours can help a lot.

Don't just encourage others to take time off for personal reasons; do so yourself. Do it visibly. Block on your calendar *Sally's soccer game* or *Billy's recital* so that people see it's okay to take time off for family needs. I know the manager of a cancer center who posts a clear folder on her office door to communicate with her staff how she can be reached (or perhaps not reached unless it is an emergency). If she is at lunch, she may put a picture of eating utensils in the folder. When she has to leave work early to coach her daughter's softball team, she uses a picture of a softball. When she is on vacation, she may place a picture of a beach or Mickey Mouse in the folder. This not only serves the purpose of informing her staff of her availability, but it's also a fun, effective way to let people know that she has a life outside of work.

It may be even more important to set these examples when times are super stressful. Here's a story to illustrate. During the height of the COVID-19 pandemic, I sent via e-mail a daily two- to three-minute video to the whole organization. It typically provided updates on the virus, rapidly changing internal factors like policy changes, words of encouragement and appreciation, success stories, and so forth. This became an important part of the communication cascade and was usually one of the most viewed e-mails in the organization.

At one point I went away for the weekend to my in-laws' lake house. I wondered if I should pre-film a few videos to have on deck while I was gone. Eventually, I decided to film the videos at the lake house. My wife took the videos on my iPhone while I stood on the dock. I made sure to say that I needed a break and had taken a couple days off. I also stated that I normally would not work on a day off, but the pandemic made this vacation an exception given the rapidity of changes and the fact that critical new information was needed as soon as possible. This turned out to be the right call. I got many e-mails thanking me for demonstrating that it's okay to take breaks.

Provide self-care resources to caregivers. Studies show that physical activity is a good coping mechanism for mitigating stress and the effects of burnout (Wolff, O'Connor, Wilson, and Gay 2021). In addition, there's plenty of evidence that points to the need to promote healthy eating to mitigate burnout risk (Esquivel 2021). Since we know there's a connection between caregiver well-being and regular exercise and good nutrition, why not make it easier for caregivers to achieve both?

I've been part of organizations that have their own gym. Some are smaller and only for employees, while others offer memberships to the community. The former makes it easier to allow a 24/7 opportunity for exercise, which is often necessary given the vastly different working hours of healthcare teams. The latter necessitates greater regulatory setup, capital, and ongoing operating costs, but can provide additional revenue through memberships as well as an opportunity to interact with the community. A third option that can be successful is partnering with an established gym to create reduced membership fees for the health system's employees.

Incidentally, partnering with other organizations can also allow you to provide discounted tickets for amusement parks, sporting events, art shows, cooking and nutrition classes, and other activities. Often, these additional partnering perks don't have any associated costs. They are a win-win-win for the employee, the health system, and the external organization.

In closing, this chapter is far from inclusive. I strongly recommend that leaders read other books and articles on burnout in healthcare. And continue to follow the research that is just starting to ramp up in the wake the last few disastrous years.

COVID greatly worsened the "sinkholes" that undermine the stability of our caregivers, the success of our healthcare systems, and the outcomes of our patients. Yet it's far from the last disruption we'll face.

As we move ahead, we owe it to those we lead to build a stronger foundation beneath them and to help them shore up their own well-being. These men and women are the heart and soul of our industry. Keeping them strong, engaged, and flourishing is not just the right thing to do—it's a cornerstone of our purpose.

Never forget: What applies to the rest of your team also applies to *you*. That's why much of this chapter has been devoted to assessing your personal wellness and strengthening your foundation. I urge to you to consider what you can do to create a healthier, happier life for yourself, and to share what you have learned with your team. You are a leader—and part of your responsibility and privilege is leading those around you in the direction of personal wellness.

REFERENCES

Abrams, A. 2021. "Languishing in the Time of Covid." Psychology Today. Published May 3. https://www.psychologytoday.com /us/blog/nurturing-self-compassion/202105/languishing-in -the-time-covid.

American Hospital Association. 2022. "Surgeon General Calls for Collective Action to Address Health Worker Burnout." AHA News. Published May 23. https://www.aha.org/news/headline /2022-05-23-surgeon-general-calls-collective-action-address -health-worker-burnout.

Covey, S. R. 2016. *Primary Greatness: The 12 Levers of Success*. New York: Simon & Schuster.

Esquivel, M. K. 2021. "Nutrition Strategies for Reducing Risk of Burnout Among Physicians and Health Care Professionals." *American Journal of Lifestyle Medicine* 15 (2): 126–29. https:// doi.org/10.1177/1559827620976538.

Fraga, J. 2019. "Why the WHO's Decision to Redefine Burnout Is So Important." Healthline. Published June 5. https://www .healthline.com/health/mental-health/burnout-definition-world -health-organization.

Goleman, D. 2022. "Can Purpose Postpone Burnout?" Korn Ferry. Accessed August 22. https://www.kornferry.com/insights/this -week-in-leadership/can-purpose-postpone-burnout.

Grant, A. 2021. "There's a Name for the Blah You're Feeling: It's Called Languishing." *New York Times*. Published April 19. https://www.nytimes.com/2021/04/19/well/mind/covid -mental-health-languishing.html.

Integris Health. 2021. "What Are the 5 Stages of Burnout?" Published November 5. https://integrisok.com/resources/on-your-health/2021/november/what-are-the-5-stages-of-burnout.

Kazi, C., and C. Hastwell. 2020. "Are You Tracking This Key Indicator of Employee Health and Productivity?" Great Place to Work. Published May 15. https://www.greatplacetowork.com/resources/blog/are-you-tracking-this-key-indicator-of-employee-health-and-productivity.

Malesic, J. 2022. "Burnout Dominated 2021. Here's the History of Our Burnout Problem." *Washington Post*. Published January 1. https://www.washingtonpost.com/history/2022/01/01/burnout-history-freudensberger-maslach/.

Mills, J. 2016. "When Your Most Motivated Employees Become Quiet." Stretch for Growth. Published May 12. https://www.stretchforgrowth.com/leadership/motivated-employees-quiet/.

Smith, M., J. Segal, and L. Robinson. 2021. "Burnout Prevention and Treatment." HelpGuide. Published November 1. https://www.helpguide.org/articles/stress/burnout-prevention-and-recovery.htm.

Wilson, S. 2020. "What Is Second Victim Syndrome and How Peer Coaching Helps." VITAL WorkLife. Published September 9. https://insights.vitalworklife.com/what-is-second-victim-syndrome-and-how-peer-coaching-helps.

Wolff, M. B., P. J. O'Connor, M. G. Wilson, and J. L. Gay. 2021. "Associations Between Occupational and Leisure-Time Physical Activity with Employee Stress, Burnout and Well-Being Among Healthcare Industry Workers." *American Journal of Health Promotion* 35 (7): 957–65. https://doi.org/10.1177/08901171211011372.

World Health Organization (WHO). 2019. "Burn-Out an 'Occupational Phenomenon': International Classification of Diseases." Published May 28. https://www.who.int/news/item/28

-05-2019-burn-out-an-occupational-phenomenon-international
-classification-of-diseases.

Yasgur, B. S. 2022. "A Tragedy of the Profession: Medscape Physician Suicide Report 2022." Medscape. Published March 4.
https://www.medscape.com/slideshow/2022-physician-suicide
-report-6014970?faf=1#1.

Conclusion: It's All About Culture

It's never been more urgent to create a great place to work. By this I mean making your healthcare organization a place not only where people want to be, but also where they can do their best work, at the top of their training. It's why I wrote this book, and it's why I'm so grateful for readers like you—readers who understand that mastering this new approach to leadership is vital to our future. Still, I know the idea of making such a monumental shift can feel overwhelming.

You may be processing everything we've covered until now—from breaking down the power gradient to mastering the 15-70-15 formula to connecting with your team and creating a sense of purpose—and thinking, *How can we make it all happen?*

Don't worry. It's not exactly easy, but it *is* doable. As with most journeys we undertake, the first step is to put it all in perspective. Getting the right mental framing is half the battle; before we can take confident, decisive action, we need to know what we're really doing. That's why I want you to understand that *all the mindset shifts, strategies, and tactics we've talked about throughout this book work together to create your culture.*

So what *is* culture? It's a bit of an elusive concept, and there are various definitions. I've heard culture described as "the behaviors that people demonstrate that are accepted as part of a norm, as well as the behaviors that are *not* demonstrated that are accepted as part of a norm." (That description is kind of a mouthful!) I've also heard it described as "the unwritten rules of behavior." (I like this definition.) Even more simply, "culture is how people act when nobody is watching." This last one is probably my favorite.

Whatever definition of culture you prefer, you can see that it all comes back to behavior. What we are really aiming for is positive behavior change—and that begins with leaders.

Modeling the right behaviors and expectations (and holding ourselves accountable for doing so, and encouraging others to hold us accountable as well) is what sets the culture. Humility, integrity, trustworthiness, empathy, respectfulness—all the qualities we want to permeate and define our culture start at the top.

Culture isn't what a leader preaches; it's what a leader demonstrates and models. Imagine a chaotic household where children are yelling. The appropriate action is calmly explaining to the kids why they should not yell and perhaps spelling out the consequences if they do. Yelling at the children not to yell is not as effective in the long term. It sends a mixed messages because you are doing something (yelling) that you are telling the children not to do. (To be clear: I'm not implying employees are children; it's just a convenient analogy.)

When leaders consistently set the right example, we establish cultural expectations across the organization. It may be even more impactful when we put those expectations in writing and get everyone to agree to them—but the leader piece is nonnegotiable. Perhaps have the caregivers (clinical and nonclinical) work together to develop the first draft of the expectations.

Be aware that there are subcultures across an organization. For example, there is a different culture in the Department of Radiology than in the Emergency Department than in the Operating Rooms than in the Pediatric Ward. The same is true for nonclinical areas. The culture of the Information Technology department may be different from that of the Legal department, which may be different from Plant Operations. These differences are fine, as long as these subcultures conform to the larger organizational culture.

Culture is foundational. It's what will determine our success or failure long-term. Some have said that "culture eats strategy for lunch." I believe that culture should be the number-one strategy of an organization. When we are intentional about and focused on creating the culture we want, we've taken the first and most important step toward cracking the code of healthcare leadership. Everything else will flow from there.

All that said, creating the right culture won't happen overnight. It can't. Changing behaviors takes time, persistence, and consistency. My advice is to break it down into bite-sized pieces.

Start with a single tactic we've described in this book and hit it head-on with full force. Set the example, model the expected behaviors, teach and coach how to do it, communicate the reasons why, and reward and recognize those who get it right. Once people have mastered this new behavior and you start seeing results, you can leverage the momentum from this and move on to the next behavior.

As the adage goes, this is how you eat the elephant: one bite at a time. Earlier in the book we discussed the risk of undertaking too many initiatives at once. Just keep moving one step at a time and don't give up. Before you know it, you'll see an incredible culture taking shape. As I said previously, it's not easy—but it's definitely worth it.

Make no mistake: This stuff works. When you understand how reducing the power gradient changes dynamics in your organization and start putting in place the tactics we've discussed in this book, amazing things happen. In my career I've seen hospitals and health systems undergo some pretty incredible transformations. Here is a snapshot of what we achieved inside one hospital and one healthcare system during my tenure, using the material in this book.

- Improved team member engagement scores to the top tenth percentile in the country
- Elevated caregiver efficiency to the top decile performance
- Improved the results of the "culture of safety" survey from the bottom quartile to the top decile
- Decreased the number of critical incident events by over two thirds

- Elevated both safety and patient experience to the top fifth percentile in the country
- Decreased hospital-acquired infections by 75 percent
- Decreased mortality to the national top decile performance
- Decreased patient care costs by 70 percent
- Tripled patient volume and revenue over five years
- Decreased anonymously filed incident reports by nearly 80 percent

In addition, here are a just a few of the awards and recognitions we received:

- Healthgrades Distinguished Hospital for Clinical Excellence (top 5 percent in the country)
- Healthgrades Outstanding Patient Experience Award (top 5 to 10 percent in the country)
- Healthgrades Patient Safety Excellence Award (top 5 percent in the country)
- Leapfrog Patient Safety "A" Rating
- IBM/Watson Top 15 Health Systems in America
- Recognition as one of the "best places to work" and "top workplaces" in Cincinnati, Ohio

Not only did all our efforts create a great place to work and a healing environment for patients, but they also created an incredibly fulfilling career for me. I can attest that getting started on this journey is the best thing you can do for your organization, your people, and yourself.

As I write these words, healthcare continues to struggle with staff shortages in all corners of the industry. This is not likely to improve any time soon. But even if it did, the best healthcare organizations will always be those who have the best people. And the best people are attracted to organizations with a great culture.

Of course, individuals (leaders, clinicians, and caregivers of every stripe) will come and go for various reasons as their life circumstances change. Collectively, though, we can create the best odds for our organization when we get our culture right. Ultimately, people who leave for better pay or a better career opportunity may return because of the culture. However, people who leave because of culture will never return for pay or opportunity.

Make sure you have the kind of culture that attracts and retains the best people. Challenge them, nurture them, and give them every reason to stay. There is simply nothing more important than an organization full of people motivated by a strong sense of purpose. I invite you to set out on this journey today. You will never regret it.

Index

Patient: consumerization, 86; feedback, capturing, 66–68; as first priority, 60–61; life changed by empowered caregivers, 195; outcomes and safety linked to service in healthcare delivery, 146; quality of care, burnout and, 267, 271; safety errors, burnout and, 271; surveys, 66

Patient care assistants (PCAs), 150, 281–282

Patient experience: experience scores, 143–144, 146; good service protocols as part of, 147–149; happiness levels and, 161; volunteers to enhance, 151

Patient priorities, 65–75; be nice to me, 71–72; budget and, 76; caregivers' understanding of, 69–70; don't hurt me, 70–71; don't waste my time, 72–73; feedback for, capturing, 66–68; heal me, 71; keep me healthy going forward, 73–75

Patients Come Second (Spiegelman and Berrett), 61

PCAs. *See* Patient care assistants

Peer interviewing, 179–180

Perceived power gradient, 116–118

Performance improvement plan (PIP), 258

Personal purpose: articulating, 18–22; finding and fulfilling, 19; Ikigai and, 21, 22

Personal strength and balance, 287–294; good health, shoring up aspects of, 288–290; healthy example, setting for others, 291–292; personal values and purpose, defining (True North), 287–288; second victim program, creating, 290–291; self-care resources provided to caregivers, 292–294

Personal values and purpose, defining (True North), 287–288

Phone call, as quick connection tactic, 228–229

Physical aspect of good health, 288

Physicians: burnout and, 270; in keeping patients healthy, 74

Pillars, 288. *See also* Good health, building blocks of

PIP. *See* Performance improvement plan

Plan-Do-Study-Act cycle, 98

Platinum Rule, 235, 278

Podcasts, 35, 214–215

Policies, in healthcare organizations, 58

Post-visit follow-up, 67–68, 149

Power distance, 115

Power gradient, 113–140; accountability of power gradient enforcers, 138–139; being accessible, 122–126; body language and, 131–132; breaking down, 3–4, 121–133; diagnostic questions to ask, 119–120; evaluating, in organization, 119–120; feedback and, 128–130; final thoughts, 139–140; formal business attire and, 131; getting stakeholders' input before making decisions, 127–129; hiring caregivers committed to flattening, 134–135, 136–137; hiring caregivers well-versed on, 135, 137; "introduce me" litmus test, 120–121; leadership tools to support and empower teams and, 137–138; low, in culture and engagement, 284; medical terminology and, proactively defining, 133; mistakes and, admitting to, 126–127; negative effects of, 118–119; perceived, 116–118; philosophy of, throughout the organization, 134–139; promptness and, prioritizing, 132; setting arrangements and, 131; small behavior tactics and, 130–133; Tenerife incident and, 113–115; term, use of, 115–116; words and, use of, 132

Predictive analytics, 58

The Primary Greatness: The 12 Levers of Success (Covey), 191

Priorities in healthcare, 57–76; awareness as a priority, 276–277; department (or division) as third priority, 62–63; healthcare organization as second priority, 61–62; healthcare workers as a priority, 63–65; to keep you on course, 59–60; patient as first priority, 60–61. *See also* Patient priorities

Prioritizing tasks, 47–55, 57–76; by deciding what not to do, 49–51; by determining what's emergent and what's not, 48–49, *49*; by keeping a written (or digital) to-do list, 48; leadership qualities for, 59–60; by learning to delegate effectively using the three-column approach, 51–54; by parking tasks in the appropriate spot, 48; spreadsheet used to help determine an optimal strategy, *52–53*; by staying on top of your inbox, 54–55

Product-to-service spectrum, 142–146; healthcare on, 143–146; industries in, 142–143

Promptness, prioritizing, 132

PTSD-like flashbacks, 291

Purpose: articulating, 18–22; breaking down the power gradient and, 3–4; connecting people to work purpose, 17; in 15-70-15 service model, 111; finding and maintaining, 1–22; Ikigai and, 21, *22*; journey, 13–18; keeping people connected to purpose, 16–17; organizational purpose statement, creating, 14–16; personal, 18–22; progression, understanding, 11–12; results, measuring, 17–18; for retention, 192

Purpose philosophy, 4–13; contributions to, role of people in, 7–9; following results of, 12–13; higher level of organizational purpose, shifting to, 10–11; leaders connected to frontline purpose, 9; of new hires, cultural fit and,

10; organization's purpose and, defining, 5–6; purpose progression, understanding, 11–12

Quick connections, 228–229

Ratings, of service in healthcare delivery, 143–144, 146

Recognition and appreciation of caregivers: by connecting, 233–239; group recognition, 234; languages of, 233–234; needing to feel recognized and appreciated, 191; for positive actions and results, 285; rewards for, 235; thank-you notes, 235–238

Redbox, 86

Redundancy, in communication, 209

Registered nurses (RNs), 281–282

Relational aspect of good health, 288–289

Relationships with caregivers. *See* Connecting with caregivers

Remote work, 188–189

Re-recruiting caregivers, 185–196; empowering caregivers to make decisions, 192–196; engaging employees after onboarding is complete, 185–186; learning sources, internal and external, 189–190; need to feel recognized, valued, appreciated, and understood, 191; turnover and, 186, 189. *See also* Retention

Respect, 285–286

Retention: external environment's impact on, 187; flexibility needed for, 187–189; purpose for, 192

Ricketts, Tom, 81

Ritz-Carlton, 88

RNs. *See* Registered nurses

Roosevelt, Theodore, 141

Rounding: benefits of, 226; burnout and, 283; connecting *vs.*, 226; to connect with caregivers, 225–228; feedback and, 67, 254; resources for, 226

About the Author

Dr. Kevin Joseph brings his broad and unusual background to this book on healthcare leadership. His experiences as a chief executive officer, chief medical officer, emergency medicine physician, and biomedical engineer, along with insights from his MBA training and work with the FBI, Secret Service, and SWAT, are distilled into critical leadership philosophies and tactics proven to make healthcare leaders and organizations successful.